24.95

DESIGNING
EFFECTIVE
COMMUNICATIONS

Creating Contexts
for Clarity and Meaning

• edited by jorge frascara •

**ALLWORTH
PRESS**
NEW YORK

10 09 08 07 06 5 4 3 2 1

Published by Allworth Press
An imprint of Allworth Communications, Inc.
10 East 23rd Street, New York, NY 10010

Cover design by Jorge Frascara and Guillermina Noël
Page design and composition/typography by Dianna Little

ISBN: 1-58115-449-6

LIBRARY OF CONGRESS CATALOGING-IN-PUBLICATION DATA
Designing effective communications: creating contexts for clarity and meaning / edited by Jorge Frascara.
     p. cm.
Includes bibliographical references and index.
ISBN 1-58115-449-6 (pbk.)
1. Commercial art. 2. Graphic arts. 3. Communication in design. I. Frascara, Jorge.

NC997.D455 2006
741.6-dc22
                                        2006016398

I dedicate this book to those whose exceptionally intelligent work has allowed me to engage in a continuing education: From Michelangelo Buonarrotti to Franz Kafka and José Hernández; from Werner Herzog to Julio Cortázar and Bertolt Brecht, including a host of people I have been lucky enough to meet in my life, in the design field and else-where. I also dedicate this book to those whose ethical position and reflections about it deeply affected me; from Jean Paul Sartre to Mahatma Gandhi; from Gérard Paris Clavel to my father Félix Daniel. The continuing education continues; with thanks.

Acknowledgments

This book is partly based on papers presented at the "Creating Communicational Spaces" conference, held May 1-3, 2003, at the University of Alberta, in Edmonton, Canada. The conference was funded by the Department of Art and Design, the Faculty of Arts, and the Conference Fund of the University of Alberta, and by the Social Sciences and Humanities Research Council of Canada. The event benefited from the assistance provided by graduate students, technicians, sessional staff, administrative staff, and academics in the Visual Communication Design area of the department.

Personal thanks go to Dr. Jetske Sybesma, department chair at the time of the conference; Stan Szynkowski, administrative professional officer; colleagues Bonnie Sadler Takach and Susan Colberg; and technicians Louise Asselstine and Dave Roles.

I thank the authors who revised, updated, and re-wrote their papers to create the present book. Special gratitude goes to Nicole Potter-Talling and Tad Crawford, of Allworth Press, for accepting this book for publication, and for keeping the press active in the design scene.

Table of Contents

Part IV: Living Spaces as Communication Spaces: From the Home to the City

Part V: The Space of Language and Graphics

Part VI: The Space of Identity

Part VII: The Learning Space

Part VIII: The Electronic Space

Prologue

Papers in this book range from the theoretical to the practical. Some writers ponder basic concepts related to human understanding, while others report on specific projects. The main point of the book is to explore the potential that the attention to contexts has for the planning of communications. Hence, the metaphor of space will appear frequently, with writers viewing the task of the designer as that of creating spaces where the public meets the messages. Notions of space discussed cover sociology, architecture, and of course, communication design and new media. Authors come from different professional fields, and from a variety of geographical places, and their year of birth varies more than forty years. Some authors were invited because they could write specifically to the point of the book, others because they could expand the range of preoccupations entertained.

The title of the book, *Designing Effective Communications*, may suggest a didactic tone. This is not the intent. The purpose of the book is to extend the range of concerns of the communication designer so that, in addition to considering all that is required for the crafting of messages, designers become conscious about the need to be fully aware of and, at times, design the contexts where the messages occur. We hope in this way to contribute to the development of both the theory and the practice of communication design.

Creating Communicational Spaces

Jorge Frascara
University of Alberta, Edmonton, Canada

"Fish are the last to recognize water."
(FLETCHER, 2)

This book is about frames, the frames that surround any and every communicational event. Normally, communication theory has been centered on the processes that take place in a communicational act. These processes have been discussed as part of the transmission of information. But today many of us are aware that for those processes to occur there are several conditions that must be in place. These conditions not only frame the acts, provide a context, a code, and a possibility, but also allow and constrain the communicational outcome.

I have elsewhere already described communication as a constructive rather than as a transmitting act. But there is more. I propose to see the communicational act as something that always happens in a setting, and the communication designer as someone who creates "a space," where the public meets the message. Designers as such have some degree of shaping power, but they must be cognizant of the many dimensions that affect the final outcome of a message. The communication designer is a designer of possibilities for communication; someone who uses existing contexts and adds to them through the best use of existing conditions—and through their modification—to strengthen the communicational power of the messages.

Traditional communication design has been based for a long time on the notion of transmission. Since the appropriation in the 1960s of Shannon's 1940s theory of communication, there has been a sustained effort to analyze the communicational process as one of transmission, so as to define the conditions that must be met to create a clear message. During the recent past, however, it has become more evident that cognitive styles, cultural backgrounds, emotional states, personal interests, intellectual development, and value systems—to name but a few important dimensions—affect the way in which people deal with information. This has led to the idea that communication hinges not only on transmission, but also, and fundamentally, on interpretation. The notion of communicational clarity has, therefore, become relative; there is no single way to make communications clear for everybody everywhere.

Some designers have come to understand that in order to craft the message they must focus on the audience for whom the message is intended. In this context, some writers have begun to talk about communication as a transaction, more than as a transmission, because a negotiation takes place. The task of the designer, therefore, is not that of translating with a view to transmitting, but that of creating "a space," a space where people engage with a message, and develop their interpretations. In other words, designers create conditions that favor the interpretation of a message in a certain—approximately—predictable direction. The task is similar to that of the stage designer: the curtain goes up. There is a certain feeling provided by the space, the objects, and the light that defines the possible, the reasonable, and the plausible. If actors are already on the stage, the cues get richer and more complex. One gets tuned in with a set of conditions within which something will happen. Goffman (496) discusses the point in his *Frame Analysis:*

"Although a stage drama involves figures who are personlike, not cardlike or checkerlike, the gamelike character of these scriptings is enhanced . . . by the tendency of the dramatist to work with a closed resource, that is, a set of characters that makes an early appearance and that provides a sufficient and necessary source for what will probably occur. As with a game, the audience can look to the interplay of these known resources for all relevant outcomes. In this way the audience can be given a sense of commanding witness of the whole of the relevant world, a sense that what turns out to happen could theoretically have been divined from the initial array of figures and forces, as in a riddle" (Goffman, 280). He also cites

Pudovkin as stating that one of the main challenges to the film director is the selection of actors, actors that in a six- to seven-second initial appearance must convey clues to the viewers as to their role in the film.

This ability to predict the future has been discussed by Theodor Lipps at the end of the nineteenth century as a source of aesthetic pleasure. He argued that pleasure is experienced in the realization of an expected activity (Worringer, 4–7). In music, for instance, tempo, melody, and key set expectations for the listeners. If the music delivers within the expected outcomes, the audience experiences pleasure. Think of any piece in particular, Beethoven's *Fifth Symphony*, Rossini's La *Gazza Ladra*, or the Beatles' *Penny Lane*: it only takes two bars for us to accommodate ourselves to what is coming. It seems that we need to create frames for our perceptions, our understanding, and our actions, and that the possibility to create these frames is central to both comprehension and pleasure. Kafka is a clear example of the same phenomenon in literature: one page is enough to get into a given atmosphere, to "understand" the tone and the codes that will take us through a whole novel—no different from the beginning of *Hamlet* or a police thriller.

One of the principles at work here is that people can only understand things that relate to things they already understand. The first time I saw a Swedish film I did not understand it. I was fourteen and tuned into Hollywood productions. The leading Swedish actor was not beautiful, and I spent the whole film waiting for the leading actor to appear. Happiness was a very passing experience in the film, and there was no happy end. I left the theatre without really understanding what had happened. I had gone with the wrong mindset, and I had not understood the clues I was given at the beginning. There seems to be a need not only for a communicational situation to be designed in ways that its language becomes understandable, but also for the audience to have the capacity to understand that language. Hence the power of the assertion: people can only understand things that relate to things they already understand. Our previous knowledge provides us with tools for building the frames that will help us to acquire new knowledge.

Prevailing frames constrain the thinking of people not only in the arts but also in the sciences. Accepted principles play active roles in support of what is considered worthwhile supporting financially or rejecting as ill conceived. The history of science is full of instances of people who "were ahead of their time," and whose ideas were only appreciated many years after their death. Isaac Newton's "Laws of Nature" were regarded as such until others redefined them, and added the conditions under which those "laws" were applicable. The relative character of scientific assertions came to the fore in the twentieth century, when they began to be understood as hypothetical frameworks. Wilden (304) reports that Werner Heisenberg coined the uncertainty principle in physics ("all observations are equally uncertain"), bringing to consciousness the need to be cautious and to pay attention to the framing theories that contextualize any individual assertion. Merleau-Ponty discusses a related topic, when he suggests that the "spirit of the time" affects the ways in which fields of knowledge are conceived and developed. He states that at the beginning of the 1900s the social sciences were in crisis. "Psychology was tending toward 'psychologism,' as Husserl called it, sociology toward 'sociologism,' and history toward 'historicism.' But in the process they were undermining their own foundations" (43–44).

Architects have been conscious of the communicational power of spaces since the beginning of civilization: the Knossos Palace in Crete, the Palace of Versailles near Paris, and the Legislature Assembly Hall in Ottawa physically express and support three different ways of understanding power and government. The Köln Cathedral, the Church of San Miniato in Perugia, and the flamboyant Rococo churches of Salzburg represent three different ways of understanding Christianity and of creating appropriate environments for the religious experience. The Intiwatana in Machu Picchu, in Peru, the Zen Stone Garden in Ryoan-ji, Kyoto, Japan, and the temple of Angkor Thom in Thailand portray three ways of dealing with the sublime. Similarly, I was surprised many years ago when I saw both the Soviet and the American space modules in the Smithsonian Institution in Washington. I went in the belief that functional constraints would force engineers to design something quite similar in both cases. This proved not to be the truth: the Soviet module looked Soviet, and the American module looked American. It seems as if the symbolic language of form powerfully informed the construction of these highly technological products, despite the technical constraints. One could say that there is no object that does not transmit an ideology, or at least, a value system, even if this is more visible in some objects than in others. In every one, however, culture is present and active, affecting the shape of manufactured objects according to expectations of the way they should—or they could—look.

The new technologies have made it quite clear that virtual "spaces" must be made understandable, because they are deprived of the physical dimensions that we are accustomed to. To do this, it is imperative that we devise systems that allow a user to "enter" into a Web site so as to learn how to navigate it, to find content, and to understand it. Some argue that these virtual spaces provide an escape from the constraints of reality. Maldonado (69), writing about the virtual and the real, shows a different view:

"It is likely that new developments in synthetic image creation will greatly enlarge the experimental possibilities in areas of design, communication and art. Theoretically, we can assume that finally the requisite creative means of production will be available with which to implement avant-garde concepts, which to date have remained impossible to implement. It is up to us to whether we decide to keep these new media at arm's length in the name of an ideology of universal immaterialization or whether we make an effort instead to make use of their extraordinary cognitive, artistic, and creative potential for socially productive interaction between man and his world. Not a *fuga mundi* therefore, rather a *creatio mundi*." (Not an escape from the world, but rather a creation of a world.)

This collection of essays discusses things that precede and surround the communicational event. Communications are always situated, that is, they are always in contexts that frame them. If our task as designers is to create communications, and if the various contexts that surround them affect them, then it is obvious that these contexts require our attention.

Life, particularly human life, is a continuing communicational act. We continually survey our surroundings, assess our situations, evaluate their potential, and respond with feelings and actions. We need so much to see what surrounds us that the sheer fact of seeing a wide panorama gives us pleasure. This was first discussed and articulated by Appleton. According to him, the enjoyment of representations of landscape in paintings is connected to those that show wide panoramas. Appleton argues that primitive human groups sought locations to settle where they could see for a distance while having their backs covered, hence, they settled up on the hillsides and in caves. This experience carries into daily behavior, making people prefer situations where a perception of the surroundings (space, time, and information) allows them to foresee what is coming. At a finer level of analysis, according to Gibson, human groups have wandered through spaces for thousands of years assessing what the environments could offer them. He calls this a theory of affordances. We always want to know what things can "afford" to us. We have in this process developed a built-in attitude to see what is there for us, in any situation. Gibson discusses the needs for shelter, terrain, water, fire, objects, tools, and other animals. We can be dealing here with different subjects, but we constantly assess whether or not moves and efforts are worth our while, just as much as our ancestors were assessing what the environments could afford them. Providing a reader with a fast possibility for assessing the personal relevance of a given text or, in the more urgent case of a warning sign, the specific nature of a danger faced, is pivotal in connection with the creation of a disposition to read the text, to understand its meaning, and to follow its contents. Seemingly, it boils down to a powerful principle: we do not perceive because we have a perceptual system; we perceive because we want to survive. Perceiving is not a sensorial act; it is an intelligent act. To survive, we need to understand what surrounds us. The topic of "priming" has been studied in cognitive psychology and in information design: when subjects know what a piece of information is going to be about, they tend to understand it more efficiently, that is, faster and better.

We are surrounded by time and space. Both dimensions can frame communication, as Hall discusses in *The Silent Language*. He reports that department heads of an organization were asked to attend interviews with him concerning non-discriminatory practices. Although these individuals reported being interested in the topic, "appointments were forgotten, long waits in outer offices were common, and the length of the interview was often cut down to ten or fifteen minutes" (2). He reports having been normally kept at a distance from the manager, and only in one case did the person come around from behind his desk. Whatever can be said in those situations is loaded by the information carried by the framing conditions. Bateson dwelled on this in an imaginary dialogue between daughter (D) and father (F):

"D: Daddy, why cannot people just say 'I am not cross at you' and let it go at that? F: Ah, now we are getting to the real problem. The point is that the messages which we exchange in gestures are really not the same as any translation of those gestures into words" (12).

Of course, this is culturally framed. Acting in a public space, one can appear obnoxious to a foreigner but cute to a friend. What might be considered a friendly gesture by a Spanish peasant could be received as an invasion of personal space by a British businessman. Kagan discusses a similar point in *Three Seductive Ideas*: "Our contemporary categories for human personality are based on contrasts that are local to North American and European psychologists in this historical moment" (37). The problem therefore is that not just cultural conditions frame our communicative behaviors; many times they are unconscious to us. The challenge to the designer is, on the one hand, to create the appropriate frames, and on the other, to be conscious of cultural differences that change the meaning of frames from group to group. The reference to cultural differences does not relate to the obvious ones between people in New York and the aboriginals in Brasil's jungle. It relates to the differences that can exist within a given location, such as between advertising executives and fast-food restaurant employees in Manhattan, or between grade-one teachers and extreme-sports fans in Edmonton.

Communication campaigns often fail because of a lack of understanding of the frames within which communications operate. A birth-control campaign in Kenya failed in the early seventies because the images chosen to motivate people to reduce their number of children were ill-conceived in relation to the local culture. What for westerners appeared as positive symbols—a couple with two children in a comfortable surrounding—was read as a sad sight by the local people. In another case, a comic strip sequence that asked illiterate South African miners to keep rocks off the railway tracks also failed, because they did not share the framing assumption that comic strips are read from left to right. One has to distinguish between given frames and designed frames. The designer has the power to prime the viewer through conscious crafting of communicational frames, but must not ignore the cultural and physical frames that already exist in a given situation.

Dixon (cited by Wright) has shown that instructions are followed more accurately when they start by giving the reader a high-level description of the task. That is, subjects understand instructions better when a global description of the task is provided at the beginning rather than at the end of an explanation (Wright, 1.9). Having a general idea of what one will confront, and having it fast, improves our ability to process information. Along the same lines, in a more recent paper, Ruecker argues that rich prospect interfaces, that is, ones that show a large number of meaningful indicators of a database content, facilitate navigation and use (Ruecker, 1). In a different vein, Barthes uses the space metaphor in *The Pleasure of the Text*:

"If I read this sentence, this story, this word with pleasure, it is because they were written in pleasure (such pleasure does not contradict the writer's complaints). But the opposite? Does writing in pleasure guarantee—guarantee me, the writer— my reader's pleasure? Not at all. I must seek out this reader (must 'cruise' him) without knowing where he is. A site of bliss is then created. It is not the reader's 'person' that is necessary to me, it is the site: the possibilities of a dialectics of desire, of an unpredictability of bliss: the bets are not placed, there can still be a game" (Barthes, 4).

Alexander explores the concept of "framing" in his *A Pattern Language*. Architecture for him functions partly on the basis of the expectations of the people. There is a pattern language, he argues, that must be alive and shared by the people who inhabit cities and buildings for those spaces to make sense. He recognizes 253 patterns in that language, something that people store in their memory and that serves to provide meaning to their experience of space. This pattern language allows us to distinguish a beer parlor from a school, from a private home, from a private room in a private home; or a bus stop from a guard's cubicle. When visiting an unknown city, we can thus find our way between residential areas and commercial centers, recreational spaces and sports facilities. Not only does the character of each space "tell" us what it is and how to behave, but also the relations between those sites communicate and condition our experience of the places and our movements within them. He writes: "The movement between rooms is as important as the rooms themselves: and its arrangement has as much effect on social interaction in the rooms, as the interiors of the rooms" (628). In a metaphor that animates the existence of spaces, he adds: ". . . The movement between rooms, the circulation space, may be generous or mean."

Laws and customs are frames. Our adaptation to the culture we live in is based on the successful understanding of the many frames that surround us, and that constantly change through the action of people. People create those frames through action, and through action they modify them. These actions come from the different ways of operating that people master, depending on their type of intelligence. Gardner explores this topic thoroughly in *Frames of Mind*. This diversity of abilities to understand and to act provides the engine for the constant change we perceive; each one of us understanding and acting in a permanent dialogue with the frames within which we build society.

And the grand frame, the global society, is today in a profound crisis of inequality. The rich and the poor have never been so distant from each other, and we have never been so conscious of that distance. But the difference between the Gross Domestic Product per capita of Norway (U.S. $29,918 per year) and of Sierra Leone (U.S. $490) is dwarfed when one looks at the distribution of that income among the actual people (UNDP HDR, 2002). Globally, people living with less than U.S. $1 a day are 1,100 million; undernourished, 831 million; school-age children not in school, 104 million; children dying under age five, 11 million; people without access to improved water source, 1,297 million; people without access to proper sanitation, 2,742 million (Human Development Indicators, UNDP HDR, 130–131). This is the world we live in today: rich and cruel. And this is an extremely challenging frame, one that offers hundreds of opportunities for developing meaningful design projects. Designing within the commercial frame of the wealthy West is fun, and is one of the strategies used to keep this wealth thriving. But there is a great need for taking design to operate within other frames, both inside the wealthy West and elsewhere.

At home in the rich countries, the challenges are stiff: 100,000 people die every year because of medical error in North America; 55,000 die in traffic incidents;

and 2.5 million suffer injuries. Twenty-five percent of the population is functionally illiterate. A culture is in reality a cluster of cultures, and, as Alexander pointed out about architecture, it is a cluster of patterns. Designers have been sharpening their ability to powerfully, precisely, and convincingly communicate the content of many complex messages, but the frames that surround those messages are crucial, and so far we have not paid enough attention to them.

This is what this book attempts to do: look at the conditions that surround different communicational acts, and then bring these conditions, these frames, and these communicational spaces, to center stage. This collection of papers aims to discuss this concept from different perspectives, thereby extending the conceptual frame of reference of the communications designer.

Jorge Frascara
Editor

October 2005

References

Alexander, C. (1977). *A Pattern Language*. New York: Oxford University Press.

Barthes, R. (1975). *The Pleasure of the Text*. New York: Hill and Wang.

Bateson, G. (1972). *Steps to an Ecology of Mind*. New York: Ballantine.

Fletcher, A. (2001). *The Art of Looking Sideways*. London: Phaidon Press, 2001.

Gardner, H. (1983, 2004). *Frames of Mind*. New York: Basic Books.

Goffman, E. (1974). *Frame Analysis*. Boston, MA: Northeastern University Press.

Hall, E. T. (1959–1990). *The Silent Language*. New York: Doubleday.

Kagan, J. (1998). *Three Seductive Ideas*. Cambridge, MA: Harvard University Press.

Maldonado, T. (1994). "Reality and Virtuality." In Meurer, M. *The Future of Space*. Frankfurt: Campus Verlag (59–70).

Merleau-Ponty, M. (1964). *The Primacy of Perception*. Evanston, IL: Northwestern University Press.

Meurer, B. (1994). *The Future of Space*. Frankfurt: Campus Verlag.

Wilden, A. (1987). *The Rules Are No Game*. London and New York: Routledge & Kegan Paul.

Worringer, W. (1911). *Abstraktion und Einfühlung*. Munich: R. Piper. Published in English (1953) as Abstraction and Empathy, New York: International Universities Press. Cited edition: Elephant Paperbacks (1997).

Wright, P. (1994). "Enhancing the Usability of Written Instructions." In *Proceedings of Public Graphics*. Lunteren, The Netherlands: Delft University and Utrecht University (26–30).

PART ONE

Conceptual Frames

Our notions of perception and cognition affect our understanding of the relation between people and their surroundings. The conventional notion of mind as something inside the head can be transformed into a dynamic notion of mind as an in-between construction, one that links people and environments through a permanent process of communication.

This communication process is social, and makes design a social practice, requiring a consciousness of the power that existing social conditions have. These conditions, to make things more complex, are not fixed, but constantly shift in response to the ongoing succession of events, including our own communicational actions. Games are a way of representing and exploring the complex structure of the communicational transactions that take place, in a constantly adjusting balancing act.

CHAPTER ONE

A Gloss on Communication

Thomas M. Nelson
University of Alberta, Edmonton, Canada

Living of life can be regarded as the sum of uniquely human opportunities to flourish and fail, lead and follow, be emotionally up and down, sick and healthy, etc., in consequence of interactions occurring within particular kinds of surround. Living transforms the surrounds in positive and/or negative ways. It has been often said that humans are a part of whatever the surround is and not apart from it. Witness the havoc that has been visited on cod populations off the east coast of Canada by over-fishing. A once magnificent biological resource is no more. The living of life must be based not only on responsible communications at the human-to-human level but at the human-nonhuman interface as well.

The individual's living of life is expressed in both cognitive and behavioral engagements that draw upon internal resources that we call "The Psycho-Biologic Agenda." The Agenda is conceived to be a general operative system having four levels of humanness. These are a) genetic inheritance, b) cultural identification/background, c) personal experience, and d) universal knowledge. Perhaps the first three are more obvious than the last. Universal knowledge refers to beliefs that are accepted by overwhelming numbers of humans everywhere. Examples of universal knowledge would be the belief in logic-mathematical commutative properties: A always equals A; when A is greater than B, B is less than A; when A is greater than B and B is greater than C, A is greater than C. Other examples are physical science's conceptions of the material world; physiological descriptions of organic structure/function; existence of sensory limitations; reality of family structure; evolutionary development of species, and so forth.

We need to recognize the staggering overlap in human agendas. In the same breath, we need to recognize that the agenda of each individual is entirely original, produced by the immensely intricate differences of human populations, which shift continually over time in response to circumstance. The agenda would represent the human being within the framework of an integrated understanding of the social sciences.

Life as lived takes the character of the surround into account. The surround varies in physical, social, and psychological ways. Other humans and social things are the dominant features encountered in most surrounds. Thus, interface with arctic and temperate climatic surrounds challenge living of life in vastly different ways. Communicating with a stranger in a riotous surround forms an interface distinct from communicating with a stranger over a cell phone. Visual symbols of hazard, prospect, and refuge identified by Jay Appleton in *The Experience of Landscape* seem to function by situation. Individual encounter of symbols of hazard in paintings hanging on the wall of a museum of art is not the same as encountering hazards in the teeth of Hurricane Katrina, August 29, 2005.

Minding

Individuals live their lives by expressing their agendas, moment to moment, in interface with their surroundings. The agenda changes so slowly, stage by stage, so that at every moment the individual seems in an equilibrium, which we recognize as "the person." The surround is diametrically otherwise. There is a vigorous dynamism going on outside of us at all times—rain to sunshine, full moon to new moon, war to peace, breakfast table to supper table, christening to funeral. It is the continual renewal of the surround that activates the individual. It is the interface with this surround that drives the living of life. Minding is the sequence of actions whereby the individual is able to make and maintain effective contact with the surround. Minding can be a momentary event or involve protracted transaction(s) such as dialogue, when surround is essentially another human being. Fundamentally, minding fixes the quality of life.

Minding depends upon what can be called the circuit of communication connecting the individual(s) to the mediums in which the individual lives life. Throughout this chapter, the medium for living life has been called "the surround" rather than "the environment" since the latter has come to have divergent meanings. By surround we mean "the physical, biological, and social context in which human life is lived." The mechanism establishing circuits of communication enabling the living of life in whatever surrounds is conceptualized as "minding."

Affordance

Affordance is a concept introduced into psychology by James Gibson in his book, *The Ecological Approach to Visual Perception*. He used the word as a reference to intrinsic properties of items or events from human perspective. Affordances for him were solely physical things communicating "invitational" qualities that prompt action. This included the sit-able property of a chair, or the grasp-able property of a steering wheel, but not socially defined things or events such as "the high five" gesture, etc.

An integrated conception of the social sciences would expand this meaning. Affordances would be made into anything that stimulates and biases the direction of minding. Affordances would enter minding taking both sensory and cognitive roots. Affordance would serve to name all communications from things originating in the physical, vegetative, animal, and human world that for whatever reasons need to be perceived by humans if minding is to be effective. Positive affordances would communicate the presence of and nature of benefits to be realized from maintaining contact and negative affordances the dangers inherent in maintaining contact.

Affordances would be uni- and bi-directional. The sound of an automobile horn at a busy intersection provides a uni-directional affordance minded as a warning. A bi-directional affordance might be the simple utterance "Look!" that directs a companion's vision to sale items in a store and that prompts the companion to say "Looks interesting."

Each affordance is dealt with as a single structure capable of triggering minding. But, an affordance possessed by an object does not necessarily stimulate the same minding in every circumstance. An ice-cream cone sign possesses a greater affordance on a summer than on a winter day. An umbrella is a stronger affordance on a rainy than clear day and more likely to trigger minding. Also, affordances can compete with one another. Availability of both lemon and apple pie on a food counter is an example. In addition, patterns of responses to affordances often are immensely complex. There are innumerable affordances that trigger a form of minding that represents ecological sensibility, that is, objects and events that elicit responses based on a sensitivity to the surroundings.

In the absence of affordances, there is no minding. Investigations of sensory deprivation show that individuals become unable to direct thought or action effectively in the absence of stimulation or where stimulation is of a very low order.

Communication of Affordance

Some affordances reflect hard-wired communication. These have been called "natural sign-tokens" (NST) by Henry Leonard in *Principles of Reasoning*. Such represent purely physical (non-cognitive) objects or events to which the individual is sensitive and which trigger minding. NST communicates affordances that lack an intended party, lack an individual engaged in token selection, and lack need of another person to convey their meaning. Thunder is an NST affordance communication. The blast from an auto horn is not.

Visual communication design depends upon creation of "deliberate sign-tokens" (DST). They are cognitive representations created within a particular social context. Systems of signage created by the International Standards Organization (ISO) have been created to convey safety information through a culture-free medium. This is a prime example of DST affordance communication. DST in common with NST is one-way communication. Usually, but not always, DST employs learned symbols. Printed letters represent culture-bound DST.

Neither NST nor DST communication encompasses dialogue, the exchange of ideas or opinions about an issue. Without stretching too far, weather with gusts of wind, rain, scuttling clouds (each of which is a NST) combine into a "natural dialogue-token" (NDT) serving to structure the minding of the series of affordances.

Conversation involves sentences structured around subject, verb, and adjective. Each such sentence element is a DST by itself but in the context of the sentence as a whole it is only one portion of a "deliberate dialogue-token" (DDT). The minding of a sentence is intended to provoke new minding on the part of the individual targeted. Minding triggered by DDT may continue for an undefined period of time. Thus, the sentence, "The weather is terrible," may induce only brief dialogue in contrast to legal dialogue released by an accident or by the question, "What should be done about poverty?"

DDT can be operational on a nonverbal level; consider the dialogue called "road rage." In the case at hand, a driver experiences discomfort from tailgating (in isolation, a DST). If the driver increases speed to increase space between the two vehicles and the tailing vehicle immediately resumes the same close proximity, the lead driver may take offense and begin minding the action as a negative DST. If the lead driver then responds by minding the action as an incivility and delivers a negative DST, such as the abusive finger gesture to the driver of the rear vehicle, a dialogue of violent character can ensue. Therefore note that the presumed road rage resulting is a DDT that is a consequent of a series of communications of negative affordance, solely.

In sum, communications of affordance guide the living of life and impart to it a qualitative character—whether it is "good" or "bad." Affordance may occur singly or be bundled together as properties of an entity or event. But, affordance is always positive or negative in valence. Affordances are never neutral since they trigger minding of the living of life. The living of life always matters to the minding individual. In addition, constellations of affordance may be a positive and negative mix, as in the case of deciding a stock market investment.

Psychological Concerns

In this final section, psychological concepts that appear critical to understanding the agenda (individual) accurately from an integrated social sciences perspective are briefly reviewed. Let's begin our survey of psychology in *The Oxford English Dictionary*. It makes "minding" a verbal form of the substantive, "mind." Etymological research reverses the order. The word has been defined as "mens," a verb meaning "to think," "to remember," "to apply oneself." Verb forms of this original term frequently appear in the other branches of the Indo-European family of languages. We employ the term minding in the original sense of being a verb but in our case the verb minding is defined as action(s) that enable the individual to make and maintain effective contact with the surrounds.

Minding is activity that takes place in the world as the human interfaces with the environment. Minding honors James Gibson's admonition "don't ask what's in your head but what your head is inside of." Psychology, as we all know, tends to seek explanations of human behavior in the interior of the body as in mind, mental states, or in the machinery of the body, as in neuro-physiological functioning. As Gibson implies, in psychology the functioning of the human individual is conceptualized as if the human is independent of the world, for the most part. This is not, of course, entirely true of all psychology. The study of sensory processing and learning reveals minding. On the other hand, the areas of personality and clinical psychology provide little apart from "in head" explanations.

Starting at the point at which the verb minding departed toward today's mind, we find the idea "nous" credited to Anaxagoras (428 BC). This ancient philosopher is said to have proposed the existence of an inexhaustible supply of a transcendent sensory/perceptual/rational awareness that humans share. He imagined this to be an actual substance originating in an ageless, external, intelligent and purposive material nous. Plato and Aristotle denied nous this material character to make it a spiritual final cause. Plato, for instance, proposed the presence of physical, biological, and spiritual realms and restated nous as a purely teleological and completely immaterial principle of human ration originating in a godhead. He proposed the human to be the scion of the deity—the godhead's favorite form of life. Thereby Homo sapiens became the only species possessing spiritual reality, an idea that has confused our identity with nature and hobbled our bond with other mammals ever since. Aristotle seems to have agreed but asserted nous to be synonymous with reason when regarded as passive in the case of sensing, and as active and creative in the case of perception. From later, highly convoluted, speculative, briefly surviving schools of philosophies reflecting Hellenic ideas of the individual, the religions Judaism, Christianity, and Islam emerged. These, while keeping the original spiritual idea intact, proceeded to build unitary but conflicting ideas of the intent of God. Theology focused upon "soul" and, secondarily, upon what it means for soul's corporeal representative "mind" to engage in saintly behavior. Religious groups have continued into the present to consider mind as an endowment of deity and support theologies that stress the obligation of each human mind to accept and obey commandments of their particular form of a transcendental power. Failing to obey commandments, they are to know what punishments to expect and the proper way to atone when shirking these.

Mind was passed on to worldly philosophers in the seventeenth century. Rene Descartes, the "father of modern philosophy," is most important. He is responsible for separation of the human into a material body and an immaterial mind. All other forms of life he left as mindless machines operating on purely mechanical principles. Thus, the mind-body distinction of Descartes continued to separate humans from other primates. Our inheritance of this is the continued controversy about whether other species think, feel pain, imagine, and other such confusions. An upside to the Descartes' bifurcation was the encouragement of biological science investigations. A downside was that Descartes' distinctions settled philosophy and, eventually, psychology, into quagmires that both still struggle to escape.

Experimental psychology is said to emerge in Leipzig, Germany, in 1879. It was to inherit mind as an object for scientific investigation. Early efforts were dedicated to temporal measurements of mental processes in some laboratories and to discovery of the contents of mind in others. Much data was obtained from the introspective analyses of consciousness. But, difficulties swiftly ensued and mind became associated with the brain or shunned entirely, as in the case of behaviorism. Then, rapid advances in neural science began mid-twentieth century. These have led some psychologists to re-visit mind in the hope that it will prove possible to identify neuro-cognitive mechanisms giving rise to mental states. This vein of exploration recently has become known as "evolutionary psychology" (EP). It assumes that at least some mental states are based on natural adaptations reflected in the brain. However, concern has been expressed that EP could be developing explanations built on sand by inadvertently linking body mechanisms to ideas of mental structure that are intellectually bankrupt (Fodor). Others deny this possibility (Barton; Thompson). It is hoped that future EP will direct attention to minding.

An integrated notion of the social sciences can have less tolerance of mind. This idea can impose culture-bound constraints on the understanding of global issues. "Mind" has been chained in large part to speculations developed within the Indo-European family of languages. Traditional Chinese science and philosophy opposed the supernatural speculations so formative of the concept "mind" (Agren). In the same era as Anaxagoras and Plato philosophized, Confucius taught anti-dualism. Also opposed to mind is the Chinese belief that the fundamental quality of the human is an organic interaction taking part of human, nature, and government (MacKay).

Chinese and other Asian explanations of human behavior thus differ fundamentally from ideas of western psychology. The Indian sub-continent is an exception to a degree. The word "minas" is close to mind and did indeed originate in the ancient Indo-European language Sanskrit. Many other religions of the sub-continent, however, create a palimpsest that defies summary (MacKay). Present-day Buddhism teaches that there is only the one reality and that it is spiritual (Goleman). This ontology puts cause out of the everyday world and all we sense and experience moment by moment becomes illusion.

Psychology is a hard nut for an integrated conception of the social sciences to crack, because it follows the age-old practice of putting the living of life in the head. It is time, we believe, to recognize where *the mind* has been located for the last one hundred years—since the time of William Morris—primarily in the brain. This information processing system is inarticulate physiology that has been and continues to be a mystification of the living of life. *Mind* must not be confused with *minding*, which relates to the interaction between people and their surrounds and therefore, puts communication at the center of the human agenda.

References

Agren, H. (1998). "Chinese ideas of mind." In *The Mind*, Gregory, R.L. (Ed.). Oxford: Oxford University Press, 243-45.

Appleton, J. (1975). *The experience of Landscape*. London: John Wiley.

Barton, R. (2005). "Letters to the editor." *The Times Literary Supplement*. London: TSL Education, 15.

Fodor, J. (2005). "The selfish gene pool." *The Times Literary Supplement*. London: TSL Education, 4–6.

Gibson, J. J. (1979). *The Ecological Approach to Visual Perception*. Boston: Houghton-Mifflin.

Goleman, D. (2003). *Destructive Emotions*. London: Bloomsburg.

Leonard, H. S. (1967). *Principles of Reasoning*. New York: Dover.

Lister, D. (2005). "Applying social science research to solving problems of modern nations: problems and pitfalls." *Psychological Reports*, 96, 779–804.

MacKay, D. (1998). "Indian ideas of mind." In Gregory, R.L. (Ed.). *The Mind*. Oxford: Oxford University Press, 357–61.

Thompson, G. (2005). "Letters to the editor." *The Times Literary Supplement*. London: TSL Education, 15.

CHAPTER TWO

Games: A Transactional Context

Sharon Poggenpohl

Institute of Design, IIT, Chicago, IL, USA, and School of Design, Hong Kong Polytechnic University

Communication was not a theorized space until after World War II, it was just something we did. Both Claude Shannon's seminal model of communication and Norbert Wiener's model of feedback dealt with the technical transmission space for communication. From the beginning of communication theory, attention focused on technical aspects and broadcast models in which the recipient of the communication was presumed to be passive. All that was necessary was to use understandable codes (language, symbols, images) with which the recipient was familiar. Since those early days, many communication models have been developed that deal with various perspectives on communication, including discourse models that seek to establish rapport; gratification models that attempt to sustain interest; innovation models that promote behavior change; and context models that seek to recognize and plan for the specific conditions in which a communication occurs. With these models the varieties of ways in which communication was received and interpreted came to the foreground, but the variables that influence any particular person's interpretation remain daunting and undiscoverable in their totality.

Since the early days of theorizing communication in which the noise to signal ratio dominated attention, the context in which we communicate has changed due to increased technical reliability, extended capability, and the proliferation of media. Now, we need to pay particular attention to the context in which communication occurs. Context encompasses the interrelated conditions in which something exists or occurs. Conditions alter context in many ways through their presence or absence, the degree or quality of presence or absence, through interaction with each other or other conditions that may occur in a range from constant to rare. The idea of context contains a multitude of dimensions, some obvious, and some obscure.

One might well ask, "What is a transactional context?" These are situations in which communicative action occurs between persons or persons and things that reciprocally affect and influence each other. For example, face-to-face conversation between people forms a transactional context of considerable complexity. Sample context conditions are presented in table 2.1.

Table 2.1 Sample conditions in a face-to-face conversational context

Personal	Inter-personal	Topical	Contingencies
Communication goal	Knowledge of the 'other'	Knowledge of topic	Time available
Interactive style	Willingness to share/negotiate	Other's presumed knowledge	Degree of privacy
Mood	Past history with the 'other'	Orientation (disciplinary)	Attention
Body language	Projected future with 'other'		Distractions
Physical well-being	Hierarchical relationship		Interruptions
	Network connections		

This list is cursory, but what is clear is the extraordinary number of interconnections between any of these conditions within and across categories. Even with this cursory list, the combinations across categories provide over a hundred particular contexts. If the communication has a critical nature, a political negotiation for example, every attempt would be made to control these conditions through removing contingencies, providing orientation to the topic through public and private media, ensuring interpersonal familiarity, and personal preparation. Even with such preparation, the outcome remains uncertain, as its transactional nature is dynamic. While there are rules of political etiquette, these rules can be suspended or ignored. The resources for possible exchange may not be fully disclosed and the real objective may be hidden. What the preparations accomplish is a smoothing out of the process so that attention is focused on substantive communication and adjustment to it based on feedback.

The key to a successful transactional event is feedback, interpretation, and the possibility of repair to misunderstandings or failures to communicate. In face-to-face conversation, the participants are simultaneously engaged in a multi-level reading of each other, while they make mental connections to new ideas, call from memory previous ones, and select words, emphasis, style, gesture, etc.

This chapter looks at games as a communicational space from three perspectives: 1) as a means to envision possible futures, 2) as a new form of prototype for complex planning situations, and 3) as an interactive space in which decision making is enhanced. In essence a game is a competitive or collaborative event that takes place within a transactional context.

Envisioning the Future

Designers envision various futures. Their instruments for doing this are scenarios, prototypes, and even the humble spontaneous drawing or diagram on a napkin. These instruments are about externalizing an idea so that it can be examined and opened for discussion (Poggenpohl). Scenarios, prototypes, and games have different attributes. What is most telling is the evolutionary nature of the game (see table 2.2).

Table 2.2   Comparisons between scenarios, prototypes and games

Instrument	Thingness	Human Connection	Nature
Scenarios	Story	Identification with characters, and situations	Discrete
Prototype	Object	Use and interaction	Discrete
Game	System	Conversation, play, and decision making	Evolutionary

Designers are not the only people who try to develop ideas for the future. Anyone constructing a budget is trying to identify income and expense to better plan how to manage resources to reach some goal in the future. Anyone planning a vacation is considering time and money, mode of transportation, accommodation, language difficulties, passport needs, sights to see, and much more to ensure future pleasure. The budget might be done by one person and have a simple set of relationships. The vacation plan has many intersecting relationships and might involve several people with competing desires. Plans for the future come in various degrees of complexity and alter from a few to a significant number of people's lives.

Prototyping with Games

Returning to scenarios and prototypes, these are, for the most part, singular ideas about the future. While there may be several of them, they tend to be discrete and not in themselves dynamic—they are like snapshots. Plans for the future often involve multiple people and the situation for which they plan might be unpredictable, full of contingency, and dynamic. No individual has god-like control in such a circumstance and often there are competing aspects within the plan—one can have more of A, but only if one is willing to give up some of B. Or one can achieve a particular goal only if other individuals compromise their goal. In such situations a game could be a more satisfying model with which to project a future, as game play is evolutionary and dynamic.

Games are found in all cultures and they have a deep history (Avedon and Sutton-Smith). They are attractive and intrinsically rewarding because they are a closed universe of possibilities defined by their objective and rules to provide a communicational frame in which skill, strategy, and chance are at play. Further, games are fabrications in which risk and alternative behaviors can be explored as the winning or losing is not forever.

Games unite thought and action, with the action prompting feedback from an opponent who recognizes a missed opportunity or envisions and acts on a revised strategy that will compensate for an earlier challenge. "Reduced to its formal essence, a game is an activity among two or more independent decision-makers seeking to achieve their objectives in some limiting context" (Abt, 7).

Enhancing Decision Making

We make decisions all the time, some small and some large, some with little impact beyond ourselves and some with substantial impact to others' lives. It is possible that big decisions, made in situations of uncertainty, can be better understood through gaming. If multiple people need to be onboard for a decision, gaming can help expose various positions: who is willing to compromise, what can be negotiated, or when consensus is viable. Ordinary citizens are called upon to participate in decision making as they serve on juries or planning and parole boards. The decisions they are called upon to make are serious and stressful. The situations in which such decisions are made involve much interpersonal influence and argument.

Having now established the perspectives from which games are investigated, we move to a sharper focus on games themselves.

Gaming and Its Technical Aspects

One scholar investigating play (Sutton-Smith) identifies types of play in terms of rhetorics. The ancient rhetorical forms of play are: play as fate, power, identity, or frivolity. The modern forms are: play as progress, the imaginary, or self-fulfillment. To these I propose a new, perhaps postmodern, category: game play as the unwinding of complexities for future projections. What is this new category based on? It is based on the need to explore the complex interrelatedness of civilization's sustaining systems such as education, criminal justice, fire and police protection, business development, taxation, political representation, civic infrastructure . . . the list could go on and on. These subsystems do not exist in isolation but have both positive and negative influence on other subsystems based on decisions made to enhance, redirect, or limit development in any one of them. Yet decisions are often made and action is taken without consideration of the interrelatedness of these systems. There is also a wealth of statistical data that shows the consequences of decisions. For example, is there a relationship between the acquisition of job skills in prison and a negative rate of recidivism? If yes, should more resources be devoted to job training? What are the comparative costs to society of job training during incarceration as opposed to the continuation of criminal activity upon release? Such relationships can be examined in terms of resource or cost or in terms of social values or how the social contract is defined. Citizens serve on planning and zoning boards, for example, and while well meaning, they may not have the experience or expertise to grasp the interrelated systems for which they will make decisions. Further, it may take significant time to understand other board members' values, allegiances, and practical perspectives.

The game play I am imagining deals with civic systems in competition for scarce resources (whether monetary or goodwill). Objectives, performance measurement, interrelatedness, patterns of past statistical performance, social values, the presence or lack of a charismatic leader, and overall strategy are present in the game. In this way decisions can be examined in terms of likely consequences, and once acted upon, feedback in terms of the reaction of other game players with other values or resources open the just recent past to amendment. The game is played on the scale of a small city or self-sufficient village.

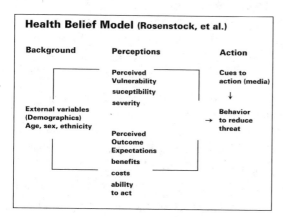

In a way, the game imagined has a deep and flexible memory of past performances (statistical resources), sharpens the present context of decision-making, and projects a future through decisions taken that elicit immediate human feedback (see figure 2.1). The game progresses on the idea that ". . . the first principle of effective decision

Figure 2.1: The game as imagined with structures moving across past, present, and future

making [is] that the decision maker must have a stake in both the costs and benefits of a decision" (Lewis). The game as imagined helps participants to make informed decisions, as they better understand the interrelatedness of various systems. There is no perfect strategy for making decisions in a dynamic context in which uncertainty and contingency are fully operational. The game as imagined is an opportunity to learn about the interconnectedness of civic systems, the outcomes of previous decisions, and the overall difficulty involved in making good decisions in a complex situation.

While the game space described may seem complex, it has credible and even larger scale forerunners. In 1969, Buckminster Fuller developed the World Game, based on a world resource inventory, behaviors, trends, "vital needs, developmental desirables and regenerative inspiration" (222) to use Fuller's own words. The goal of the game was to provide a sustainable physical and metaphysical success for all humanity. This is in contrast to war gaming, predicated on the British Empire's first inventory of vital statistics of the world assembled by Thomas Malthus, professor of political economics, in 1805. War gaming assumes an inadequacy of life support on the planet and also assumes Darwin's survival only of the fittest as its evolutionary model. The World Game's accounting system is not monetary but instead is based on the universe's own time-energy intertransforming requirements (Fuller). It is interesting to note that Fuller recognized the World Game as a continuing scientific research complemented by physical prototyping (Fuller).

The greatest attention in Fuller's game is to physical resources and energy. Fuller was an engineer and technologist and a self-described design-science revolutionary. An optimist and big thinker, his position was that "spaceship earth" had adequate resources for life support for everyone on the planet, if only we would think big and give up the nation-state as an outmoded form of governance. His book *Critical Path* includes a description of the World Game; there he briefly recognizes human fear of the unfamiliar (Fuller) as a problem for his projected future. Like many utopians, Fuller hungered for a totalizing conception of the good, which if enacted could well be oppressive. We are now critical of twentieth-century totalizing schemes, even if framed in the most benign and well-meaning way.

World Game, as developed by Fuller, is a game in support of decisions to enhance human life on this planet in a technical sense. Technical decisions can be accepted or overturned based on rationality, logic, or scientific evidence. What Fuller avoided was the human component of game play that is essential and complex.

In contrast but also at a large scale, the Model United Nations is an interactive role-playing game in operation worldwide at universities, high schools, and online. In this game, students represent a particular country after absorbing the country brief. They learn the procedure within the security council, develop skill in resolution writing, caucusing, and consensus building. Based on human interaction and persuasion, issues are argued, coalitions are formed, and decisions are made within the simulated structure of the United Nations. The game is very fluid and dependent on the knowledge and communication skills of the players.

World Game and the Model United Nations are at opposite ends of the gaming spectrum. The former is based on physical-technical information and on a top-down approach to decision making, while the latter focuses on human communication and interaction and is based on a bottom-up approach to decision making through negotiation and consensus building.

Recognizing Human Aspects of Game Space

Games can be approached as containing technical skills one wishes to master or as opportunities to interact socially. For example, some chess players prefer to play the computer (remember "Big Blue") and some prefer to play a human adversary. The experience is different as the computer may play an intellectually challenging game, but cannot effectively stall, bluff, or look for sympathy.

Games provide a conversational space in which we try on behaviors that perhaps don't come easily to us: for example, aggression or collaboration, negotiation or nondisclosure. In the context of the game we get immediate feedback from others in terms of their social response or game response, both of which are revealing and dynamic. Games can be a structure in which we get acquainted as they require participation and they provide a ritual to sustain interaction. Through this participation we learn something about the values and strategies of our opponents and even ourselves.

What exactly can we learn from games? On a personal level, we learn how to adapt to circumstances and be flexible in how we think. We also learn to develop strategy and consider alternatives and their impact on short- and long-term goals. Anticipation of our opponent's response also figures prominently in play. On a human level we have an opportunity to become more sensitive to human interaction and exchange—to pay attention to the goals of others and look for opportunities to compete or collaborate. Games can also foster recognition of the variety of human motivations and possible behaviors. On a technical level, we develop the ability to assess the impact of various moves. We also develop an overview of the game through seeing the interconnectedness of its elements (see table 2.3).

| **Table 2.3** | Games and social and technical learning |

Personal Actions	Human Interactions	Technical Skills
• adapt to situation	• be sensitive to others	• assess strategies
• be flexible	• observe other's goals	• develop overview
• think long & short term	• recognize variety of	• understand
• anticipate	motivations	interconnectedness

Constructing Games

Information is no longer scarce—we are awash in it—there is too much to process. Once it was thought that good and reasonable decisions could be made if only there was sufficient information. Now a great deal of information is available, but it still requires interpretation, pattern-finding, and synthesis to be useful. The game concept under discussion moves in this direction.

Games appear to be simple constructions only when they are complete. The number of closely intersecting variables makes them difficult to construct. Games consist of an objective, the goal of the game; a structure of play, the possibilities for skill, chance, and strategy to develop; rules, the contract for play; and content, the ideas at play. These basic game elements are not just technical, they condition the social space within which players interact. The objective provides a unified focus for all players; the structure of play reveals game possibilities and combinations; the rules provide a foil against which misunderstandings or conflicts can be decided; and the content gives meaning to the event (see figure 2.2).

It is often a good idea to begin with a known game structure (board game, cards, etc.) and then to modify it. The benefit of this approach is that the game is playable at an early stage (see figure 2.3). Because game development is necessarily iterative and interactive with users, getting something playable early is important (see figure 2.4). Tuning the content so that it is not too easy or too difficult, and has some dimension of surprise can be another challenge. Structuring the relationship and balance between chance and skill requires fine-tuning. Both of these relate to the game's timing. Too much information to process (cognitive load), too long an interval between turns (pace) courts boredom. Likewise, infrequent surprise or a game

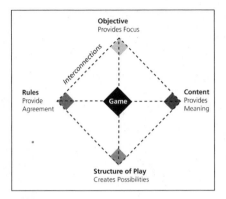

Figure 2.2: Basic game structure

Figure 2.3: Image of an early prototype with recognizable borrowed game elements

Figure 2.4: Early play with a quickly conceived physical game form

that is too predictable also brings boredom. Games cannot be constructed in a vacuum; their development requires frequent play and its observation. We learn from the game players—the users—their engagement and frustration. The constructive process fairly demands iteration and user interaction. Game construction requires an interesting combination of systems thinking and off-the-wall creativity.

Given the rich communication context of games, their necessity to be progressively prototyped and played by novices in order to improve, I gave a graduate workshop on games in the spring of 2003 at the Institute of Design, IIT in Chicago.

Designing Specific Games

The goal of the workshop was to consider and develop games as an exploration and communication space in which future plans can be entertained. Games are typically either competitive or collaborative. The former has a clear system of measurement and a winner or loser with psychological benefit or cost attached. In the latter, the game has increased social interaction and possibility for social learning through negotiation. Games are motivating because they deliver fast feedback and can deal with interrelated, reciprocal processes. They engage players in working with incomplete information, complexity, and uncertainty that characterize life situations.

Two game outlines were offered: one for adults and one for middle school children. The adult game addressed the complexity and interrelatedness of civic spending and possible social outcomes. It is related to both Monopoly and the economic idea that you can have guns or butter, but often not both. The adult game dealt with competition for scarce resources, i.e., money and goodwill. Social decisions whether to support more spending on education or the development of increased law enforcement, for example, are the kinds of decisions to be made. A list of social systems for consideration on the level of a small city was provided along with the proviso that taxes must be collected to fund development.

The children's game addresses the future through considering who they are and what job they might have as an adult. The number and character of possible jobs was overwhelming, so locating the game geographically was entertained as a way to limit and focus the search for jobs. An example of each is given: NewLondon, an adult game, and Sitka, a children's game.

NewLondon

NewLondon is a board game that explores the interrelatedness of social decisions and their consequences as made through negotiation. In this way various behaviors and decisions are tied together and possible outcomes are sampled. Continuous decision making and strategy development make the game challenging; every move positions the player closer toward winning or losing. Collaboration and negotiation figure in the game action as individuals need to trade game elements (see figure 2.5).

The game has a role-playing aspect in that the four players take on different roles: futurist, capitalist, spiritualist, and environmentalist. Each has a mission to fulfill that is different from the others and sometimes comes into conflict with the others. The goal is to build a city through strategically using taxes, money, people, service infrastructure, and the leader's particular building mission. For example, in the case of the environmentalist, such things as parks, public transportation, and a zoo are to be constructed.

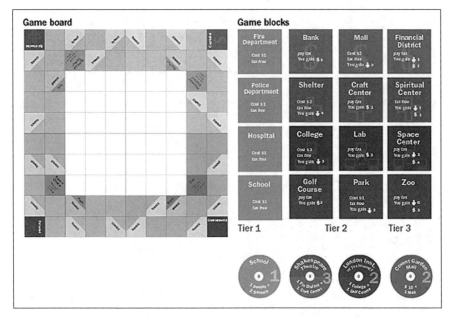

Figure 2.5: Game elements for NewLondon

There are four tiers of building that the player must move through progressively with prerequisite buildings in each previous tier. The tiers structure progressive achievement and play. And play gets personal as the current player can adjust the tax rate for the next player.

Many adjustments were made to the game as it was played, based on a changing prototype. One of the most continuous adjustments was what can be called the "economy" of the game. What is something worth, how much money does a player need to operate, how many people are needed, etc. In this way the closed universe of the game is established—challenge is maintained, things are not too easy, but they are not impossible either. Drawing an analogy to communication space, it is like establishing a conceptual frame for a discussion in which certain topics and perspectives are expected while others are excluded; how often discussion is summarized; in what ways participants receive recognition for their contribution. Pace and cognitive load is a more subtle aspect of the economy of the game as played. If a turn takes too long, opponents may lose interest—if there are too many factors to tally or too many discrete actions in a turn, players may get confused, edgy, or frustrated. Likewise in a communication, using an obscure vocabulary or jargon, developing an intricate logical argument that few can follow, or generalizing out of context may stop communication completely. Another subtle aspect of economy is the relationship between strategy and chance—if either dominates, gamefulness is lost (see figure 2.6). In a communication space, partic-

	FIRST TIER ▶		SECOND TIER ▶			THIRD TIER ▶			CAPITOL
	You need to provide basic services to your town. They don't cost too much and they don't generate money or people. The services you build will help your community from adversities. You will need to have at least 2 services on your community in order to start building Tier 2 things.		Now that you have your services built, you want to start building your community based on your leader type. You should have the cards of the things you are able to build. They are color coded and you also have them written on your leader card. In order to start building your third tier item you should have built the two items from this tier. (with two of this you can build one third tier item)			Now will earn people and money.. You have noticed that you need items you don't have in order to start building in the capital. You will have to start negotiating with other leaders in order to get them. Make sure you get a good deal. remember that the stuff you have no one else has so you can set a good deal to sell them!			This is the last stage.. Only by building things in the capital you will gain capitol points. The one who earns more capital points is the one who wins. In order to build in the capital you will need to have some items built in your community. You can look at the board and see the requirements needed
	It costs		**It costs**	**By building a**	**You will earn**	**It costs**	**By building a**	**You will earn**	
Capitalist ($)	$1 Fire Department $1 Police Department $1 School $1 Hospital		$2 $4	Museum tax free Bank pay tax	= [person] 6 = $12	$9	FACTORY pay tax	= [person] 2 $20	
Spiritual (+)	$1 Fire Department $1 Police Department $1 School $1 Hospital		$2 $2	Seminary tax free Public TV tax free	= [person] 6 = $4	$5	CHURCH pay tax	= [person] 10 $4	
Technologist	$1 Fire Department $1 Police Department $1 School $1 Hospital		$3 $4	College tax free Hotel pay tax	= [person] 8 = $8	$8	LABS pay tax	= [person] 3 $16	
Environmental	$1 Fire Department $1 Police Department $1 School $1 Hospital		$2 $3	Park tax free Public Transp pay tax	= [person] 4 = $6	$5	ZOO pay tax	= [person] 6 $12	

Figure 2.6: The economic structure of NewLondon

ipants who stay too close to an expected script become boring, while those who use an analogy or who have a unique perspective on it challenge or enliven the discussion.

The physical nature of the game, its various prototypes as it developed, were not inconsequential. The game must represent the player's achievement, the opponent's development, and the score as it unfolds. Whether this is represented clearly is at issue. Interaction between the physical game and the players prompt-

Figure 2.7: An early NewLondon prototype

Figure 2.8: The final NewLondon prototype in play

ed other kinds of adjustment: the score for each player needed to be visible to all; the scoring system needed to be simple and automatic; negotiation needed to be open and exploratory, but tied to a player's turn. The free-form style of negotiation revealed in surprising ways how different players perceived what is valuable. Deciding on what is visible and what is hidden is another way to tune what is important in the game, i.e., what the players must think about and attend to. The changing game prototype altered the communication space in visible ways (see figures 2.7 and 2.8).

Sitka

Sitka is a card game for fourth to sixth grade students that could be used in a social studies class, since it is based on Alaskan traditions. It provides a humorously competitive atmosphere in which students think critically and creatively about real regional issues in a socially interactive setting. Game content is based on actual current events drawn from online news media. The goal in this game is to balance information set in an unusual context with surprise and fun—to differentiate it from card games that are either trivial or bluntly scholastic. Sitka immerses players in the trials and tribulations of an unfamiliar society. Storytelling is an important element in Alaskan culture because it saves and enriches native language as it passes important stories between generations. Players accomplish challenges by assembling Skill cards that consist of people, skills, and tools, and from these the player tells a story of how these components meet a challenge.

Game Elements

Community: this is the primary structural element of the game—it is an abstraction of people, tools, and challenges that are present in the setting (see figure 2.9).

Figure 2.9: Card layout as Sitka's "community"

Skill cards: these are the people, skills, and tools that comprise the units of action in the game. Players hold Skill cards in their hands and use them to fulfill challenges. For example, a challenge may require a participant (a fisherman), skills (navigation), and tools (knife) for completion (see figure 2.10).

Challenge cards: these are situations in Sitka that need the players' help.

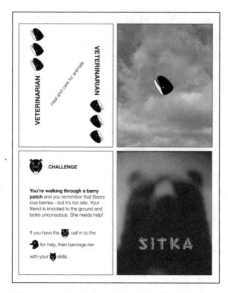

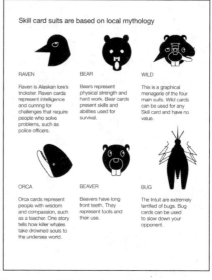

Figure 2.10: Varieties of "help" to be found in Skill cards and the nature of a Challenge that sets the stage for action

Figure 2.11: Sitka's suits and their meaning in relation to play

Calamities are Challenge cards that are always bad luck for the player who draws them. Winning is determined by adding up the number of heads in a particular suit as represented on the Skill cards that a player uses to accomplish their Challenge. The game ends when a player accomplishes three Challenges.

The cards are divided into four suits based on local mythology. The Raven is Alaskan lore's trickster. These cards represent intelligence and cunning for challenges that require people to solve problems. For example, a police officer appears on a Raven card. Orca cards represent people with wisdom and compassion, such as a teacher. Bears represent physical strength and hard work; these cards are skills and abilities used for survival, for example, hunting. Beavers have long front teeth—these cards represent tools, for example, a tranquilizer gun.

In addition to the four suits, there are two other cards: *Wild cards* are a graphic menagerie of the main suits and can be used in place of any Skill card. They have no value. *Bug cards* can be used to slow down opponents—the Inuit are terrified of bugs.

The game was developed through numerous prototypes with play observed by the game creators as a means to refine the possibilities of play. Game validation pushed the game to further refinement through play by age-appropriate children.

Sitka demonstrates how many different kinds of jobs help to create a community able to address its specific challenges. For more information regarding the game's development and rules for play see *http://id.iit.edu/*

Conclusion

Games create a communication space in several ways: the nature of games themselves are a constructed communication space; the interactive creation and refinement of games by teams of designers and multiple players engages a communication space analytically as individuals act as observer, listener, creator, collaborator, player, opponent, etc.; and finally the nature of the two game examples discussed that focus either on competition and collaboration (NewLondon) or competition, cultural exploration, and storytelling (Sitka) reveal some of the specifics of game space. Games structure communication and provide a ritual for shared exploration, learning, and discovery. As a scaled-down model of some aspects of life, games can reveal aspects of reality that may remain hidden in everyday life or in the serious context of "real" decision making. "Games" are a prevalent metaphor used to describe situations of subtlety or complexity in many aspects of life. What is suggested here is that games should be seriously considered as an exploratory tool for making complex decisions.

References

Abt, Clark C. (1970). *Serious Games*. New York: Viking.

Avedon, Elliot M. and Brian Sutton-Smith (1971). *The Study of Games*. Huntington, NY: Robert E. Krieger.

Fuller, R. Buckminster (1981). *Critical Path*. New York: St. Martin's Press.

Lewis, H.W. (1997). *Why Flip a Coin? The Art and Science of Good Decisions*. New York: Wiley.

Poggenpohl, Sharon (2002). "Design Moves: approximating a desired future with users." In Frascara, Jorge (Ed.). *Design and the Social Sciences: Making Connections*. London: Taylor and Francis.

Sutton-Smith, Brian (1997). *The Ambiguity of Play*. Cambridge: Harvard University Press.

PART TWO

The Space
of Information

Our experience of the world is mediated by codified information. The shape of a drop of water as we know it is not physically accurate: it is a cultural icon coined on the basis of a perceptual illusion. The information designer explores the spaces created by existing information, evaluates them, and constantly extends them, in search for improving the accuracy of the information exchange. Sometimes this is done on the safe terrain of existing codes, aiming at international and cross-cultural communications, but sometimes the call is for highly customized, individualized tools that open possibilities for populations with special needs.

CHAPTER THREE

Where Am I?

David Sless
Communication Research Institute of Australia, Melbourne, Australia

The purpose of this book, to discuss the importance of contexts in communication and explore the metaphor of "communicational spaces", struck a chord. In 1985, just as I was setting up the unit that eventually became the Communication Research Institute of Australia (CRIA), I finished a book—*In Search of Semiotics*—in which I wrote: "My search for an understanding of communication has led me to consider . . . a metaphor based on the idea of a landscape within which are located both the researcher and the object of study. How the landscape appears to the researcher depends very much on the position from which he views it; as the position he occupies changes so does the scene, and as certain views become visible, others disappear." (Sless 1986, 31)

I used this metaphor throughout the book, developing what I called a Logic of Positions to describe the strict inexorable relationship between the texts we create (using the term "text" in a broad generic way) and the texts we read. My principal interest was in the academic study of semiotic systems, but as I became immersed in the practical research, which CRIA was commissioned to undertake—redesigning forms, insurance documents, etc.—I discovered the very real practical relevance of the Logic of Positions in helping us at CRIA understand and influence the communication landscapes in which we found ourselves working. At the time, I had very little opportunity to write a major paper documenting this discovery, but I managed a brief critical exploration of some of the implications of the Logic of Positions as it affected Cultural Studies, Social Semiotics, and Social Survey Research (Sless 1987). I returned to the topic in a later joint paper (Sless and Shrensky) in which we teased out how the Logic of Positions came into play at the boundary of what is and what is not communication. But I have never given an account of the relevance of the Logic of Positions to communication and information design. This book offers the ideal opportunity to do so.

The Beholder's Experience

The beholder's experience of a work of art—what the beholder sees—is not a result of separate items: the artist's presentation, then the beholders' share, then the experience. On the contrary, it is an indivisible unity—a whole that is more than the sum of its parts. Moreover, it is a logical and psychological unity. Just as there can be no flight without air—air making the flight possible—there can be no experience of a work of art without the joint contribution of the artwork and the beholder. This logical and psychological unity manifests itself in a compelling way. Look at the image in Figure 3.1.

If you have seen this demonstration before, you may have the necessary beholder's share to bring to the experience. If you have not seen it before, you may not see what the artist is presenting you with. Figure 3.2 will give you the schema (to use Kant's term) that you can bring to what you are being presented with, and return to Figure 3.1. The resultant experience is compelling, vivid, and, importantly, persistent. You can no longer see the incoherent blobs of black and white, only the coherent image. The fact that its coherence is a product of the share or schema you have brought to it is not separable from the overall experience. Moreover, you cannot return to your state of innocence. There is no going back. Despite your memory of a previous innocent experience you cannot undo what has been done. This is the compelling magic of the commonplace. But like all magic, it is a mixture of good and bad. Good, because it means that once you have

learnt to look in a particular way, you don't have to relearn it. This gives your experience coherence and meaning. Bad, because its persistence makes it very difficult for you to see things anew or from the point of view of others who may bring their own distinctive share to their experience. Quite literally, you cannot see things from somebody else's point of view.

Figure 3.1

Using the metaphor of a landscape, each of us occupies a slightly different position in the landscape because of our differing social and psychological histories. And, from these different positions, the landscape before each of us is different.

From Art to Communication

It struck me, and many others, that, if this is true of a work of art, it is also true of other forms of communication. Our reading of a book, for example, is a combination of what the writer presents us with and our own expectations. The same is true of a movie, a poster, a timetable, a map, indeed any form of communication. Thus Gombrich's insight following on from Kant is relevant at the most general level of our description of communication. Indeed Kant was referring to all types of experience, not just communication. People each bring their own expectations—their share—to experience in general.

But there is something distinctive about communication as an experience that separates it out from other forms of experience. To tease out what this might be, my colleagues and I looked at a number of cases that hovered at the boundary between communication activity and naturally occurring phenomena. The most famous of these was the discovery of pulsars (Hewish; Sless 1981). Because the pulses generated by the astronomical phenomena are so regular, the researchers who first discovered them speculated that the pulses might be a signal from a distant civilization. However, once they accepted that there was a satisfactory physical explanation, they abandoned the idea of a signal.

Sometimes, fascinatingly, things hover ambiguously between communication and non-communication, as in the case of the wink/twitch (Sless and Shrensky). Imagine sitting in a train and the man opposite you closes and opens one eye quickly while looking straight at you. Is he winking at you or twitching? By analyzing this example carefully, we have been able to show the subtle nature of the boundary between communication and non-communication. The difference between treating the phenomenon as communication or as non-communication turns out not to be a characteristic of the phenomenon itself but rather a characteristic of our description of the phenomenon. Put another way, it is what we—experiencing the phenomenon—bring to its apprehension: the beholder's share again.

In the case of communication, when we read something as a text, we apply a quite specific schema that implies a notion of an author. We do not need a clear idea of who the author may be, what their purpose or intention was, or the nature of the message they wanted to present. If we believe something to be the product of an author then we treat it in a distinctive way. We try to make sense of it in a special way, quite different from the way we would try to make sense of it if we regarded it as a natural phenomenon. Treating something as communication leads us to ask questions about intention and semiotic systems. Treating something as a natural phenomenon leads us to ask questions about causes and effects, a quite different type of inquiry leading to quite different descriptions and explanations.

Equally, as the author of texts (using the term "author" in a broad generic way), we imply a notion of a reader. Again, this notion can be quite vague, and often is, but the presence of this implied or inferred reader is a defining characteristic of communication from the author's point of view. There is thus a symmetry between the author and reader positions. But, importantly, these are different positions in the communication landscape, and the presence of the text both joins and separates them.

An Emerging Logic

So far, the logic that emerges has two components: an author/text with an implied reader, and a reader/text with an implied author. One of the basic characteristics of these two components is counterintuitive—their irreducibility. Even though we can talk as if authors, texts, and readers were separate entities, in the emerging logic the smallest units of analysis are the author/text/implied reader on the one hand, and the reader/text/implied author on the other hand. Claiming the irreducibility of these entities marks a radical departure from our normal way of talking about these things and conducting research into the nature of communication. In ordinary conversation we talk about authors, readers, and texts as separate entities. In research we traditionally distinguish between studies that focus on the creators of texts, such as biography; studies that focus on an analysis of texts, such as social semiotics; and studies that focus on readers of text, such as psychology. The logic of positions slices the cake in an altogether different manner and in many ways challenges the validity of these traditional discipline boundaries.

But the logic of positions goes further. As there are only two basic positions, and no outsider position, there is no scholarly position of neutrality or objectivity: one is either an author or a reader already embedded within the process. I have undertaken a number of studies to illustrate this as it has been applied across a range of modalities in the published communication studies literature (Sless 1980, 1981b, 1983a, 1983b, 1985, 1986a, 1986b, 1987, 1988, 1994). Even when researchers claim to be studying text on its own the shadowy implied authors and readers are always present plus a little old fashioned magic in which inanimate objects make people do things. For example Hodge and Kress make the following observation about a billboard: "The text itself is of a scale and kind which *implies* the use of significant material resources. The availability of such resources *is understood by the reader* to be a precondition of the production of such a text and that *gives the text* a particular status . . . and places the reader in a particular position" (Hodge and Kress, 9, my italics).

Notice how Hodge and Kress make the text itself vaguely animated, as if capable of action—doing things to people. The text "implies," and it "places the reader." Hodge and Kress also tell us how the billboard is "understood by the reader." This illustrates one of the common rhetorical devices that researchers use to imply their own neutrality; they introduce another shadowy persona into their study of texts: the implied other reader. This is a fascinating construction that appears to do the work of reading for them. Sometimes in social semiotics these implied entities take on the persona of an entire culture. Far from being scholarly and detached, such research is populated by fictional (implied) other readers and authors. It is easy to demonstrate that these are highly subjective works of fiction, more so than a personal account of one's own reading of a text. Scholarship more subjective than personal accounts—a radical claim! But the question that we need to answer in any study of communication is not whether we are being more or less subjective—we have no choice but to be subjective, in a sense—rather, what position we are in and how explicitly and rigorously do we give an account of the implied readers and authors that inevitably populate our accounts.

The Designer's Position

All the above thinking was done before I began my work investigating through CRIA the application of communication and information design processes in large organizations. When I began this later work, I was well primed to look for these shadowy implied readers and authors. I was also keenly conscious that as a designer I was already embedded as a part of the authoring process.

The work we were asked to undertake by both government and industry was to make their communication with the public more user friendly. Thus right at the heart of our work is a highly explicit construction of an implied reader. This is not new; large organizations are used to working with other implied readers. For example, many bureaucrats when drafting a form for public use ask themselves what a judge in court would make of a particular usage, what the internal information processing needs require, or what their superior's point of view might be. But "the public," "citizens," "consumers," "customers," or "clients" are new implied readers requiring a new outlook. First, there is the political issue of a formerly unrepresented constituency having a voice at the table. Second, there is the equally political issue of whose notion of the implied reader is to prevail? Third, is how to demonstrate that the new implied reader is being catered to. To many in politics and the bureaucracy the third issue has been dealt with by introducing plain language. We are skeptical (Sless 1993–1996); the plain English style or writing genre, like any authoring process, contains an implied reader. In the case of plain English it is a simplified construction of the reader and the reading processes. But what constitutes evidence that plain English is an inadequate solution to a complex communication problem, and more generally what kind of evidence is acceptable from the designer's position within the communication landscape about the user-friendliness of a document?

Using the Logic of Positions we analyzed the various types of data and data collection methods available to us. As suggested above, the data from semiotic analyses provided some interesting speculation, useful perhaps at a preliminary stage, but not useable as evidence. In government and business, focus groups and surveys are popular sources of data on how people react to documents, but how useful are these types of data? If one looks from our position as information designers relative to this type of data, the first thing we notice is that we typically have access to the data via a report. In other words, there has been a chain of author/text and reader/text relations between us and the data. It is possible to open this up a little further in detail. If we start at the point where the data is collected we can notice first that the person being interviewed is often being asked to give an opinion of a document, but not necessarily using the document at the time. Thus the person interviewed creates a text, an account or story about their use of the document. Moreover, because they are creating their story for the benefit of the interviewer, there is an implied reader of their story. The interviewer takes this text— the person's story about their use of the document—and constructs another text— their report of the interview. This report of interview is a text with an implied author—the original storyteller—and an implied reader—the person who will compile all the interviews into a report for the client, the next implied reader in the chain.

Finally, the information designer reads the report from the other end of this long chain of invented entities, which may or may not in some respects correspond to the actual readers and authors. From the designer's position in the landscape, most of these entities are invisible and it may be tempting to imagine that reading the report gives the designer direct access to the people who use the document. As this analysis shows, this is far from the case, and it makes no difference whether the data is qualitative or quantitative—a flowing set of narratives or a collection of mini narratives that have been classified and counted—the result is the same: fiction is built on top of fiction, construction and reconstruction occurring at every point. In the typical survey or focus group there are some five opportunities for such construction and reconstruction to occur between the reading of the document in the first instance by the public and the reading of the account of that reading by the information designer. Not much good data here from the point of view of the information designer.

Some researchers, in an informal attempt to give their clients a more veridical sense of the data, encourage clients to view research behind a one-way-mirror. Leaving aside the ethical issues involved in watching people in this way—issues which we take seriously and hence never allow to come up—there is a technical problem created by the Logic of Positions. Interviewees in this situation usually know that they are being observed. They construct an implied reader—an imaginary audience for their performance. Yet again, there are multiple opportunities for construction.

After considering these alternatives we eventually came to the view that the best type of data for us to collect was of individual people actually using the documents in our presence with our prompting, asking them to use them in specific ways that interested us and talking with them about their experience as it unfolded in our presence.

We would make no claim that such a process is somehow objective or neutral. We are in these conversations engaging directly with people as part of a conversation, not as part of some scientific experiment. But we would argue that there are fewer opportunities in this type of conversation for constructing implied authors and readers. Moreover, there is the direct opportunity to correct the quality of one's data before using it to take action. We would, therefore, want to claim that this type of data is of better quality than any other available to us. It is important to emphasize that it is we, as information designers, who are collecting these data. This in itself marks a break with the traditional division of labor between studio-based designers and researchers. Ours is no longer only a studio-based practice.

Position and Politics

As I have already suggested, the Logic of Positions enables us to analyze a political aspect of information design. This goes beyond recognizing that there are different views of implied readers and authors within organizations, to helping us develop ways of managing these differences in the interest of an appropriate outcome for the public. One of the perennial issues we deal with in large organizations is the diverse range of persistent schema that people use in reading texts and constructing implied readers and authors. Many of these schemata are unhelpful in developing documents that the public can use. But as we saw with Figure 3.1, the effect is compelling. Once people "see" something in a particular way, it is very difficult to change, even more so if they are unaware of what they are doing in terms of applying schema with implied authors or readers. If dislodging a schema is important, we will invite a client to sit in as observer in our conversations with the public. This can often be a turning point, an epiphany.

Where it is not possible to do this, we try to deal with each interest separately. If we bring everyone together in a committee, they will argue about what each one "sees" without a capacity to "see" from somebody else's point of view. The result is often poor decision making. Nonetheless, sometimes these unhelpful schemata prevail and the resultant decisions can seriously jeopardize the outcome.

Position and Humility

Finally, the Logic of Positions imposes a strict discipline on our decision-making. The communication landscape we inhabit allows us to see some part of the landscape but not all. We do not have a god's eye view, only ever a partial view from which some things are not visible and can only be inferred, and whatever we do see is constructed by the assumptions and expectations we bring to the act of seeing. This requires us to proceed with great professional humility. The steps we take across the landscape of communication must always be careful, measured, and cautious. But our work in this landscape is often a direct intervention into its fabric. We not only inhabit the landscape but through our designs we change and transform it. It is as if our footsteps reshape the landscape as we walk across it—

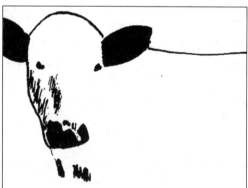

adding hills and valleys. Here the metaphor of the landscape becomes distended, literally! Nonetheless the metaphor serves us well, and by analogy reminds us that we need to look after the diversity and values of our communication landscape in the way we might look after the physical landscape we inhabit.

Figure 3.2

References

Gombrich, E. H. (1968). *Art and Illusion*. London: Phaidon Press.

Hewish, Antony (1968). "Pulsars." *Scientifc American*, vol. 219 (4) 25–35.

Hodge, R. and Kress G. (1988). *Social Semiotics*. Cambridge: Polity Press.

Kant, Immanuel (1781). *Critique of Pure Reason*. Translated by Norman Kemp Smith London: Macmillan 1929.

Sless, D. (1979). "Image design and modification: an experimental project in transforming." *Information Design Journal* 1 (2) 74–80.

Sless, D. (1980). "What is the meaning of the message?" *Science for a Sustainable Society:* Communication Papers given during the 50th Jubilee Congress of ANZAAS 1980. Adelaide: ANZAAS 34–46.

Sless, D. (1981a). *Learning and Visual Communication*. London: Croom Helm.

Sless, D. (1981b). "Photographic meaning: an introduction for teachers." *Working Papers on Photography* 8, 7–18.

Sless, D. (1983a). "Discourse, speculation, and the media." *Media Information Australia* 28, 16–17.

Sless, D. (1983b). "What we make messages do." In Smith III, T. J. (Ed.) *Communication in Australia*, Selected Papers from The Second National Conference of the Australian Communication Association. Warrnambool: Warrnambool Institute Press and Australian Communication Association.

Sless, D. (1985). "Whose image?" In Smith III, T. J., Osborne, G. and Penman, R. (Eds.) *Communication and Government: Issues Policies and Trends*. Canberra: CAE Press 120–136.

Sless, D. (1986a). *In Search of Semiotics*. London: Croom Helm.

Sless, D. (1986b). "Whose agenda? Whose meeting?" *Media Information*, Australia 40, 21–23.

Sless, D. (1987). "A matter of position." *Australian Journal of Communication* 12, 9–28.

Sless, D. (1988). "Forms of control." *Australian Journal of Communication* 14, 57–69.

Sless, D. (1993–1996). "Problems with plain language." Communication Research Institute of Australia Web site. Downloaded 6 April 2005 from: *www.communication.org.au/cria_publications/publication_id_52_187155692.html*.

Sless, D. (1994). "Who am I, Where am I, What do I Understand?" In Borland, H. (Ed.) *Communication and Identity: Local, Regional, Global*. Selected Papers from the 1993 National Conference of the Australian Communication Association Canberra: ANZCA 6–16.

Sless, D. and Shrensky R. (1995). "The boundary of communication." *Australian Journal of Communication* 22 (2) 31–47.

CHAPTER FOUR

Visual Information about Medicines for Patients

Karel van der Waarde
Brussels, Belgium

This article illustrates the relevance of visual design in relation to the provision of information for patients about medicines.

Situation: Four trends in medicine-taking are: an increase in medicine use, an increase in costs, unsatisfactory compliance rates, and an increase in the number of medication errors. The combination of these four trends shows a gloomy future: medicines will become even more expensive and even less effective.

Question: Could the provision of visual information affect these trends?

Approach: Information about Prescription-Only Medicines that is currently provided to patients was analyzed and discussed with patients. The aim of the discussions was to establish the differences between what is factually provided and what is actually needed.

Results: Patients identified twelve different activities that must be undertaken to take prescription-only medicines at home. These twelve activities need to be optimally supported by relevant, clear, and memorable information. The current supply of information does not achieve these criteria. This poor performance can be explained by reference to economic, social, technological, legal, and historical factors. It is necessary to reconsider some fundamental assumptions about patient information in relation to these five factors in order to improve visual information for patients.

Scoping the Issues

The main aims for taking medicines are to cure disease, to manage chronic conditions, to prevent ill-health, and to enhance the quality of life and well-being. Taking medicines has become an integral part of human life in the Western world. Four sets of figures point to the future of medicine-taking. These are related to demographics, costs, compliance, and medication errors.

In coming decades, it is very likely that consumption of medicines will increase. More medicines are taken by each individual, more people are taking medicines, and a greater variety of medicines will become available. Medicine use will be increased further by demographic trends: an increase in the percentage of people aged sixty-five and older, due both to an increase in average life expectancy and an increase of the number of elderly people.

A second set of figures shows how much medicines cost to society. In Europe, the cost per person differs from country to country: from 201 euro (U.S. $240) in Denmark to 445 euro (U.S. $535) in Switzerland. Expenditure on medicines as a percentage of the health budget varies from 7.8 percent in Norway to 25.0 percent in Portugal (Tinke and Griens). It is expected that these costs will increase by about 9 percent per year. Direct costs are exacerbated by hospital admissions due to non-compliance, or adverse drug reactions (Col, Fanale, and Kronholm; Heath). Of course, taking medicines has major benefits as well: people are able to continue their normal activities, and medicines improve the quality of lives; these factors should be considered in relation to costs to provide a more balanced economic perspective.

A third group of figures is variously described as adherence, concordance, compliance, or persistence. It provides an insight into the "actual use" of medicines. These figures indicate what proportion of medicine is taken in such a way that optimum benefit is achieved. The Cochrane Collaboration and the World Health Organization have published figures about compliance, which suggest that 50 percent of medicines for chronic conditions are not taken according to the instructions (Haynes, McDonald, and Garg). Even medical professionals (301 interviewed) only follow the prescribed regimen in about 80 percent of the treatments: 77 percent for short-term medications, and 84 percent for long-term medications (Corda, Burke, and Horowitz). It should be noted that there are several different kinds of non-compliance, and there is no standard for measuring it (Vermeire, Hearnshaw, Van Royen, and Denekens). The research was neatly characterized in 1992: "After decades of compliance research, very little consistent information is available, except that people do not take their medications as prescribed." (Morris and Schulz). This is still true today.

A fourth group of figures concerns errors with medicines. The report *To err is human* has once more focused the attention of the medical profession on this topic (Institute of Medicine), pointing out that between 44,000 and 98,000 people in the U.S. die every year because of medication errors. Although these extrapolated figures may need to be verified, they clearly indicate that medication errors are fairly common and very costly.

All four groups of figures still need substantial research into methodology as well as into validity-related issues. Differences between EU countries and between different groups of patients especially need attention. But even if these figures are wildly incorrect, they show a worrying trend.

The Role of Information

The importance of the relations between medicines and information started to be taken seriously from around 1970 onwards. Before that time, the medical world was skeptical about any possible benefits of providing patients with information, and was scared of the potential dangers. Information is now seen as an integral part of treatment (Haynes, McDonald, Garg, and Montague) and good information is part of good communication between healthcare providers and patients.

Providing appropriate information is likely to have several effects. Despite the variation in quality, topics, methods of delivery, and evaluation criteria, some conclusions about the effects can be drawn (Kenny et al).

- Information increases knowledge about medicines. Better informed patients can participate more actively in their own treatment, and better informed patients ask better questions (van Haecht, Vander Stichele, and Bogaert).

- Patients simply like to receive information (Trewin and Veitch). Patients are happier when they are given information. The supply of information increases patient satisfaction.

- The counter-arguments that providing patients with information has detrimental effects, such as the exchange of medicines among patients, or inducing side effects by suggestion, or increasing inappropriate use, have not been found to be correct.

However, information is only one of the factors likely to influence medicine-taking behavior and it must be understood that the supply of information on its own does not modify compliance. Examples of other factors are: physician-patient communication, patient anxiety, the complexity of the regimen, forgetfulness, ignoring medication when feeling better, and apprehensions about side effects. A meta-analysis of sixty-four studies showed that not a single strategy appeared to be best (Peterson, Takiya, and Finley). In other words, it is worth looking at visual information, but it should be realized that it will only be a part of a possible positive development.

User Experience Diagrams

User experience diagrams are used to map actions of users in different contexts. The actions of patients in relation to their medicines can be analyzed in this way. Figure 4.1 shows the five steps that patients experience when they have to obtain and use Prescription-Only Medicines (POM). This diagram was developed as a meta-analysis of around 300 patient interviews undertaken between 2000 and 2003 (Van der Waarde).

There are many other contexts in which medicines are used. This diagram shows only one particular situation: it is only for those medicines that are used at home. Other contexts of use, such as hospitals or emergency situations, are not included. Figure 4.1 only shows the perspective of patients. The views of other stakeholders, such as doctors, pharmacists, pharmaceutical industry, and regulators, are not dealt with in detail. And figure 4.1 is only applicable for POM. Other types of medicines, such as medicines that can be bought without a prescription, herbal medicines, and medicines bought without a prescription via the Internet, are not included. The user experience diagrams of these other situations are very different.

Patients receive information in each of the steps. In step 1, there might be advertising or items on television, radio, or in printed media. Brochures are sometimes available and patients could consult Web sites or telephone help lines. The doctor and pharmacist give information in both oral and written formats in step 2 and 3. The visual information that is available in step 4 is presented on both the outer pack as well as on the patient package insert. Each step in this diagram is interesting from an information design point of view, and each step can be investigated.

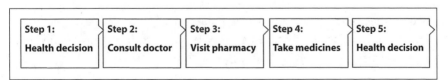

Figure 4.1: The process of obtaining and using prescription-only medicines consists, according to patients, of five consecutive steps.

What Do Patients Really Want to Do?

This article focuses on step four of the diagram in figure 4.1. A patient has been to a physician who prescribed a medicine, or multiple medicines. These medicines have been collected from a pharmacy and a patient has returned home. Usually, the medicines are put onto the kitchen table or dining table and the visual information is observed.

At this point patients should be able to take medicines correctly. Doctors (mainly oral advice), pharmacists (mainly oral advice and labeling) and pharmaceutical industry (packaging and leaflet) have all provided information. After arriving home, patients need to read, remember, recall, and transform this information into actions. Although physicians, pharmacists, and industry do their utmost best, it is still not certain that patients can take medicines correctly.

These problems have been reported in a recent study in the United States, which concluded that it is necessary to address the unmet needs of physicians, pharmacists, and patients (Law, Ray, Knapp, and Balesh). This study did not describe these unmet needs in detail.

The interviews with patients revealed the reasons why this supply is not optimal, and what the actual needs of patients are. During the interviews, patients mention several activities that they want to do, and they clearly indicate what kinds of information are required. At least twelve activities need to be undertaken. These are listed below.

Activity 1: Familiarizing and Identification

One of the first things patients need to be able to do is to find out what a medicine is for: the therapeutic indications. Unfortunately, at the moment, these are rarely mentioned on the outer packaging of prescription-only medicines. Only the name of the active ingredient and the proprietary name of the medicine are provided.

Secondly, there needs to be a relation between the medicine, the package, and the package leaflet. Especially when patients receive more than one medicine, it is essential that patients are able to keep product, package, and insert together. If there is no visual relation between these three artifacts, it is unnecessarily difficult to see them as a group.

Activity 2: Locating a Starting Point

It is not very clear where to start reading. There is not an obvious sequence in which information can be read. Neither on the packaging nor on the package insert is a clear starting point indicated. This becomes even more complex if the oral information from both doctor and pharmacist need to be compared with the visual information. The reliability and trustworthiness needs to be considered. In other words, the starting point needs to be made clear and an information hierarchy needs to be established.

Activity 3: Checking

A patient needs to be able to check whether a specific medicine is suitable and applicable to an individual situation. The contra-indications ("Do not use if . . . ") and the precautions ("Be careful if . . . ") need to be checked. Although most of these points should have been discussed during the consultation with a physician (step 2 in figure 4.1), it is unlikely that all details are dealt with in sufficient detail. Information about contra-indications and precautions needs to be provided to patients as an opportunity for an additional safety check.

Activity 4: Deciding

A patient has to make at least two decisions. The first decision is to weigh the benefits and the potential risks of side effects of taking a particular medicine, or combination of medicines. Jungermann states that there are at least two elements that influence this decision: the ways in which things can go wrong, and the incidence with which this occurs. For this reason, it is necessary to mention the frequency indicators, such as "rare," "seldom," and "very rare." A second decision is to consider the risk of "not taking" or "postpone taking." This depends, amongst other factors, on the type of medicine. Medicines with direct personal risks such as oral contraceptives, or medicines for which the risk is not directly obvious, such as insulin injections, need to be treated in a different manner.

Activity 5: Taking Medicines

Taking a medicine itself can consist of many separate activities. It is clear that patients organize their medicine-taking around their own priorities (Britten). Both the integration of a regimen into daily life, as well as the actual detailed actions, need to be considered. Preparing a glass of water to swallow tablets, blowing a nose before a spray, preparing an inhaler for the next dose, diluting an aerosol solution are all examples of different activities that need to be done correctly before a medicine can be taken. All these activities depend on the personal situation, location, and convenience.

Activity 6: Learning and Understanding

Understanding the way the medicine is effective in treating or preventing illnesses is the educational value of information. Patients want to know how a medicine works. This type of information is beneficial and highly appreciated by patients (Vander Stichele).

Activity 7: Recognizing and Noticing

A separate activity is the recognition of symptoms if and when they occur. This should also include information about experiences that indicate that a medicine is working. Again, this is not appropriate for all medicines, but if it can be told, it should be.

Activity 8: Remembering

Patients have to remember many relevant details about their medicines. Examples are: remembering to take, remembering side effects ("Which ones are so important that I should call my doctor immediately?"), remembering interactions with food ("Can I drink grapefruit juice?"). Although it is likely that important information is emphasized by doctors, pharmacists, and the leaflet, is unlikely that patients would remember all information.

Activity 9: Consulting and Referring

Patients need to be able to consult information again to check details. Patients expect normal visual pointers, such as a clear visual hierarchy, prominent headings, and a clear paragraph structure. When package inserts get longer, a contents list and an index need to be considered. Cross references to Web sites, brochures, telephone help lines, and the addresses of patient groups are considered essential, and their absence in the current information supply is not appreciated by patients.

Activity 10: Reacting

Patients need to be able to react appropriately. Patients do not want to disturb either physicians or pharmacists unnecessarily, but it is not easy for a patient to decide the relevance of professional advice in uncommon circumstances. "Inform your doctor" or "tell your pharmacist" are common phrases, but they do not express how urgent such advice is, or how immediately it should be sought.

Activity 11: Storing

Storing medicines safely is necessary, especially if the collection of medicines becomes larger. The current packaging and multiple-folded, lightweight paper insert makes it difficult to store. Repacking a medicine and its insert into its original package is nearly impossible.

Activity 12: Disposing

Not all medicines are used until the packaging is empty. Many medicines are stored in bathroom medicine cabinets for future use. Eventually, these need to be discarded and it is at the moment not clear how to do this. Some pharmacists offer this as a service, but there is no indication on the box how to dispose of medicines safely.

It is clear that not all activities are equally important for all types of medicines. It is also clear that this list is not in chronological order. It is likely that both the order of importance, as well as the chronological order, change according to the type of medicine.

Until we support patients in these twelve activities, information for patients about medicines—when patients take prescribed medicines at home—is not optimal.

Influential Factors and Assumptions

The underlying reasons that patients receive poor visual information at the moment can be traced back to five influential factors: economic, social, technological, legal, and historical. These five factors have an indirect influence on the information supply to patients and the way in which this information is visually presented.

Economic

The combination of low-compliance and increasing costs creates a negative financial balance. Ideally, the costs should go down and the compliance should go up.

The costs are currently controlled by a combination of several insurance-systems and governmental institutions deciding on medicine prices. These systems vary from country to country and from product to product. The result of this is that large parts of a population do not pay the full price for their medicines.

On the other side of the equation is low-compliance, which means that a substantial part—up to 50 percent—of medical products are not used to their optimal effect. Providing accurate and supportive information might increase the correct use of medicines. And, at the same time, information about the pricing systems of medicines might make people aware of the real costs.

Social

The relation between patients and health-care systems is shifting from a paternalistic mode (patients should obey prescription and be compliant) to a team approach (patients are part of the treatment team). In order to participate successfully in these teams, patients need to receive suitable information and be able to provide information. Expressing the experience of symptoms and telling healthcare providers about the integration of medicine taking in daily life has become essential. Patients need to be supported in this area.

Technological

Technology has altered the ways in which patients search for information about medicines. Telephone help lines, Web sites, and e-mail user groups are just a few examples. These developments are hardly acknowledged in the current legal framework, and very often are severely criticized by the medical and pharmaceutical profession. Despite this, patients use these "new" technologies to search for information about their medicines.

Legal

The developments in the European Union and the development of a worldwide pharmaceutical industry have increased the number of regulations. Most of these regulations favor accurate information for patients about medicines. For example, EU Directive 2001/83/EC states: "*The provisions governing the information supplied to users should provide a high degree of consumer protection, in order that medicinal products may be used correctly on the basis of full and comprehensible information.*" The basic regulations are in place, but unfortunately, this law is not enforced. Patients simply have a right to be informed, but the enforcement of this law proves difficult in practice.

Historical

A fifth factor that influences the quality of information for patients is related to the historical development of information about medicines. The tradition has not favored clear information for patients. Breaking with these traditions takes a lot of time and effort.

Approaching these Issues

In order to provide patients with good information, and taking the above mentioned five factors into account, it becomes possible to redefine some assumptions. Five of these starting points are:

a: Start from the Perspective of a Patient

It is essential to see the provision of information as a single process from a patient's point of view. The trustworthiness, reliability, and accuracy of sources are changing in such a way that it becomes essential for all stakeholders to provide transparent information. Patients need to know who the originator is and what the motivations for providing information are. The information seeking behavior of patients should be the basis for any development.

b: Not a Single Stakeholder Approach: Cooperation

Industry, patients, doctors, pharmacists, and regulators need to coordinate their efforts. A good example of this is provided by the recent developments of regulations in Australia (Sless and Wiseman; Sless).

c: Not a Single Step: Consider the Whole Process

The solutions need to be integrated into a larger scale. It is necessary to look at the whole process of obtaining and using medicines (figure 4.1). It is also clear that situation (home, hospital, emergency), duration of use (single use, continuous use, intermittent use), pharmaceutical form (inhaler, tablet), age (children, elderly), personal situation (pregnancy, family) all affect the way information is required. Information about medicines needs to consider all steps in every context. This implies that blanket regulations that are valid for all medicines are unlikely to be effective for all contexts.

d: Not a Single Development: All Areas Need to Be Considered Together

Relying too heavily on a single factor might not be beneficial. All five factors need to be considered and balanced. Ignoring the current factors that hinder the development of adequate information for patients leads to failure.

e: Not a Single Artifact: All Information Artifacts Need to Be Coordinated

The current supply of information is presented on a host of artifacts: leaflets, boxes, brochures, Web sites. . . . None of these is suitable to provide all information at all times. It is necessary to decide which artifacts are most suitable and consider the combination.

Monitoring Changes

One of the essential elements in any process of change is to monitor vital criteria. Three relevant and measurable outcomes are costs, appropriate use, and errors. All three are notoriously difficult to measure accurately. Methods to accurately describe these criteria need to be developed further.

It should be noted that none of the list of influential factors, nor the list of starting points is directly related to the design of visual information. These lists provide the reasons and excuses for the poor state of affairs at the moment. These reasons are, however, not valid for patients who want to take their medicines properly. Visual information is essential to support patients in all twelve activities. The suggested starting points indicate that it is possible, but that it will take substantially more effort of all stakeholders to achieve an acceptable standard.

Conclusions

In order to modify the visual presentation of a single leaflet, it is necessary to consider both the requirements of patients and the underlying reasons for the current presentation.

Interviews with patients revealed that information is not treated as a single experience. If we want to support patients in their decisions about using medicines, it is essential to provide this information at the most suitable time, in the most suitable format. At least twelve activities need to be supported. The importance of each activity and the sequence in which these activities are presented need to be carefully developed. Not all activities are equally important for all medicines and it is likely that the sequence of these activities depends on patients and the type of medicine.

The underlying reasons for the current presentation need to be considered. All five factors—economic, social, technological, legal, and historical—must be taken into account before any changes can be made. Taking these factors into account will lead to an adjusted set of starting points in which patients are put in the center of the development of visual information.

References

Britten, N. (2003). *Does a prescribed treatment match a patient's priorities?* British Medical Journal. Oct 11. 327 (7419), 840.

Col, N., Fanale, J. E., and Kronholm, P. (1990). "The role of medication noncompliance and adverse drug reactions in hospitalizations of the elderly." *Arch Intern Medicine.* 150(4), 841–845.

Corda, R. S., Burke, H. B., and Horowitz, H. W. (2000). "Adherence to prescription medications among medical professionals." *South Medicine Journal* 93(6), 585–589.

Directive 2001/83/EC (2001). "On the Community code relating to medicinal products for human use." Official Journal of the European Communities. L311, 67–127.

Haynes, R. B., McDonald, H., and Garg, A. X. (2002). "Helping patients follow prescribed treatment: clinical applications." *JAMA.* 288(22), 2880–2883.

Haynes, R. B., McDonald, H., Garg, A. X., and Montague, P. (2002). "Interventions for helping patients to follow prescriptions for medications." Cochrane Database System Revised 2000. (2): CD000011.

Heath, I. (2003). *A wolf in sheep's clothing: a critical look at the ethics of drug taking.* British Medical Journal. 327, 856–858.

Institute of Medicine (2000). *To err is human. Building a safer health system.* Report available from: http://books.nap.edu/books/0309068371/html/index.html

Jungermann, H., Schultz, H., and Thuring, M. (1988). "Mental models in risk assessment: informing people about drugs." *Risk Analysis* 8(1), 147–155.

Kenny, T., Wilson, R. G., Purves, I. N., Clark, J., Newton, L. D., Newton, D. P., and Moseley, D. V. (1998). "A PIL for every ill? Patient information leaflets (PILs): a review of past, present and future use." *Family Practice.* 15(5), 471–479.

Law, A. V., Ray, M. D., Knapp, K. K., and Balesh, J. K. (2003). "Unmet needs in the medication use process: perceptions of physicians, pharmacists, and patients." *Journal of the American Pharmaceutical Association* (Washington DC). May–June; 43(3), 394–402.

Morris, S. and Schulz, R. M. (1992). "Patient compliance—an overview." *Journal of Clinical Pharmacy Therapy.* 17(5), 283–295.

Peterson, A. M., Takiya, L, and Finley, R. (2003). "Meta-analysis of trials of interventions to improve medication adherence." *American J Health Syst Pharm.* 60(7), 657–665.

Sless, D. and Wiseman, R. (1997). *Writing about medicines for people. Usability guidelines for consumer medicines information.* Canberra: Australian Government Publishing Service.

Sless, D. (2004). *Labelling code of practice. Designing usable non-prescription medicine labels for consumers.* Canberra: Communication Research Press.

Tinke, J.L., and Griens, A.M.G.F. (2003). *Data en Feiten 2003.* Den Haag: Stichting Farmaceutische Kengetallen (http://www.sfk.nl)

Trewin, V. F., and Veitch, G. B. (2003). "Patient sources for drug information and attitude to their provision: a corticosteroid model." *Pharmacy World Science*. October, 25(5), 191–196.

Vander Stichele, R. (2004). *Impact of written drug information in patient package inserts*. Gent: Academia Press Scientific Publishers.

Van der Waarde, K. (2004). "Visual information about medicines. Providing patients with relevant information." *Proceedings of the Information Design International Conference*, Recife, Brazil. September 8–11, 2003.

Van Haecht, C. H., Vander Stichele, R., and Bogaert, M. G. (1990). "Package inserts for antihypertensive drugs: use by the patients and impact on adverse drug reactions." *European Journal of Clinical Pharmacology*. 39(6), 551–554.

Vermeire, E., Hearnshaw, H., Van Royen, P., and Denekens, J. (2001). "Patient adherence to treatment: three decades of research. A comprehensive review." *Journal of Clinical Pharmacy Therapy*. 26(5), 331–342.

Extending the Boundaries of Communication

Interactive Iconic Communication to Help Those Who Suffer from Aphasia

Rosemary Sassoon
Sevenoaks, England

This chapter is more about bridging a communication abyss than creating a communication space. It concerns a system of interactive iconic communication to help people who have lost the power of speech. Aphasia is often the result of a stroke and it is possible that sufferers will, at least temporarily, be paralyzed down one side (hemi-pariesis), and therefore may have impaired use of their natural writing hand. Such patients may also have some degree of cognitive impairment.

Where can a precedent be found when personal communication disintegrates? How can we begin to help when the capability to communicate by speech, which we take for granted, is lost; when words make no sense, and even letters are no longer recognizable?

It should be possible to re-establish communication by returning to the origins of human development when facial expression and gesture were used. Initially, even these strategies do not always work for those traumatized by the sudden onset of aphasia, with stiff bodies in a state of shock and depression. A better strategy would be to use the origins of written communication: very simple symbols.

The accepted way of dealing with this condition involves pictorial aids with sub-titles for recovering aphasics to point to and indicate what they want. One of the best known of these schemes is Canadian: *Pictographic Communication Resources, Enhancing Communicative Access*, by Kagan, Winkel and Shumway. It is dedicated to helping stroke survivors communicate. Such schemes allow some degree of communication, control, and choice, especially when handled by expert thera-pists, who themselves are few and far between. Even allied to gesture and facial expression such aids do not cover all an individual may want to communicate. Sometimes these schemes for supported conversation may be too complicated, slow, or clumsy for a patient or caregiver to manage. Moreover they do not always filter down to where they are needed in small or isolated hospitals or in the home. What I am suggesting augments and in no way conflicts with those resources already in general use, or more complex methods such as Bliss Symbolics that are sometimes used at later stages for patients with unimpaired intellectual capacity. It is primarily meant for the early stages post-stroke, when depression and frustra-tion are so hard to deal with.

If a person cannot speak it does not always mean that he/she cannot write or maybe produce some kind of mark. This possibility is often ignored. It is a basic human need to make your own mark, and is of psychological importance not only to read or recognize something, but to have some fast personal means of having an input into your care or daily life. Ideally you need a way of expressing your thoughts and feelings, negative as well as positive.

The seeds of this project were sown some twenty years ago when Alan Wing, then at the MRC APU, knowing of my interest in handwriting problems, asked me to join his team. My first project was to investigate those who had lost the use of their natural writing hand, predominantly due to stroke, writer's cramp, and other neu-rological disorders. This work highlighted the importance of the personal trace to those who had lost that capability, and the effect on motivation and returning opti-mism when patients were led in stages to producing some sort of signature. Without a signature you are a non-person in society.

Simple iconic communication suggested itself when I was investigating icons for special needs. It was reinforced when I was myself a patient on a geriatric ward and saw of the plight of aphasics: "Talked about and talked over but never talked at," as one recovered patient described it. Small wonder so many become severely depressed. Professor of Rehabilitation DL McLellan asserted that stroke affects people in many different ways and that while two strokes may appear much the same, two people with strokes never are (Sassoon 2002). Then their remaining skills, their characters, and their environment compound the differences. For example, when researching for my book about stroke I heard of a man who could neither speak, read, nor write, but, being a talented artist, could communicate through detailed drawings.

To have a means of graphic communication restored by one way or another has important implications for a patient's overall rehabilitation. Let me cite just one case. Several years ago, in Singapore, I was asked to see an eminent public figure who had suffered a stroke. He had laid like a log in his hospital bed and would not cooperate with his therapist. I asked if they had some kind of indicator board so he could have some choice even in food and drink. The reply was that they could not afford such extravagances. Extravagance—all that would be needed would be a piece of paper with squares and a few simple pictures. The patient's eyes livened up. Then I asked for paper and pencil to see if he could write—after all one hand was undamaged. The reply was chilling (and I have heard similar utterings since)—something like: "He is so muddled in his head he will never be able to get his thoughts together again." The paper was produced under protest, and I put a pen in his left hand. The result: a line of Chinese characters which none of us could read! I heard through the grapevine that after that he made an almost complete recovery.

The value of an iconography is to be understandable by everyone concerned. That is why iconographies worked well in the ancient world where small groups shared the same experiences—but not always so well in today's global village. Between two people any mark can become an understandable icon. A very simple two-way, open-ended, and interactive iconic communication between patient and caregiver would not need to be comprehensible to anyone else other than those two, but could be extended within a family.

Although patients might be unable to write or to draw, they could probably make some kind of mark, even if that means supporting the damaged hand with the unaffected one. A dot, a wavy line, a circle or a cross, anything might became imbued with a relevant meaning. An approximate question mark for "I do not understand; tell me what is wrong" would be a start. If the counterchange movement of a question mark was too complex for the hand, then an upright wavy line would do. A way of indicating thanks and something to express "stop," "slow down," or "it hurts" are the kinds of things that could follow as well as more practical needs.

This "vocabulary" could be extended as manual dexterity and comprehension developed. It should be adapted imaginatively to meeting individuals' particular needs and should aim at encouraging patients wherever possible to make their own mark. There is an additional benefit to this: using the damaged hand for something so positive helps restore function. This is an important point. The retraining of the affected hand is often neglected in the need to restore mobility. It is often left too late or considered unnecessary—after all we have two hands but for life we need both. Harnessing this urge to make a mark, then progressing to the person's name, can have unexpected benefits towards rehabilitation, stimulating hand function and comprehension at the same time.

This is a concept only, without a product. The difference between my idea and accepted practice (apart from combining hand function with recognition and communication) is that there is no intention of permanently imposed icons. I have never forgotten the words of a teacher of learning disabled adults when I was researching for a book on iconic communication (Sassoon 1997): "My patients can be taught to recognize an icon once but seldom remember it as they often cannot relate to a designer's conception of any particular object. The ones they produce themselves work best."

Shortly after I met Guillermina Noël she became involved in this kind of work. Her father suffered a stroke and has been, up to now, unable to speak. Working to his requirements, she developed some imaginative stacks of icons. In my opinion the emoticons are perhaps the most original: e.g., frustration, thanks, love, tiredness, etc. So much has come out of this joint project with her family working together with her father. She discusses her project in the next chapter, but I would like to use a few of the comments that have arisen to illustrate another point: the psychological effect of such work on all concerned. "Within the whole family it has become a focus of hope and positive action. Optimism is contagious." These are vital issues for a family at such traumatic times. Another comment backs up the benefit of trying to get a patient to make some sort of mark with the affected hand: "My mother is fascinated with the changes in my father after he started to work with his right hand. Now he wants to use his knife." This is the same feedback that I have had from previous patients. It is also pertinent to mention that Noël's stepfather's speech therapist does not approve of what we are doing despite the positive results.

I have discussed this concept of an interactive iconography with many people in the field. Some speech and language therapists have disputed its use, unwilling to recognize it might be helpful; that the written trace, however unskilled, could be combined with the methods they are trained to use. I heard the comment from those who think their own resources adequate: "You are reinventing the wheel," they say. Others are excited at the prospect but unsure how they could put it into action. I accept that this would not be appropriate in all cases—or for all therapists to use—and that is why I am introducing it for patient and caregiver in the early days. On the other hand there have been some positive comments: an Australian research therapist said that she liked the concept, suggesting that it takes what capabilities a patient still has and uses them.

However, the system needs to be tried with a variety of patients, particularly those who cannot manage words or letters but can master their own thoughts and make some sort of mark of their own, whatever it may be, and have it given meaning. Some may come to making their own icons, after commencing in a more traditional way. Some may even find that beginning with the production of icons, as well as improving hand function, they may later progress to drawing letters.

What Guillermina Noël has done is perhaps more easily comprehensible—to introduce the idea of a very personal iconography exactly tailored to a patient's needs and developed with him and his family's participation. Not every daughter can produce icons of this standard but that need not be a handicap. Empathy and warmth are more important than perfect icons. By empowering the patient through even a limited method of communication this simple method could provide the vital motivation to move from despondency to hope.

Figure 5.1: The written trace is an ideal diagnostic tool. It reveals the state of mind and body of the writer at any given time. In this case it will provide a baseline for a record of the progress of written communication and hand function.

References

Kagan, Aura, Winkel, Joanne, and Shumway, Elyse (1996). *Pictographic Communication Resources, Enhancing Communicative Access.* Toronto, ON: The Pat Arato Aphasia Centre.

McLellan, D.L. (2002). "Different Doctors, a Personal View." In Sassoon, R., *Understanding Stroke.* Dorchester, UK: Pardoe Blacker Publishing.

Sassoon, R. and Gaur, A. (1995). *Signs Symbols and Icons.* Exeter, England: Intellect.

Sassoon, R. (2002). *Understanding Stroke.* Dorchester, UK: Pardoe Blacker Publishing.

CHAPTER SIX

Creating Possibilities for Communication

Guillermina Noël

University of Alberta, Edmonton, Canada

This chapter, which continues the theme of the previous one, is about the design of a customized system of forty-two icons to help AM, my stepfather—who suffers from aphasia because of a stroke—to communicate. It is also about a personal experience and it is about the creation of possibilities. The system of icons was designed according to the individual's needs, and taking into consideration his level of education, age, background, personal interests, personal objects, and preferences for styles, among other considerations. It was also designed according to the needs of the caregiver.

To understand the project, it is necessary to understand the individual and the family situation. AM was seventy-two years old when he suffered the stroke. He used to be a lawyer, specializing in legislation, and in the history of the Constitution. Although retired, AM was still working as a consultant. One of his hobbies was reading, and the subjects of the books that he read were usually related to his profession. His professional life, however, ended after the stroke.

As a result of the stroke, AM suffers from Broca's aphasia, a nonfluent aphasia. Individuals with this kind of aphasia have their speech reduced to a few words, which are produced with effort. When trying to articulate a sentence, the effort is such and the result is so poor, usually just one or two words, that the individual becomes tired and frustrated. Auditory comprehension in AM is good, and he can "participate" in a conversation by just listening, but he is not able to respond to questions or to make comments. It is not that he doesn't want to, he can't. He is able to talk on the phone, answering with brief sentences (for example, "hello," "I feel fine").

In the case of AM, the right side of the body is also affected. Even though the arm is not paralyzed, it has become weak. Writing is also affected, and he is not able to sign a form, but he is able to do a mark. His reading comprehension is generally good, and he is able to read the titles in the newspaper, but not a complete article. In general, " . . . individuals rarely read for recreation because of the slowness and the effort required" (Goodglass, 210). His ability to gesture is lost. To survive the stroke, AM had to have surgery in a main neck artery, and after the surgery he needed to avoid moving his head and neck for a brief period.

The whole family situation is altered because the individual should not be left alone. If he needs something, he is not able to communicate his needs by phone or to explain his situation. Someone has to be at home to care for him. Because of the weakness in his right arm, for example, AM is not able to prepare his own lunch.

It is important to try to understand the psychological aspects of the situation. It is, in part, because of language that we are human. Through language, we express our feelings, we communicate our thoughts, we acquire and accumulate knowledge, and we understand each other: We are alive. How does someone feel after suffering a stroke? How is it to wake up in the hospital unable to speak, unable to move the right side of your body, and unable to communicate your basic needs?

Literature on the subject highlights the important role that significant others and close friends play in the treatment intervention. The "partners play a critical role in defining communicative success" (Garrett and Beukelman, 255). It is the partner who will help the individual to satisfy his or her needs. It is the partner who will provide information about interests, abilities, educational level, and other related background information.

Even though AM is not able to speak, he will try to tell the caregiver something about a friend who came to visit him, or try to remind the caregiver to pay the rent, etc. In this case, the caregiver was my mother, and she was able to comprehend my stepfather's needs. Together, they became a team, the users of the icons that I designed. The icons helped them to make communication possible, while avoiding AM's frustration. From the designer's point of view, it was fundamental to be part of the situation that they were living in, as well as able to work with them.

The system that was developed comprised a set of forty-two icons to cover the individual's basic needs during the first stage of his language disorder. When AM needed to communicate a need, he pointed to the icon.

The "aphasiboard system," as Rosemary Sassoon calls it, is a set of seven sheets of A4-size paper (ISO standard equivalent to letter size). There are six icons per sheet, and each icon is framed by an 8x8 cm square. The icons are to be not only visible but also legible. The paper and the size were chosen because these are easily handled by the individual, who has, we should remember, a weak right arm. To avoid spending time shipping the set by courier, it was sent by e-mail from Canada and printed in Argentina.

The icons are black and white, and red is used as an accent. They were originally designed in both color and black and white, and then tested with AM, who preferred the last option. It was Rosemary Sassoon who suggested that the reduced color variation would work better. Rosemary is herself a stroke survivor and has been researching in the stroke area for several years, resulting in her book, *Understanding Stroke*.

In the cases where the icon is a person, that person is a man, just like AM. If the icon had represented a girl or a boy, it could have made the individual feel under-

Figure 6.1

Figure 6.2

Figure 6.3

estimated or unable to relate to the picture. The features are simple, but detailed enough for the individual to recognize a person. The person is not a cartoon of AM, but hair, eyes, eyebrows, mouth, and neck help him understand the icon. When the icon is an object, the objects are generally similar to AM's objects.

For some speech therapists, this did not seem necessary, but I believe that this decision provides some kind of pleasure for the individual.

It is fundamental that each area of the icons be distinguished from another. To facilitate this, the icons are designed with visible outlines and solid areas. If, for example, one area is dark gray, the following one is light gray, and the line that separates both areas is black. The line thickness varies from one to three points.

A word or a written description of the meaning is included below each icon. This allows the individual to keep on seeing text and helps the partner to be sure about what the individual is trying to communicate. The word without the icon is impossible to use because, among other things, AM has vision problems that were caused by the stroke, and sometimes he can confuse letters such as *b*, *d*, and *p*. The text was set in Frutiger, upper and lower case, 23 points, and printed in black. This typeface is well known for its legibility and readability. It has a good balance between the weight of the strokes and the counters, and the length of the ascenders and descenders is appropriate in relation to its x-height. The selection was a mistake, however, because it is essential when working with brain-damaged individuals to have a good differentiation between the letters. In this case, the uppercase "I" (as in "India"), and the lowercase "l" (as in "laundry") are similar, as is the case with the counters of the letters *b*, *d*, *p*, and *q*. It was also a mistake because, considering AM's background, probably most of the books that he has read were set in serif typefaces, which usually have more differences between the letters because of the serifs and endings.

Instead of using just the name of the object or action to communicate, I decided to use the whole sentence. For example, under the icon of music, instead of saying "music" it says "I want some music." A friendly tone of voice is important, and used well it brings positive associations to the individual.

The aphasiboard was used for a specific period of time, from the first week in the hospital until the first week at home (two months). For that period, the material worked extremely well. Then, after AM recovered some ability to communicate through gestures and shorts words, what the device mostly provided was hope; it brought a lot of optimism to AM and the family, it brought a possibility.

After two months, it was used sometimes by the speech therapist for activities such as naming. The icon most used was the one for music, followed by the one for the "f . . ." word. After the third week, the icons for "yes" and "not" were unnecessary.

There are probably several details that need to be improved, as is the case for the icon for "thanks," but the purpose of the aphasiboard was achieved and communication was made possible. For that specific period of time, AM was able to communicate his needs and my mother was able to satisfy them.

Three people made this project possible: Rosemary Sassoon, a typographer who has researched the medical aspects of handwriting, such as those in the stroke patient; Jorge Frascara, a designer and researcher who has worked in the area of signs for many years; and my mother, whose stamina and smiles made my stepfather improve his abilities and thereby have a better life.

After having done this project, I think that this is what design is essentially about: the creation of possibilities for communication.

References

Garrett, K. L. and Beukelman, D. R. (1992). "Aphasia: Augmentative Communication Approaches for Persons with Severe Aphasia." In Yorkston, K. (Ed.) *Augmentative communication in the medical setting* (245–303). Tucson, AZ: Communication Skill Builders.

Goodglass, H. (1993). *Understanding Aphasia*. San Diego, CA: Academic Press.

Sassoon, R. (2002). *Understanding Stroke*. Dorchester, UK: Pardoe Blacker Publishing.

PART THREE

Exploring Tools and Frames

The consciousness of the need to attend to content and context in order to plan effective design responses pushes designers to reconsider their knowledge, their tools, and their ways of working. The very notion of the object of design needs reassessment: we used to design objects, but now we have to think more about activities, the activities that people engage in, sometimes as a result of the objects and services we design. The commercial push for innovation calls for methods to evaluate the possible futures that these innovations could bring. New conceptual tools are required. The tools required must always place people at the center, sometimes observing them from very close quarters, sometimes bringing them into the design development loop.

CHAPTER SEVEN

Scaffolds for Building Everyday Creativity

Elizabeth B.-N. Sanders
MakeTools, Columbus, Ohio, USA

New information and communication technologies have changed the ways in which we live, learn, and play. How we communicate with one another has been particularly affected. We can reach others and be reached by them anytime and anywhere. And this is not always a good thing.

Where Is Communication Design Now?

The new information technologies afford nearly instantaneous feedback. Consequently, communication design has moved from being a one-way transmission of the message to being an interactive scenario that unfolds rapidly over time. But we, as designers, do not yet have the knowledge, processes, or tools to deal with the unfolding of the interactive flow of information.

The design education system is struggling to keep up with the demands of these new challenges. Students want to be prepared to live and work in the interactive world, but those who teach them are struggling even to learn the new tools. How can we teach the next generation of designers when we don't understand the tools or the media?

We are at a crossroads in communication design. Design and marketing professionals sell "experience design." Some Web design firms proudly claim to be able to "manufacture experience." Do they really think they have the ability to design or to manufacture an experience for someone else? Do they think they have the right to determine what other people experience? Unfortunately many claim to be doing so.

Who Are We Serving through Design?

The people who buy and use the products of design are the people that we serve. I will refer to them from here on as "everyday people" to distinguish them from others such as designers or engineers who have been specifically trained to design and develop goods and services.

The labels we use to refer to everyday people have been changing. We are slowly becoming sensitive to the fact that they are first and foremost people, as opposed to users or consumers.

Looking at Figure 7.1, one can see how the labels we have used to refer to the people we serve through design have been changing over the last twenty years. For many years, we referred to them as the "customer" or "consumer" (i.e., the recipient of the "product" at the end of the design and production process). We changed to thinking of them as "users" in the 1980s and 1990s as the move toward user-centered design processes gained acceptance in response to more advanced products of technology. As users, people are still recipients of artifacts of the design process, but they play a more active role in their interactions with such products. The user-centered design approach is still prevalent today in communication design circles.

In other areas of design (e.g., software in particular), there are preliminary signs of other ways to see the people we serve through design. We are beginning to see them not only as recipients of the artifacts of the process, but as active participants in the design and production process itself. We see that they are capable of adapting products to better meet their own needs.

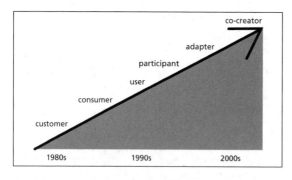

The need to be directly involved in the creation and production of goods and services is pointing toward a human-centered design revolution, with the act of co-creation between designers and everyday people being the end goal.

Figure 7.1: A human-centered design revolution is underway

The Emergence of More Creative Ways of Living

In the generative research I have conducted over the last three years for many different clients, it has become increasingly evident that everyday people are no longer satisfied with simply being "consumers." They want to be "creators" as well. This unmet need for creativity is being expressed through the use of participatory toolkits (Sanders and William) whether we are conducting research with people about their home experiences, their learning experiences, or their work experiences. Their examples of what constitutes creative behavior are surprisingly varied. For example, some people say they feel creative when they are exercising or when they are cleaning out the closet. Others feel creative when making scrapbooks from family photographs. And others feel creative when they are cooking "freestyle," making up the recipe as they go from whatever ingredients they have on hand.

The interest in more creative ways of living can be seen also in the recent spate of new books dedicated to the topic. Two good examples include Ray and Anderson's *The Cultural Creatives: How 50 Million People are Changing the World*, and Florida's *The Rise of the Creative Class*.

New forms of creativity in art and design are emerging as well. *Postproduction* (Bourriaud) refers to the increasing number of recent artworks that have been created based primarily on pre-existing works of art. Artists today are interpreting, reproducing, and re-using the art originally created by others. Similarly, "ad hocism" is the idea that describes the trend in industrial design whereby old products are salvaged and recombined to create new ones. The new products are often humorous, such as cheese-grater lamps and scrub-brush coat racks (Thompson).

The Need for Convivial Tools

Why are people expressing their unmet needs for creativity now? One explanation is that the tools we have made to "improve" our lives have, in fact, taken creativity away from us. A concern that this might happen was voiced over thirty years ago by Ivan Illich, one of the radical theorists of the 1960s.

Illich defined tools as anything made by man. "I use the term 'tool' broadly enough to include not only simple hardware such as drills, pots, syringes, brooms, building elements, or motors, and not just large machines like cars or power stations. I also include among tools productive institutions such as factories that produce tangible commodities like corn flakes or electric current and productive systems for intangible commodities such as those which produce 'education,' 'health,' 'knowledge,' or 'decisions'." (Illich, 20). In other words, all the artifacts of the design process are tools, according to Illich.

Illich described the difference between two basic types of tools. "*Convivial tools* allow users to invest the world with their meaning, to enrich the environment with the fruits of their visions, and to use them for the accomplishment of a purpose they have chosen. *Industrial tools* deny this possibility to those who use them, and they allow their designers to determine the meaning and expectations of others."

He argued in *Tools for Conviviality* for the exploration and use of convivial as opposed to industrial tools. He described eloquently how a balance between consumptive and creative activities was necessary for human survival. "People need not only to obtain things, they need, above all, the freedom to make things among which they can live, to give shape to them according to their own tastes, and to put them to use in caring for and about others" (Illich, 20).

The Need to Balance Consumptive and Creative Ways of Living

Just as Illich had predicted, today we are feeling the weight of living for many years with the output of industrial tools.

The diagram at the top of Figure 7.2 shows how much the industrial tool mindset predominates today, overshadowing the convivial tool mindset. The diagram at the bottom of Figure 7.2 shows how the situation could be in the future with a better balance between the use of industrial and convivial tools leading, as you will see, to a balance between consumptive and creative mindsets.

Figure 7.3 shows the everyday activities that characterize the consumptive and the creative mindsets. The consumptive mindset is characterized by the activities of "customers and consumers" who shop for, purchase, and use goods and services. The creative mindset is characterized by a different set of activities that will be described shortly.

What does the contrast between consumptive and creative living reveal about the field of design? It shows that currently we are far better at serving consumption than we are at serving creativity.

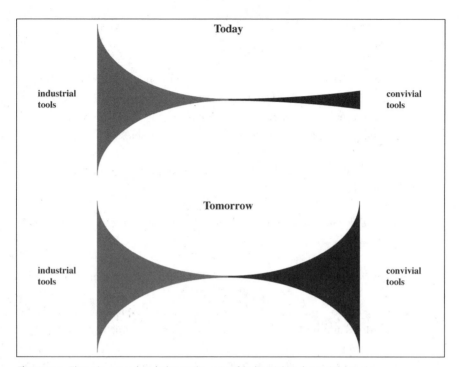

Figure 7.2: There is a need to balance the use of industrial and convivial tools

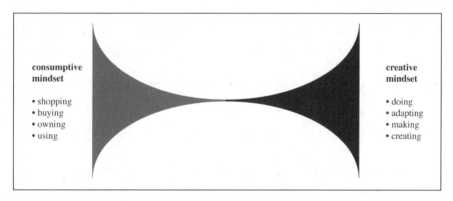

Figure 7.3: Everyday activities of consumption and creativity

We already know how to use our design skills to fulfill the demands of the consumptive mindset.

- We know how to design brands and create retail environments to promote shopping and buying.

- We have learned how to evoke and sustain purchase behavior through advertising, naming, and packaging design.

- We know how to do user-centered design and conduct usability testing in order to make interfaces and Web sites that are easy for people to use. In fact, we can even make inhuman combinations of technology (such as a combination cell phone/PDA/video camera) somewhat usable.

- We know how to design objects, artifacts, and spaces that people desire to own or live in.

But we don't yet know how to use our design skills to fulfill the needs of the creative mindset.

- How can we use design to make people's productive activities more fulfilling?

- Can we learn to "under design" so that everyday people can continue the design process and make the product, artifact, or space suit their needs?

- How can we encourage everyday people to move to higher levels of creativity? Will they need to be encouraged to do so?

- How do we build scaffolds (Sanders, 2002) or frameworks on which people can make their own experiences? What is a scaffold? What does it look like?

- What are convivial tools? How will they be different from the tools we have on hand today?

- Will new technology be used in the creation of convivial tools? How?

- What will everyday people come up with when convivial tools are put in their hands?

The Development of Everyday Creativity

There are at least four levels of creativity that everyday people seek. The four levels follow a developmental path from doing to adapting to making and finally to creating. The chart below shows the primary differentiating characteristics of each level.

Table 7.1 The four levels of everyday creativity follow a developmental path

Level of creativity	Motivations	Requirements
Doing	To get something done / to be productive	Minimal interest Minimal domain experience
Adapting	To make something on my own	Some interest Some domain expertise
Making	To make something with my own hands	Genuine interest Domain experience
Creating	To express my creativity	Passion Domain expertise

The most basic level of creativity is doing. The motivation behind doing is to accomplish something through productive activity. For example, people have told us that they feel creative when they are productively engaged in everyday activities such as exercising or organizing their homes. Doing requires a minimal amount of interest. The skill requirements are low as well. Many of the goods and services offered to "consumers" today can be said to satisfy the doing level of creativity. They come to the consumer readymade. For example, in the food preparation domain, a doing activity would be to buy or select a prepackaged microwave entrée and prepare it for a meal.

The next level of creativity, adapting, is more advanced. The motivation behind adapting is to make something one's own by changing it in some way. People might do this to personalize an object so that it better fits their personality. Or they might adapt a product so that it better fits their functional needs. We can see adaptive creativity emerging whenever products, services, or environments don't exactly fit people's needs. Adapting requires more interest and a higher skill level than doing. It takes some confidence to go "outside of the box." In the food preparation domain, an adapting activity might be to add an extra ingredient to a cake mix to make it special.

The third level of creativity is making. The motivation behind making is to use one's hands and mind to make or build something that did not exist before. There is usually some kind of guidance involved, e.g., a pattern, a recipe, or notes that describe what types of materials to use and how to put them together. Making requires a genuine interest in the domain as well as experience. People are likely to spend a lot of their time, energy, and money on their favorite making activities. Many hobbies fit in this level of creativity. In the food preparation domain, an example might be to create an entrée using a recipe.

The most advanced level of creativity is creating. The motivation behind creating is to express oneself or to innovate. Truly creative efforts are fueled by passion and guided by a high level of experience. Creating differs from making in that creating relies on the use of raw materials and the absence of a predetermined pattern. In the food preparation domain, for example, making is cooking with a recipe, whereas creating is making up the recipe as you go and having to improvise along the way when you discover that you have run out of a key ingredient.

The path from doing to adapting to making and finally to creating develops in the individual over time and through experience. All people are capable of reaching the highest level of creativity, but they need the passion and the experience to do so. Consequently, people differ in the level of creativity they attain in different domains. In fact, they may find themselves at all four levels of creativity simultaneously in different domains. For example:

- Someone may be perfectly satisfied with being at the doing level in the area of food preparation, e.g., eating take-out food or heating frozen entrées;

- While at work they have modified their workspace with many items that speak to their personality; and

- At home they spend much of their spare time building their own online gaming community.

The Emergence of New Design Spaces

We cannot use the design tools and methods that have served the consumptive mindset for so many years to serve the needs of the creative mindset. New design spaces are evolving and are now beginning to emerge. Table 7.2 shows this transformation.

Table 7.2 New design spaces are emerging in response to people's needs for everyday creativity

Design spaces	Everyday activities
Design for consuming	Shopping, buying, owning, and using
Design for experiencing	Doing and using
Design for adapting	Adapting, modifying, or filling in
Co-creating	Making and creating

We are currently in, and have been for the past fifty years, a design space focused on consumptive activities such as shopping and buying which leads to owning and using. The Design for Consuming Space will always exist, but will be joined by new design spaces along a continuum of creativity.

Companies tend to be fixated at some point along this developmental continuum. Many manufacturing companies are positioned in the Design for Consuming Space, with a focus on producing products that people will choose to buy. In fact, this emphasis on consumptive activities has resulted in products such as multi-functional technology devices (e.g., a cell phone/PDA/video camera) that have so many features and functions that they are difficult to use. In the Design for Consuming Space, it is important for your products to have more bells and whistles than your competitors' products, whether people will use these features or not.

A Design for Experiencing Space is emerging now, most notably in the domain of interactive media. A new class of practitioners who call themselves user-experience designers claims to be able to "design experiences." Although this is highly unlikely (Sanders, 2002), the movement is nevertheless leading to the emergence of new design tools such as personas and scenarios. For example, personas are fictional people or user archetypes that can be used throughout the design development process to represent real people (i.e., real "users"). Storytelling and scenarios are being used to bring everyday life experiences to the personas. These user-centered design tools help the design team to keep the user top-of-mind and in the center of the design development process. Although the new tools often suffer from superficiality (e.g., personas may be based on very little research), they are at least a step in the right direction.

At the edge of practice are the newer Design for Adapting Spaces that are being discussed mainly in research-based universities, large software companies, and on design-oriented Weblogs. Design for Adapting has been referred to as "under design" (Moran), meta-design (Fischer, 2003), and as "loose fit" design (Rapoport). The idea is that people can and will fill in the designed artifact to meet their own needs and dreams. In fact, the less you give them, the more they fill in (McCloud).

How do you design for people to "fill in?" This does not mean simply leaving a product unfinished and then putting it out as a Beta test version so that lead users can find and report the bugs. It goes way beyond that. It means learning how to build scaffolds for experiencing. A scaffold is a special type of communicational space, one that supports and affords creative behavior.

- How do we build scaffolds for experiencing?

- What is "enough" to serve as a scaffold?

- What is "too much" such that creativity is dampened?

- How can we use the inherent properties of ambiguity (Gaver et al.) to serve the adaptation process rather than to confuse it?

Design for Adapting is a new design space that begs to be explored. It is a space where we must acknowledge the creativity on the part of everyday people. Beyond the edge of practice are the Co-Creating Spaces where designers and everyday people work collaboratively throughout the design and development process. Co-Creating Spaces will be especially important in highly complex domains in the future. Designers can make a significant contribution toward these domains if they are open to new forms of collective creativity and if they respect the levels of creativity of the domain experts.

Frequently Asked Questions

When designers consider the emergence of these new design spaces, they tend to ask questions such as those that follow.

Are We Losing Control of the Design Process?

Yes, we are losing control of the traditional design process, but we are at the same time opening it up to others. We are entering new design spaces where we let go of our control in order to amplify the creativity of other people.

Designing in the new spaces will require new design processes and a new attitude about everyday people. We will learn to acknowledge that they are creative and especially so when they are working with us in their areas of expertise or passion. We must learn to be humble in our interactions with everyday people since they are the experts on their own experiences. We must become comfortable in our humility.

How Much Do We Want Everyday People to Drive Design?

Everyday people should drive the design process to the extent that they are capable and willing. If they are at a high level of creativity in a domain, then they should drive the design process. If they are at a low level of creativity, on the other hand, they will probably be content to consume what we deliver.

What Will We Need to Know for Designing in the Future?

The design team needs to fully understand the experience domains of everyday people (Sanders, 2001). This understanding includes their relevant past memories and experiences, their thoughts and feelings about their everyday experiences, and their dreams and fears for the future. To the extent that we are co-designing with everyday people, however, they can represent themselves directly in the design process.

How Will the Composition of the Design Team Change?

It is the attitude more than the academic training of the design team members that is crucial. If the team members do not believe that everyday people are creative and can contribute at the front end, the new design spaces will not grow. People trained in the social sciences are often more open to the potential creativity and abilities of everyday people. We can expect the proliferation and integration of social scientists into the new design spaces. This is already apparent in the Design for Experiencing Space.

If Everyone Is Creative, Then What is the Role of the Designer?

Designers will learn to use their own creativity to amplify the creativity of other people. Scaffolds are communicational spaces that support and serve people's creativity, enhancing the conviviality of their lives. In the future, designers will be the creators of scaffolds upon which everyday people can express their creativity.

How Will the Tools and Methods for Research and Design Change?

As we invite everyday people into the design process, the tools, rules, and methods for research and design will begin to blur. For example, personas and scenarios are tools of both research and design. In the future, research will become more creative; design will become more rigorous.

How Will We Evaluate the Results?

The ultimate way to evaluate the effects of design is in the betterment of people's lives. If we, as designers, can improve the conviviality of human experience, then we will have succeeded in our efforts.

What Is Next?

We are entering new design spaces. The old design space will be surrounded by new human-centered communicational spaces. The communicational spaces of tomorrow will be filled with everyday people co-designing with us. These spaces will be living, thriving, diverse, and probably somewhat messy. And that is OK.

References

Alexander, C., Ishikawa, S., and Silverstein, M. (1977). *A Pattern Language: Towns, Buildings Construction*. New York: Oxford University Press.

Alexander, C. (2001). *The Nature of Order: An Essay on the Art of Building and the Nature of the Universe. Book One: The Phenomenon of Life*. New York: Oxford University Press.

Bourriaud, N. (2002). *Postproduction. Culture as Screenplay: How Art Reprograms the World*. New York: Lukas & Sternberg.

Brand, S. (1999). *The Clock of the Long Now: Time and Responsibility*. New York: Basic Books.

Dunne, A. and Raby, F. (2001). *Design Noir: The Secret Life of Electronic Objects*. Birkhauser.

Fischer, G. (2002). "Beyond 'Couch Potatoes': From Consumers to Designers and Active Contributors." *FirstMonday: Peer-reviewed Journal on the Internet*. *www.firstmonday.dk/issues/issue7_12/fischer/*

Fischer, G. (2003). "Meta-Design: Beyond User-Centered and Participatory Design," *Proceedings of HCI International 2003*, Crete, Greece.

Florida, R. (2002). *The Rise of the Creative Class: And How It's Transforming Work, Leisure, Community and Everyday Life*. New York: Basic Books.

Gaver, W. W., Beaver, J., and Benford, S. (2003). "Ambiguity as a Resource for Design." Paper presented at CHI, *Computer Human Interaction 2003*.

Hoinacki, L. and Mitcham, C. (Eds.) (2002). *The Challanges of Ivan Illich*. New York: State University of New York Press.

Illich, I. (1975). *Tools for Conviviality*. New York: Harper & Row Publishers.

Jensen, R. (1999). *The Dream Society: How the Coming Shift from Information to Imagination will Transform your Business*. New York: McGraw-Hill.

Koestler, A. (1964). *The Act of Creation*. London, England: Hutchinson & Co.

McCloud, S. (1994). *Understanding Comics: The Invisible Art*. New York: HarperCollins.

Moran, T. (2002). "Everyday Adaptive Design." Invited presentation at *Designing Interactive Systems*, London, June, 2002.

Ray, P. H. and Anderson, S. R. (2000). *The Cultural Creatives: How 50 Million People are Changing the World*. New York: Harmony Books.

Rapoport, A. (1990). *The Meaning of the Built Environment: A Nonverbal Communication Approach*. Tucson: The University of Arizona Press.

Sanders, E.B.-N. (2001). "Virtuosos of the experience domain." In *Proceedings of the 2001 IDSA Education Conference*.

Sanders, E. B.-N. (2002). "Scaffolds for Experiencing in the New Design Space." In *Information Design*, Institute for Information Design Japan (Editors), IID.J., Graphic-Sha Publishing Co. (In Japanese).

Sanders, E. B.-N. and William, C. T. (2001). "Harnessing People's Creativity: Ideation and Expression through Visual Communication." In Langford, J. and McDonagh-Philp, D.

(Eds.) *Focus Groups: Supporting Effective Product Development.* London and New York: Taylor & Francis.

Thompson, H. (2003). "(Re) Appropriate Behavior." *Dwell: At Home in the Modern World,* Vol. 3, September, 2003.

CHAPTER EIGHT

Design-Driven Innovation:

Scenario Building as a Tool to Facilitate the Communication Flow within Complex Design Processes

Simona Maschi
Ivrea Design Institute, Italy

Scenario building can be defined as a communication tool that can drive innovation in complex design processes. The object of this contribution is to investigate how the design practice could promote and guide convergence dynamics amongst a plurality of stakeholders. The involvement of a plurality of stakeholders faces the need to set up a platform of interaction based on the management of multi-disciplinary knowledge and on the use of a common language through the path of innovation. This contribution premise addresses four areas: the scientific background, the approach, the tool, and the result.

This contribution refers to a research project called HiCS (Highly Contextualised Solutions), which concerns the definition of a methodology that companies may effectively implement to help agile and dynamic networks of partners produce and deliver new solutions for people with reduced mobility.

HiCS. is a research project coordinated by the Politecnico di Milano and co-financed by the European Union. The research partners are four academic institutions: Cranfield University (UK); INETI (Portugal); Politecnico di Milano (Italy); and TU Delft (Netherlands). There are also four industrial partners: Philips Design (Netherlands); Bosch-Siemens (Spain), Biologica (Italy); and DeSter ACS (Belgium).

System Innovation: the Scientific Background

System innovation is a dynamic process that simultaneously calls into question all of the various elements of the system (market and social stakeholders, processes, products, and services), and their interconnections.

The approach to the system is internal to the discipline of industrial design: all the design actions display, more or less consciously, dynamics of cause and effect with the system within which they occur. What has become obvious today is that the nature of information phenomena, of production and consumption, has reached such levels of complexity and pervasiveness that an action at the system level leads to a simultaneous combination of results. This, moreover, makes it admissible that design driven system innovations can have the goal of achieving advantages at an economic, technological, environmental, and social level.

Strategic Design: the Approach

Strategic Design is a design activity concerning the product system, i.e., the integrated body of products, services, and communications with which a company presents itself to the market and sets itself in society, so giving form to its strategy.

Within this kind of design activity, practices, attitudes, and methods of traditional design shift from the dimension of a product, of a service, or of a technology, to the dimension of a complex system. In particular, because of the complexity of factors involved within the product system, strategic design requires a cooperative activity involving different groups of stakeholders with different capabilities, strategies, and organization approaches. As a consequence, a strategic design approach requires the establishment of a strong synergy between management and design practices.

Scenario Building: the Tool

Given a certain system, scenario building is the tool to generate eventual future systems. In the practice of design, scenario building is aimed at generating visions of potential future systems of products and services together with their supportive social, technological, and business strategies. Within system innovation, scenario building is a planning tool, which is able to go over the individual actor view-point, and to produce a common language which makes the communication between all the stakeholders easier.

Nowadays organizations and industries are facing structural change, uncertainty, and decisions with huge opportunities and risks. The future anticipation in this environment requires both systematic analysis and creativity, as well as insight and intuition. Regarding this, scenario building enables an organization to learn, adapt, and enrich the ongoing decision-making processes while bringing together a deeper understanding of the external environment with the organization's goal and competences.

Platform of Interaction: the Goal

A platform of interaction is created when several stakeholders converge, aiming at the co-production of the value within the market (added value in both products and services) as well as within society (social, cultural, environmental values).

There can be several criteria on which basis markets and society stakeholders can reshape their relationships. The traditional convergence logic, based on techno-logical processes and market segmentation opportunities, shows weaknesses with-in the social, technological, and environmental changes that we are witnessing today. Recent studies within several disciplinary fields (industrial design, knowl-edge management, and business innovation) prove that the convergence towards the context of use turns out to be a promising criterion in order to generate new partnership logic. Within this framework, the context of use places itself as a cat-alyst of all the logic tied to the project, therefore reshaping the relationships between stakeholders (including customers), processes, strategies, and knowledge.

Based upon these concepts, within a complex system, strong innovation must nec-essarily base itself upon a reconfiguration of the elements the system itself com-prises and, to do so, it is necessary to establish a new order of these elements and a new equilibrium of their relationships. One of the necessary conditions to establish this new order is to create a platform of stakeholders who agree on a shared vision. *The generation and the identification of this shared vision is a pure act of design.*

Given a reference system, what emerges nowadays is the necessity to define new methodological tools capable of supporting the generation of shared visions and, consequently, of rendering them clear and explicit. This is due to several contin-gent factors: compared to the past, processes of innovation are based on highly accelerated information and material flows. The relative periods of settlement are no longer only progressive and incremental, but bound to much more interactive dynamics that always follow briefer periods of time. Within this context, the more the platforms of stakeholders are articulated, the more co-design activities are generated, the more complexity is created, and the more the construction of a common language and a method capable of organizing the ideas and marking the stages along the path of innovation becomes necessary. In other words, given that every design process presents the strong subjectivity of its promoter, in the case of a complex system, the generation of shared visions allows for the superceding of the limits of individual interpretation of phenomena and leads to the establishment of a "platform of interaction" amongst the various stakeholders involved. In this way, by means of the ability to generate shared visions, the design activity promotes the "convergence" of the points of view of the various stakeholders and, auspiciously, catalyzes their design and organizational energies.

References

Barnett, Steve (1994). "Futures, Probable and Plausible." *Anthropology Newsletter*, October.

Bonnett, Thomas W. and Olson, Robert L. (1993). *Scenarios of State Government in the Year 2010*. Washington, D.C.: Council of Governors' Policy Advisors.

Carroll, J. M. (1995). *Scenario-based design*. New York: John Wiley.

Churchman, C. West (1971). *The Design of Inquiring Systems*. New York: Basic Books.

Christensen, Clayton M. (1997). *The Innovator's Dilemma: When New Technologies Cause Great Firms to Fail*. Boston, MA: Harvard Business School Press.

Collyns, Napier (1993). Chapter Six, in Griffin, E. (Ed.) *The Reflective Executive*. New York: Crossroads.

De Geus, Arie (1988). "Planning as Learning." *Harvard Business Review* 66, no. 2, 70–74.

Douglas, Mary (1986). *How Institutions Think*. Syracuse, NY: Syracuse University Press, 1986.

Dutch Central Planning Bureau (1992). *Scanning the Future*. The Hague: SDU Publishers.

Forrester, Jay Wright (1961). *Industrial Dynamics*. Cambridge, MA: MIT Press.

Jégou, F., and Manzini, E. (2000). "Scenario Building." In *Strategies Towards a Sustainable Household*, Research EU DG12. Milan: Politecnico of Milan.

Kahn, H. and Wiener, A. (1967). *Toward the Year 2000: A Framework for Speculation*. New York: Macmillan.

Kolb, David A. (1984). *Experiential Learning: Experience as the Source of Learning and Development*. Englewood Cliffs, NJ: Prentice Hall.

Leemhuis, J. P. "Using Scenarios to Develop Strategies." *Long Range Planning* 18, Vol. No. 2, 30–37.

Lundvall, B. A. (1988). "Innovation as an interactive process: from user-producer interaction to the national system of innovation." In Dosi, G. et al, *Technical Change and Economic Theory*, London: Pinter Publishers.

Manzini Ezio and Jègou, Francois (2000). *Design Orienting Scenarios*, SusHouse project.

Manzini Ezio (1997). *Design of Convergence*, SMAU, Milano.

Mason, David H. (1994). "Scenario-Based Planning: Decision Model for the Learning Organization." *Planning Review* (March-April).

Michael, Don (1973). *On Learning to Plan and Planning to Learn*. New York, NY: Jossey Bass.

Ogilvy, James (1992). "Future Studies and the Human Sciences: The Case for Normative Scenarios." *Futures Research Quarterly* 8, no. 2: 5–65.

Quinn, Lucia Luce and David H. Mason (1994). "How Digital Uses Scenarios to Rethink the Present." *Planning Review* 22, no. 6: 14–17.

Schoemaker, Paul and Kees van der Heijden (1992). Integrating Scenarios into Strategic Planning at Royal Dutch/Shell. *Planning Review* 20, no. 3: 41–46.

CHAPTER NINE

From Communication Design to Activity Design

Stefano Maffei and Daniela Sangiorgi
Politecnico di Milano, Italy

The worldwide shift of product-oriented firms toward a more complex productive framework is characterized by the progressive introduction and integration of services within their businesses. Services introduce an immaterial and interactive dimension that increases the possibilities of physical products to create relationships between providers (firms) and customers (users). Services can support the communication with customers; they represent a potential medium through which companies, in a commodities market, can build their peculiar value creation strategy (Norman).

Service as a Situated Action

We can observe a shift from a design/sale of only "physical" products, to the design/sale of systems of products *and services* all able to satisfy specific customers' needs. In this service-oriented economy, communication issues cannot be analyzed in an isolated way, but should be considered and evaluated as a part of the whole service design process. Considering services as interaction spaces characterized by complex social and communication interfaces (Mantovani), there is the need for new conceptual models to help evaluate and design services.

This chapter considers services in their social and systemic dimension, presenting an activity-based approach that could be used as an analytical tool for communication design practitioners to improve the design of service communication interfaces. Our approach interprets services as purposeful actions, using as theoretical reference two main research frameworks: the theory of *Situated Action* (Suchman) and the *Activity Theory* (Engeström et al.). The *situated action* research perspective was developed in the social science field, in a branch called *ethnomethodology* (Suchman; Coulon) that looks for a descriptive model to understand human action.

Suchman thinks that our actions are developed through an interaction between actors and environments, and that the action process strictly depends on the material, social, and communicative circumstances in which it happens. The action itself, therefore cannot be interpreted through a rational modeling process, but should be considered as a situated process that has a precise aim. The meaning of each action is simultaneously developed both in the physical and material world of artifacts and in the communicative and social sphere in which actors are engaged in the action.

This seems to be the real *action space* that coincides, according to our hypothesis, with the *service space*.

The service space is an interactive space, mediated by material and cognitive artifacts, which can enable or facilitate purposeful actions, and it is also the encounter place in which the participants in an interaction produce a series of events and performances throughout time.

In the world of contemporary services, the *service* space is radically changing as the *information and communication technologies* are increasingly empowering the potentialities of service action and communication. The *contemporary service action* happens within environments and contexts in which the presence of remote interaction enablers (the *mediating artifacts*, i.e., the interactive interfaces) is getting more and more fundamental. We need, therefore, to analyze the physical dimension of these artifacts and the service supply system, and the potential space of action—that is what we call *service space*.

The definition of service deriving from this change is that of a mediated experience where the relationship between user and his or her action possibilities is based on an interactive system, the service interface.

The design as well as the evaluation of the service interface requires conceptualizing the man-artifact interaction as a part of an interaction path located in the service space; this interaction path is interpreted as a series of service encounters (Czepiel et al.), i.e., a sequence of contact moments of the customer with all the visible elements of the service company (the staff, the physical support, and the environment). The interface should, therefore, be understood as part of the over-all service supply system, including the social sphere as a relevant part of the whole interaction context.

These considerations help us to focus on the main issue of this chapter: to improve the design of service interfaces. The traditional design approaches, generally inter-ested in information processing and human computer interaction, should be inte-grated into a wider understanding of the social and communicative processes involving the actor and its community in specific contexts (the service spaces). For this reason, we propose an analytical model for the evaluation of the service space that has been tested with a concrete example of a mediated service, *Pay x Use* of Merloni Elettrodomestici. Our aim is to support a shift from a design culture based on the peculiar actor-interface interaction, to a design culture able to look at situ-ated interactions within a precise experiential context. The new perspective also generates a shift from a service (and communication) design to what we call the design of activity systems. The adaptation of *Activity Theory* framework (Engeström et al.) to service design represents a first step in this direction.

Activity Theory and Service Evaluation: The Encounter Model

Considering services as situated social and communication activities, we see Activity Theory as an interesting research framework because of its systemic and artifact-mediated (tools and signs) conception of human activity.

Activity Theory is a framework that offers a set of perspectives and orienting con-cepts to study human activity focused on practice as the way to understand the

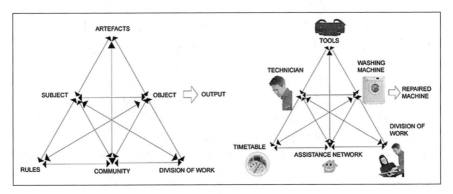

Figure 9.1: Engeström's Activity System model and its application to the washing machine service case.

unity of consciousness and activity. In particular, Activity Theory suggests a unit of analysis of human activity, defined as Activity System (Figure 9.1), where the activity, described as intermediary between an acting-subject or a group, and an object (physical artifact or problem), is always mediated by artifacts (physical or cognitive) and takes place within a specific community characterized by rules (formal and informal) and by a work organization (roles and tasks).

Starting from this analytical model, we made a first hypothesis: that the systemic dimension and situated nature of the service action could be represented through the elements of the *Activity System*. Services could therefore be described as *Activity Systems* oriented toward goals, carried out by people with different roles, competencies, and expertise, which use various tools and information, and behave in relation to rules and particular habits.

To develop an evaluation method of the service and communication space, we have extracted some key concepts from the Activity Theory framework:

- *Systemic and contextual approach*: each service element should be interpreted within a situated context (Activity System model) and in relation to the other service elements, because the variation of a single element can change the perception and fulfillment of the activity as a whole; and

- *Focus upon the interactions between different activity systems*: the analysis of human activity should not be considered on its own, but in its encounter/relationship with other Activity Systems as they can produce possible contradictions and encourage adaptation processes of the involved communities. The Activity Theory model should then comprise (at least) two Activity Systems that interact with each other to reach their goal. The service action (using and supplying) can therefore be evaluated as the encounter/relationship space or service encounter between two activity systems originally separated, such as that of the supplier and that of the user.

Therefore, by applying these principles, the service space and the concerned communication issues can be described as a situated activity, comprising different encounter moments (service encounters), accountable as Activity Systems co-produced by the interaction of the user with the supplying system. The representation of this idea can be defined as the encounter model (Figure 9.2).

The derived service design model looks at moments of encounter between service suppliers and user Activity Systems as the main focus to describe and analyze

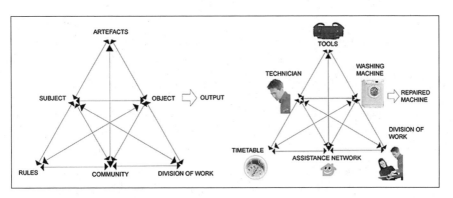

Figure 9.2: The service encounter model as a situated action.

service (and communication) spaces. Our methodology, therefore, is based upon two main levels of analysis: the reconstruction of the user's and the supplier's Activity Systems, and the consequent observation/evaluation of situated service interactions read as the result of the encounters between the originally separated user's and supplier's Activity Systems.

The service design model and the related analytical approach imply the necessity of a first phase of field analysis—based on ethnographic techniques and filtered by the use of the Activity System model—whose aim is to study the contexts of the communities involved in the service performance.

The Activity System model is used as a guiding framework that suggests the main elements and relations/contradictions to look at during the analytical phases: interacting subjects, objectives, physical artifacts (products and environment), cognitive artifacts (explicit and tacit knowledge used during the interaction), norms (procedures and habits), roles and tasks.

The analytical method can therefore be divided into five main phases:

1. *Pre-understanding of the service and selection of the service encounters to be analyzed*: to identify critical service encounters and the related interacting actors, a pre-understanding of the service is necessary. This pre-understanding should collect information about the design and implementation processes, the service offering, and the supplying system;

2. *Reconstruction of the Activity Systems of the involved actors*: the reconstruction of the Activity Systems of the selected service encounters mainly requires the collection of documentation (pictures, maps, organizational charts, procedures, etc.) and of information through interviews carried out with the

actors directly (direct participants) or indirectly (i.e., designers of the supplying systems) involved in the service interactions. The collection of documentation and the interviews aim at identifying and evaluating the elements
of their Activity Systems;

3. *Observation and analysis of the selected service encounters*: the analysis of the
service encounters is carried out through interviews with the service participants (internal point of view) and through the researcher's direct observation
of the action (external point of view). Both the observation and the interviews are driven by analytical filters that help evaluate the single elements of
the Activity Systems in relation to the other elements (systemic reconstruction of the action). Moreover, they are double-faced filters because they evaluate the same elements of the Activity System, considering the complemen-
tary and antithetic point of view of the user and the supplier. For example,
considering the Activity System element of the service rules, the analytical
filters could be: from the supplier's point of view, the level of flexibility of the
service rules to the users' habits and needs, and from the user's point of view,
the user's level of adaptation to the service rules;

4. *Organization of the information and identification of critical nodes*: comparing the
different points of view on the same service encounter with the information
collected on the interacting Activity Systems, the researcher should be able
to identify and understand critical nodes and represent them in a systemic
way; and

5. *Focusing of design issues*: the systemic representation of the origins of the critical nodes is the starting point to identify existing design issues and to propose
possible new design directions.

The Interface as Service Encounter Enabler: The Case of Ariston Digital Pay X Use

A preliminary evaluation of the described approach has been carried out on a
domotic service case study (**Editor's note**: Domotics is the use of computer and
robot technologies in domestic appliances and household systems. It derives from
domus [Latin for house] and *informatics.*): the Pay per Use (PXU) of Merloni-
ENEL; Merloni is a multinational household appliances producer, and ENEL is
the main Italian electric energy supplier.

The PXU service foresees a washing machine rental that enables the consumer to
pay for each washing load and to be continually connected with the Contact

Centre Merloni through a modem, allowing the automatic recharge of the user's available credit, the tele-diagnosis, the alarm in case of breakage, the mailing of promotional messages of usage advice, and statistics.

This case study represents an example of the recent ICT-based services that are bringing relevant changes to family life activity. The PXU analysis and evaluation have followed the above-described methodological steps, choosing as starting point the main service encounters where problems related to activity change and learning processes could more easily emerge. PXU is a mediated service, where users interact with the supplier mostly through artifacts (washing machine, telephone, etc.), and where the service encounters tend to coincide with the users' interactions with the interface of the artifacts themselves.

The evaluation of these kinds of service-communication spaces asks for the analysis of these interfaces seen as the places of encounter among different communities; because the analyzed service implies a high degree of social innovation (introducing new behavioral models), we have also considered, among the interacting communities, the PXU design team, to be able to compare the design process objectives and choices with the actual customer service action. In the PXU case, the encounter model can therefore be described as the convergence of three Activity Systems, as figure 9.3 illustrates.

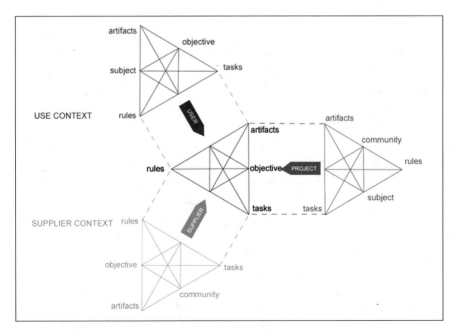

Figure 9.3: The encounter model: the user/supplier activity systems and their relationships with the design team activity system

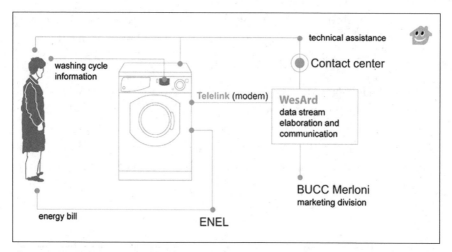

Figure 9.4: PXU functional scheme: the washing machine interface as a mediating tool with different Activity Systems: users, ENEL, Merloni Contact Center and Business Unit Customer Care

The big effort of Merloni Elettrodomestici has been to create the complex technological and service infrastructure necessary for the supplying of PXU service, and then to simplify its interface for both clients and people involved in the supplying system (figure 9.4).

The Margherita Dialogic therefore becomes the physical device around which the service space is materialized. Consequently, the evaluation of the service-communication system that happens through the PXU interface cannot be based upon the observation of the mere man-machine interaction, but should include the evaluation and the comparison of the activity systems of the involved actors through the observation/reconstruction of their encounters during the installation, use, and management of the washing machine itself.

The Pay per Use has been analyzed focusing on the interface of the Dialogic and on the two main service encounters that it enables: the installation of the PXU, which directly involves the user and the technician, and indirectly the design team (figure 9.5), and the daily use of the machine, which directly involves the user and the contact center, and indirectly the design team (figure 9.6).

The analysis has been mainly carried out through interviews that aimed at investigating, respectively:

- the Activity System of the user before the renting of the PXU (family life and modalities of use and maintenance of the traditional appliance), as well as related to the activation and use of the new washing machine;

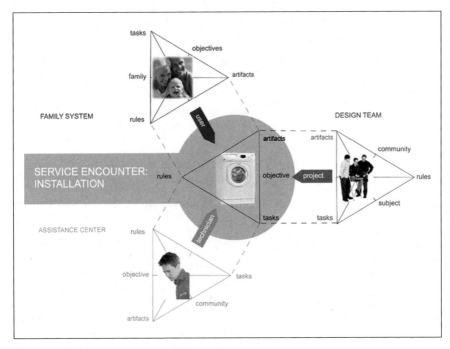

Figure 9.5: Service encounter model: installation

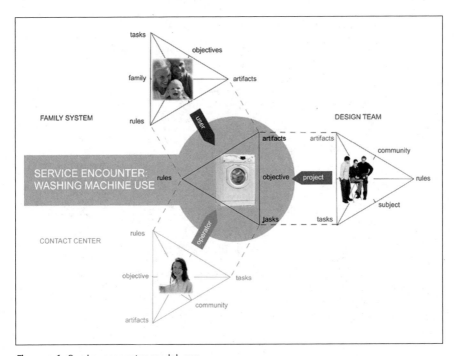

Figure 9.6: Service encounter model: use

- the Activity System of the supplier's main actors: the contact center (modality of data management and interaction with the user), and the technician (assistance center and machine's installation Activity Systems); and

- the Activity System of the design team that followed the interface design (aims, assumed interaction model, technological constraints, and design process).

Two central issues emerged from the systematization and comparison of the collected information (figures 9.7 and 9.8): 1) the activity change and learning issues associated with the introduction of the new artifact, and 2) the usability issues, such as readability and flexibility of the suggested interaction model, that always compare the pre-existent user's Activity System and the whole supplying system.

Activity Change and Learning Issues

Users of the *Dialogic* have a limited perception of the impact of the changes associated with the introduction of the new PXU functions, but they seem to understand better the changes associated with the new management of the washing programs (now based upon the choice of fabric) and the renewed range of choices and functions that users have to learn.

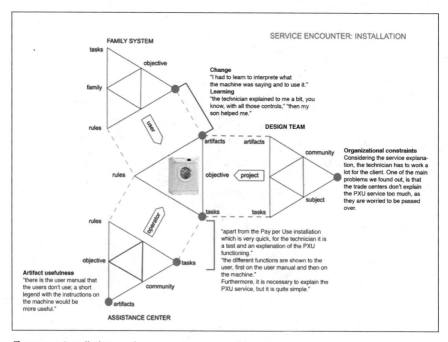

Figure 9.7: Installation service encounter: some evidences

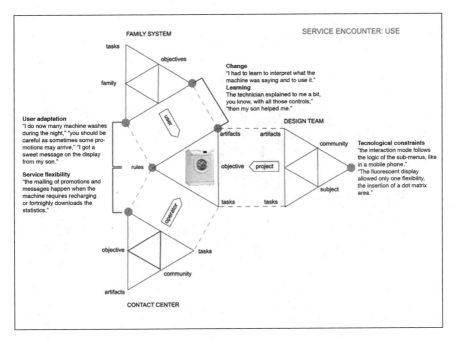

Figure 9.8: Use service encounter: some evidences

Users showed an initial resistance to the way that the machine communicates the information and drives the interaction (user: "all those knobs," "be able to read what the machine was saying"), and to the novelty of the meaning of some functions (*Ironless, Pay per Use, etc.*). The human support during the learning process, therefore, plays a central role (technician: "the different functions are explained to the user, first through the user manual, and then on the machine [. . .] this is the best way to explain it, as in this way it remains clear in the customer's memory"). In the absence of a socially assimilated use model (technician: "the user can't go ask a friend: *how do you do it?*") and of an effective support from the selling network, the technician plays a central role in introducing and explaining the innovative services offered by the machine.

These brief considerations highlight the importance, within interface and communication design, to look at the wider Activity System, comprising the different encounter moments among the different actors involved in the action; the learning of the Pay per Use cannot be in fact imagined focusing exclusively on the man-machine interaction, as it is actually supported by the wider service Activity System, comprising actors, artifacts, and pre-existent behavioral models (rules and tasks), of which the washing machine is just a part.

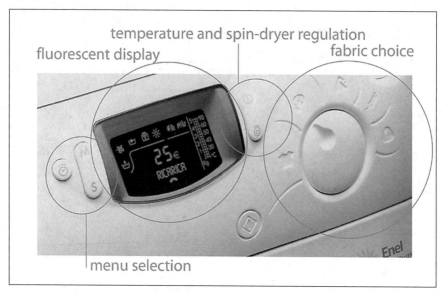

temperature and spin-dryer regulation

fluorescent display   fabric choice

menu selection

Figure 9.9: PXU interface main interaction areas: fabric choice knob, menu and functions selection knobs, and fluorescent display with fixed icons and sliding text

Usability Issues

The wider dialogue potentialities offered by the digitalization of the washing functions, by the connection with the contact center, and by the PXU service introduction require the proposal of a new model for interacting with the washing machine, which should supersede the traditional one without disorienting the user. Merloni seems to have adopted an intermediate interaction solution by drawing upon an existing interaction-communication model, the mobile telephone, which is now assimilated in contemporary society. The adoption of the mobile phone interaction model proposes, in addition to the application of the menus and submenus choice logic (figure 9.10), a terminology that is related to a recognizable semantic universe, with words such as *recharge, promotion,* and *messages receipt.*

On the one hand, the adoption of a socially acquired communication model simplifies the comprehension and the approach to the PXU system because it proposes well-known behavioral habits; on the other hand, though, it can generate some incomprehension when it is integrated with a more traditional model such as that of the washing machine. The resulting solution is unavoidably a hybrid one.

Comparing the PXU interaction model with the ones of the mobile telephone and of the traditional washing machine (figures 9.11 and 9.12), one can find contradictions that derive from the overlapping of two originally distinct Activity Systems.

PAY PER USE FUNCTIONS
pushing more than one time the M button, the PXU menu is activated, while pushing the S button the six submenus can be visualised:

1. CREDIT: it indicates the available amount of credit (in euros)

2. PROMOTION: it visualises the last promotion sent

3. COST OF THE LAST WASH: it indicates the cost of the last wash done

4. DATE OF THE LAST RECHARGE: it indicates the date of the last recharge

5. NUMBER OF WASHES: number of washes done since the first installation

6. MESSAGES: it visualises the last message received

Figure 9.10: The main interaction functions of the PXU interface

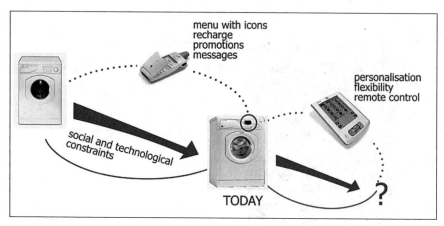

Figure 9.11: The evolution of the washing machine interaction model

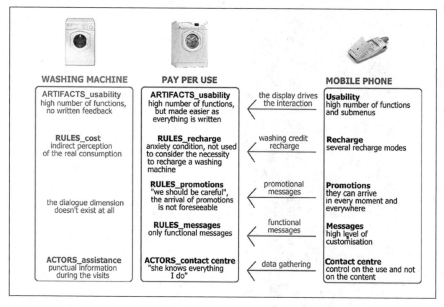

Figure 9.12: Comparison among interaction models: traditional washing machine, PXU machine, mobile phone

Despite the high number of functions and knobs, the introduction of the sliding words on the display enhances the dialogue potentiality, supporting the interaction with the machine (user: "everything is visualized, even the less educated person can read it [. . .] it is all so simple, so clear, everything is written"). Although in the traditional washing machine the exactness of the washing choices could be checked through a visual (apparent functioning and knob movement) and sound control of the machine itself, the *Dialogic* really supports and simplifies the use by giving detailed information upon the single functions and carried-out operations.

The effect of the introduction of functions such as the recharge and the mailing of promotions and messages is a bit different and can sometimes disorient the user. Compared with the telephone field where the payment modality is proportional to the effective use, and the possibility to visualize this consumption are acquired use models, in the appliance field there is the need for a behavioral change, because the use cost is generally associated more with purchase than with use.

The possibility to pay for the washing and the necessity to recharge the available credit, even if completely automatic, can generate perplexity reactions in front of the message "reserve credit recharging" or anxiety reactions if the recharging time is longer than expected, or the recharge itself has some problems (telephone or line problems). This can happen because the PXU interaction modality implies the use of a not yet assimilated behavioral model (user: "once it happened that I had loads of washing to do and after the first cycle the machine told me 'disabled cycle, non sufficient credit'").

The introduction of promotions and messages aims at personalizing the offering and creating a closer link with users. The technological constraints of the fluorescent display, with a small area for sliding words, and those of the connection modalities with the contact center (possible only during the recharge or the statistics download) make the mailing of messages limited in time and length. The limited interaction with the washing machine during the day and the limited mailing time of the contact center have highlighted the unpredictability of the messages reception (user: "it is necessary to be careful as a promotion could arrive"), even if in this way the communication system seems to be less invasive.

Users perceive the customization in terms of assistance and total control on the use modalities of the machine. If the user has, on the one hand, the clear perception of being continually monitored in his or her consumption habits, on the other hand, he or she interprets the control as a continual assistance (user: "the young lady [Business Unit Customer Care, Merloni marketing] knows everything I do, how many washings, how I use it [. . .] it doesn't annoy me, as I feel free [. . .] and then if there is so much attention, I know that if there would be any problems they'd sort them out"). There exists then a delicate equilibrium between the company's interests and the costs and advantages on the users' side. The big potentiality of this service solution has to be carefully implemented to safeguard this equilibrium.

As shown through the analysis of this case study, the evaluation of the PXU interaction models and communication system acquires new meanings when the analytical model, which is used to interpret the service interaction, is applied to real-use situations (situated action) and when it compares information coming from the whole *Activity Systems* made up of actors, physical and conceptual artifacts, pre-existent and acquired behavioral models.

Final Considerations

The key points that emerged from the interpretation of the Merloni case are:

- The change of users' *Activity System* should be evaluated comparing users' perception with what the design team and the supplier had foreseen as a support to this change;

- The users' level of adaptation (to service rules) should be evaluated considering the design team's and the supplier's level of flexibility (to user's needs); and

- The users' level of learning depends upon the supplier's adequacy in enabling communication with the users and upon the level of transparency of the service system features (level of systemic usability).

The way in which users interact with the machine seems to be perceived, in the PXU case, as the main change; the users considered the PXU interface as a sort of new communication language they had to learn, made up of a digital display with menu selections, sliding prescriptions for action, totally new functions such as the credit charge, and the mailing of messages and promotions.

From the supplier's point of view, the support to change is related to the adoption of an existing model of interaction, the mobile phone—one that should facilitate the comprehension of the machine's new functions.

This hybrid solution of PXU interaction model (washing machine + mobile phone) can present some contradictions: washing activity, unlike mobile's use, has a limit in terms of the effectiveness of the messages and promotions sent.

From the supplier's side, there is still a lack of flexibility in terms of capability to fit user's experience. This kind of limit depends both on the limited features of PXU technology and on a limited communication spectrum in the machine interface.

A possible design direction could be the widening of the communication perspective that includes the overall washing activity system in the interface design. This can be translated as better interaction modes, functions, and usability of the overall service system. We think that possible design directions could be imagined in terms of improving the general service system's flexibility as a gradual system adaptation to users' real capabilities of action and task understanding.

This implies that the whole question of communication in service design must be reconsidered from a more systemic point of view; we should build new approaches and tools that are really effective in controlling contextual fluxes of communication related to *Activity Systems* in the service domain.

In conclusion, we can say that to evaluate the quality of the service space, it is necessary to define an analytical model that considers communication activities in a systemic way.

This presents some issues about potential changes in designers' roles and competencies; in particular, communication and interface designers should acquire an Activity System approach to enrich their practitioner background with activity-based analytical tools and competences.

Our perspective merges an interactive vision with a contextualized vision: the generative process that builds the action-service is in fact based upon a series of negotiated interactions ruled by a specific real, social, and cognitive context. This seems then to be the precise identification of what we define as the *space of the action-service-communication*, which is, according to our hypothesis, the *service space*.

The service space is an interactive space mediated by material and cognitive artifacts, which can enable purposeful actions; it is the encounter's place, in which the participants in interactive actions constantly produce and reproduce a series of events or performances. A fundamental condition for the effective development of the encounter is that the actors participating in the interactive process are able to reach the mutual intelligibility of their roles through the understanding of how their actions are appropriate to the service situations. Garfinkel thinks that this condition could be obtained through the tacit use of an interpretative method (that verifies the coherence of the relation between actions and situations); this allows the actors to participate in the objective, which is hidden in the intentions of the other agents.

Making explicit what is tacit is therefore the basic condition that allows a dynamic participatory condition in the encounters within the service space and becomes the basic condition to imagine a design action.

This condition enables what we call the *design of the Activity Systems*. We think that design should be oriented toward this rich and complex frontier to design effective and systemic service actions.

References

Barley, S. R. (1996). "Technicians in the workplace: Ethnographic evidence for bringing work into organisation studies." In *Administrative Science Quarterly*, 41.

Coulon, A. (1995). *Ethnomethodology*. Thousand Oaks: Sage.

Czepiel, J., Solomon, M. and Suprenant, C. [Eds.] (1985). *The Service Encounter. Managing Employee/Customer Interaction in Service Business*. Lexington, MA: Lexington Books.

Engeström, Y., Miettinen, R. and Punamäki, R. [Eds.] (1999). *Perspectives on Activity Theory*. Cambridge: Cambridge University Press.

Garfinkel, H. (1967). *Studies in Ethnomethodology*. Englewood Cliffs, NJ: Prentice-Hall.

Lave, J. and Wenger, E. (1991). *Situated Learning: Legitimate Peripheral Participation*. Cambridge: Cambridge University Press.

Maffei, S. and Sangiorgi, D. (2003). "Service design as the design of activity systems: From a theoretical model to applied tools within an industrial project." *Sustainable product-service system "state of the art."* Conference Proceedings, Amsterdam, 5–6 June.

Mantovani, G. (1995). *Comunicazione e identità. Dalle situazioni quotidiane agli ambienti virtuali*. Bologna: Il Mulino.

Manzini, E., and Vezzoli, C. (2000). *Designing a new product-service mix*. Expert-Meeting on Product Service System, EU.

Mead, G. H. (1934). *Mind, Self, and Society*. Chicago: University of Chicago Press.

Nardi, B. [Ed.] (1996). *Context and Consciousness. Activity Theory and Human Computer Interaction*. Cambridge, MA: MIT Press.

Normann, R. (1999). *La gestione strategica dei servizi*. Milano: Etas.

Orsingher, C. (1999). *Il servizio dalla parte del cliente. Un approccio cognitivo all'esperienza di consumo*. Roma: Carocci.

Rullani, E., and Romano, L. [Eds.] (1998). *Il postfordismo, Idee per il Capitalismo Prossimo Venturo*. Milano: Etas.

Sangiorgi, D. (2004). *Il Design dei servizi come Design dei Sistemi di Attività. La Teoria dell'Attività applicata alla progettazione dei servizi*. Industrial Design PhD thesis, Politecnico di Milano.

Schutz, A. (1962). "Common sense and scientific interpretations of human action." In *Collected Papers*. L'Aia: Martinus Nijhoff, vol. I.

Strauss, M. (1978). "A social worlds perspective." In Denzin, N. [Ed.]. *Studies in Symbolic Interaction*. Greenwich: JAI Press.

Suchman, L. (1987). *Plans and Situated Actions: The Problem of Human-Machine Communication*. Cambridge: Cambridge University Press.

CHAPTER TEN

Behavior Change Theory and Visual Communication Design

Zoe Strickler
University of Connecticut, Storrs, USA

This chapter discusses several models and theories of behavior change, developed within the field of psychology, that have particular promise as conceptual tools for strengthening visual communication design. Visual communication design (graphic design) as a discipline has tended not to study behavioral outcomes that result from audience or user interactions with designed artifacts, or even to explicitly identify user behavioral change as an end goal for our work. However, behavioral impact is implied in many of the claims we make for our profession. A promotional text from the AIGA states: "Designers are incredibly powerful. We have a hand in creating the communications, experiences and artifacts that shape our world and [have] growing influence on decisions affecting the quality of life for millions of people. We make the mundane easier; we can delight the spirit; we can make things function better; we can help others understand the implications of choice by the way we see problems; and we can help all people to communicate among themselves better." This chapter proposes that we should begin to consider behavioral outcomes that result from end-user contact with designed communications to be an important area for study within design academic investigation and professional practice.

What follows is a (necessarily brief) overview of five important models of behavioral change that have gained acceptance among social and health scientists working across a range of disciplines concerned with health behavior. Each model or theory contains elements that would appear to have considerable relevance for visual communication design aimed at reducing injury and disease in targeted populations. This body of literature is typically not taught as part of visual communication design educational curricula, but the concepts investigated may have implications for our profession well beyond the obvious health applications.

The Health Belief Model

The *Health Belief Model* (HBM) was developed in the 1950s by psychologists at the U.S. Public Health Service (Janz and Becker), and has been associated for decades with the work of Irwin Rosenstock and Marshall Becker (Rosenstock et al.), among others. The Health Belief Model was widely adopted and refined through the 1970s, and it has since served as the basis for a large number of public health initiatives in the U.S. and elsewhere (Murray-Johnson). The model was developed during a period in which social psychologists were beginning to focus on beliefs and attitudes as presumed precursors for behavior, with a particular emphasis on understanding factors that cause people to perform, or not perform, preventive behaviors regarding their health.

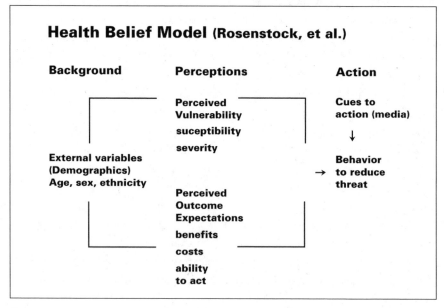

Figure 10.1

The Health Belief Model (figure 10.1) proposes that, in addition to socio-demographic factors in people's lives, there are two types of beliefs that influence whether people will avoid an unsafe behavior and/or adopt a safer health behavior. These are *people's perception of vulnerability to harm* and their *outcome expectations* regarding a health-related behavior (Rosenstock et al.).

Within the model, *perception of vulnerability* is understood to be the extent to which people believe that they are personally *susceptible* to contracting a particular disease or condition, modified by their perception of the *severity* of the condition (the *perceived threat* of the ailment). For example, whereas individuals may believe that they are *susceptible* to contracting gonorrhea during sex with a casual partner, they may choose not to use condoms because they believe gonorrhea can be controlled with antibiotics (and assume, therefore, that it does not pose a serious, long-term *threat* to their health). On the other hand, individuals may fully believe that HIV/AIDS is a life-threatening and incurable disease, but if they believe that their partner is unlikely to have it, they may choose not to use condoms because they do not believe that they are personally *susceptible*.

Outcome expectations within the Health Belief Model are the anticipated *benefits* and *barriers*, or costs, of enacting, or not enacting, a particular health behavior. These can represent financial, social, or physiological rewards or barriers believed to be linked to a particular action (Rosenstoc, et. al.). The model proposes that the decision to change a behavior (i.e., to cease a risky behavior, or to adopt a recommended behavior) will be based on the extent to which individuals believe that the benefits from making the change will outweigh the costs. For instance, young people may know that recreational drug use can lead to long-term adverse health effects and/or risk of addiction, yet many use them anyway because they believe that the perceived immediate advantages—peer approval, group identity, or access to desired persons and experiences—outweigh potential long-term health hazards.

Despite its extensive use in the public health sector, studies over several decades have yielded inconsistent empirical support for the HBM as a basis for effecting behavioral change (Janz and Becker; Fisher and Fisher 2000). In some studies where the HBM was used as the guiding theoretical model, relations between HBM constructs and behavioral outcomes have showed significant, but small, changes in desired behavior in targeted populations (Janz and Becker). In other studies, relations between HBM constructs and behavior have been found to be minimal, or were not found (Gerrard; Wayment et al.). In general, the HBM has been used more successfully as a predictive model in studies where the health behavior under consideration is a one-time, relatively simple action, such as obtaining a cancer screening or immunization (this is the kind of health problem for which it was developed). For health behaviors that involve complex social interactions or difficult actions that must be maintained over time, such as weight loss or preventing HIV/AIDS, the model has generally been less successful at adequately predicting behavioral change or demonstrating effect (Rosenstock et al.; Janz and Becker).

Despite its status as an older model with sometimes equivocal or weak scientific support, I have included the HBM in this discussion because it has been highly influential in public health communications for decades, and from the standpoint of visual communication design practice, it has strong intuitive appeal. The HBM was developed around the same time that graphic design was forming as a profession in the U.S. (the 1950s and 1960s), and some of its constructs are consistent with assumptions that have guided work in our profession for decades. These shared ideas include, first, the premise that if people are provided with persuasive and powerfully delivered information they will act on it in desired ways. Second, the model invokes the classic economic assumption that people will logically weigh the costs and benefits of choices they face, and that they will make rational behavioral decisions based on what should benefit them most, according to presented information.

Particularly the first assumption is consistent with claims long put forward in the writings of prominent figures in graphic design. The books of Paul Rand (Rand), for instance, are still cited and are found on recommended reading lists for courses in beginning through graduate graphic design education programs (Heller). Rand's writings (which must be understood as collections of personal essays), and the books and articles of many subsequent designers, imply that a designer's subjective, intuitive processes will produce efficacious designs through use of aesthetics (visual properties selected by the designer) and, in some instances, clear organization. These writings assume—like the HBM—that people will interpret our work as we think they will, and will act on it as we intend, so long as the visual presentation is strong, but without explaining how this will occur, and without providing supporting empirical evidence.

A seminal work used in design education for decades is *Thoughts on Design*, by Paul Rand, originally published in 1947. With respect to the end-user Rand wrote, "because advertising art, in the end, deals with the spectator, and because it is the function of advertising to influence him, it follows that the designer's problem is twofold: to anticipate the spectator's reactions and to meet his own aesthetic needs" (13). The matter of influence or effectiveness is dropped at this point in the book in favor of discussions of fine art, aesthetics, and image-making accompanied by extensive examples of the designer's own work, and quotations from artists, art historians, and philosophers. The book does not provide supporting evidence for claims of design's influence on audience beliefs or behaviors. This format and approach has served as a model for books by well-known design educators for decades, such as *Graphic Design Sources* by Ken Hiebert. While such texts have been inspirational for young designers entering the field (and they have strongly influenced the knowledge and skills sets that are considered necessary for a design education), their assumptions have not been challenged or tested in any meaningful sense by our field. The confident, yet unexamined, tone of early literature produced by the profession continues to be present in writing by designers about design today (as can be seen in the text for the AIGA national conference). *Teaching Graphic Design*, edited by Steven Heller, is a reference consisting of forty-five course syllabi, and class projects, submitted by graphic design faculty from prominent graphic design programs in the U.S. While most, but not all, of the courses include some requirement of reading, the recommended texts tend to be about graphic designers, typographers, and architects, or works of contemporary cultural analysis. Few readings represented are in the social sciences. Most courses and projects in the book invoke a purpose such as to "create excellent portfolio pieces that visually communicate through the embodiment of form and function" (9), but stated objectives such as *communication* and *function* are not defined or evaluated in terms of outcomes beyond a subjective class critique. The design process is often mapped as a variant on "Research > Analysis > Design Intent > Methodology > Fabrication > Documentation" (130), but verification procedures such as testing and evaluation, or even qualitative contact with representative end-users, are largely absent from assignments, readings, and process. Two exceptions in the book are 1) Sharon Poggenpohl's graduate course, the *Future of Learning Workshop* at IIT, which integrates user observation, testing, and evaluation processes directly into the development of prototypes, and requires background reading in cognitive science, and 2) an exhibit design project by Lisa Fontaine of Iowa State University which involves field trips to local museums where students observe museum visitors interacting with exhibits before designing their projects.

In sharp contrast, the social sciences, including clinical, experimental, educational, and social psychology, have exhaustively challenged theoretical precepts developed in the formative years of their professions. Each generation of research produced in these fields has become more rigorous than the work that preceded it (particularly with respect to matters of the validity and reliability of study designs, measures, and theoretical constructs employed in research), and investigators are more cautious in claims that are made for their findings (Brinberg and McGrath; Kirk and Miller).

The Theory of Reasoned Action

A second influential model, the *Theory of Reasoned Action* (TRA) (Fishbein and Ajzen; Ajzen and Fishbein), developed in the 1970s by social psychologists Martin Fishbein and Icek Ajzen, is a theory of behavioral change that, in its basic formulation, addresses factors that are weakly addressed in the Health Belief Model. Fishbein and Ajzen were concerned with identifying specific relations between beliefs, attitudes, and behaviors, toward the goal of being able to predict behavioral change in individuals based on their expressed attitudes. Whereas the Health Belief Model does not specify clear relations between its component constructs (Fisher and Fisher 2000), the TRA was developed to be quite clear in this regard.

Attitude research prior to the work of Fishbein and Ajzen had generally demonstrated weak correlations between people's beliefs and attitudes about particular issues, and their actions relative to them (McGuire). Fishbein and Ajzen, however, found that whereas people's general beliefs and attitudes toward a situation or "object" are unlikely to predict their behaviors, certain types of attitudes can be highly predictive of behavior (Ajzen and Fishbein). One factor they found to be strongly predictive of behavior was a person's stated *intention* to perform a behavior. Within the TRA, the formation of *intention* is related to two specific kinds of attitudes and beliefs: 1) a person's *attitude toward the behavior* (e.g., the person's belief that a behavior will lead to certain outcomes, as in the HBM) and 2) a person's *subjective norms* regarding the behavior (beliefs held by the person about what others think the person should do).

Within the TRA, attitudes are understood to be functions of beliefs. For instance, if a person believes that mostly favorable outcomes will result from a behavior, then the person is said to have a "favorable attitude" toward the behavior. If anticipated outcomes are believed to be negative, the person will have a "negative attitude" toward the behavior. However, within the model, these attitudes toward the behavior are further modified by a person's perception of what influential others think about the behavior (social norms), and by the person's motivation to comply with the perceived expectations of others. The theory suggests that if the relative weight or importance of attitudes and norms held by individuals or populations can be determined, behaviors can be predicted with greater accuracy.

For instance, a young person may fully believe that smoking leads to harmful health outcomes later in life, and may also believe that his or her parents disapprove of smoking. However, if the young person perceives that key individuals within his or her peer group regard smoking favorably, and that smoking is expected within that peer circle, a strong motivation to comply with peer expectations may overwhelm negative beliefs and parental expectations. Ajzen and Fishbein expressed the relations between these constructs in a multiple regression equation: $(B \sim BI = [A_{act}]w_1 + [SN]w_2)$ where a person's behavior (B) is a function of his or her behavioral intention (BI). Behavioral intention is determined by the weight of attitude toward the behavior (A_{act}) and the weight (w) of the subjective norm (SN).

While it would be rare for designers to need to predict or measure behavior in individuals in this way, the TRA is a useful conceptual model for designers who work on problems in which target populations are not receptive to institutional messages or authority, and for whom peer influence and perceived social norms play a strong role in behavioral decision-making. The constructs within the TRA have been shown to be particularly strong predictors of behavior across a number of studies and situations (Ajzen and Fishbein; McGuire). In that these constructs deal directly with beliefs, attitudes, and perceived norms, the potential of the TRA to explain the role that certain beliefs may play in shaping behaviors— including beliefs derived from interpersonal and mass communication—should be of considerable interest to communication designers.

Social Cognitive Theory

From the 1950s through the 1990s (and with continuing influence on the field), Albert Bandura studied behavior change from the perspective of how individuals model the behavior of others when learning skills are needed to perform tasks. By studying processes of learning and social interaction across a wide range of environments that included athletic and artistic performance, as well as interpersonal aggression, academic learning, and health, Bandura produced the *Social Cognitive Theory* (SCT) (figure 10.2).

A key construct within SCT is the notion of *self-efficacy*, or the belief that one will be *able* to perform a particular task. Self-efficacy is related to the self-reflective and self-regulatory mental processes that determine whether a person will try to perform a behavior and how it will be attempted (Bandura 1986, 1997; Strecher et al.). Bandura's work suggests that whereas *knowledge* (or expertise) regarding a task or skill is an important component of successful execution of the task, knowledge

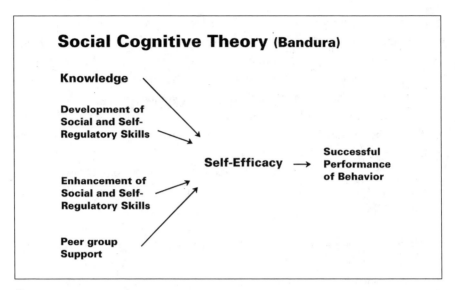

Figure 10.2

alone is not sufficient to ensure that it will be performed (or performed well)—an individual must also believe that he or she is capable of performing it successfully.

Self-efficacy is not a fixed personality trait like self-esteem (the perception of self-worth). Whereas a person's base level of self-esteem remains relatively constant across situations, self-efficacy is sensitive to particular environments and tasks. People can believe themselves to be competent in one task or skill area (for instance, math), but inefficacious (incompetent) in another (such as drawing).

For communication designers, the theorized role of *self-efficacy* in human behavior can, and should, be present in nearly every project we undertake. For instance, a basic precept of product design for many decades has been that designed objects should be created to be easy and intuitive for people to use. Through the lens of social cognitive theory this implies that by reducing social, cognitive, and psychological barriers to actions such as use of a product or practice of a safer behavior, communication design may help people to feel greater confidence that they can perform a skill successfully when they need to.

The Information—Motivation—Behavioral Skills Model

The Information—Motivation—Behavioral Skills (IMB) model of behavior change (figure 10.3) was developed by social psychologists Jeffrey D. Fisher and William A. Fisher in the late 1980s in response to the emergence of HIV/AIDS as a global public health crisis. Fisher and Fisher developed the IMB model (Fisher

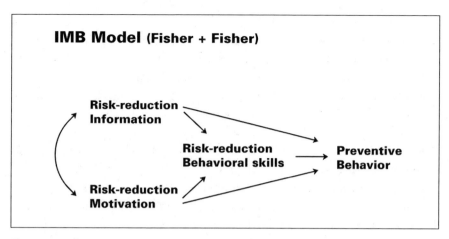

Figure 10.3

and Fisher 1992; Fisher and Fisher 2002), as a framework for designing health risk interventions for use in real world environments by employing well-supported, extant theories of behavior change. As such the IMB model defines theorized relationships among concepts, and provides guidelines and methods that are intended to translate behavior theory into effective action.

The model evolved from a review of the literature on HIV intervention efforts available up to that time (Fisher and Fisher 1992) with an emphasis on those that measured behavioral outcomes. The search showed that interventions that focused on existing deficits in a population's knowledge about specific HIV prevention behaviors, and/or that modeled or taught enactment of preventive behaviors, and/or that addressed people's motivations to enact (or not enact) risk prevention behaviors, were more effective than those that only attempted to increase participants' knowledge of the HIV/AIDS disease, or that dealt with other factors. The model holds that effective health risk behavior change intervention requires three components: 1) *information* regarding the disease and specific behaviors that can prevent its transmission; 2) elements that address people's beliefs and attitudes regarding preventive behaviors and that provide *motivation* to change risk behaviors or enact protective behaviors; and 3) elements that describe and *model* specific, effective, risk-preventive *behavioral skills*.

Fisher and Fisher found that many prior HIV prevention interventions had been designed primarily to increase participants' knowledge regarding HIV/AIDS. In particular, school-based interventions aimed at young people had tended to focus on increasing students' scientific knowledge of the disease, such as sources of transmission, t-cells, and viral replication. However, studies did not consistently demonstrate that gains in participant knowledge of this sort led to enactment of safer behaviors. In some of these, significant, but slight, relationships could be demonstrated; in others no relationship was found (Fisher and Fisher 1992). However, where interventions delivered both information about sources of disease transmission and behaviors that could be enacted to prevent such transmission, desired behavioral correlations were stronger.

The IMB model holds that risk-prevention *information* and risk-prevention *motivation* work primarily through risk-prevention *behavioral skills* to effect safer behavior. Information is understood within the model to be a necessary precursor for behavioral change, but one unlikely to be a sufficient condition for change. Likewise, motivation is assumed to be strongly correlated with preventive behaviors, but in the absence of relevant preventive skill acquisition and self-efficacy to enact acquired skills, behavioral change will be unlikely to occur.

Finally the model holds that learned behavioral skills must be specific and appropriate to the environment and social situation in which participants live, or they will not be enacted. Toward this end the model specifies that extensive elicitation research with a target population is necessary to design and implement effective health behavioral interventions. Where behavior modeling is present in an intervention, participants must be able to identify with the role models, and to imagine themselves successfully using the protective strategies in their own lives.

The model was developed specifically within the arena of HIV/AIDS risk-reduction, but its constructs have been applied and supported in health areas beyond HIV (Byrne, Kelly, and Fisher; Misovich et al.). Because of the model's focus on specific elements necessary for effective intervention in natural settings it is especially relevant for designers collaborating with public health organizations. In particular, designers working on communication projects intended to change health behaviors should review whether all necessary factors that promote health behavior change are present in the programs they design.

Trans-Theoretical Model

Clinical psychologists James O. Prochaska and Carlo C. DiClemente began work in the late 1970s to try to identify a common set of processes—distilled from an already broad range of approaches used in addiction research—that could be applied to the problem of smoking. At the time there were over 300 theories of psychotherapy in the literature (Prochaska and Velicer). The original insight was to try to identify common elements across that body of work that could be found

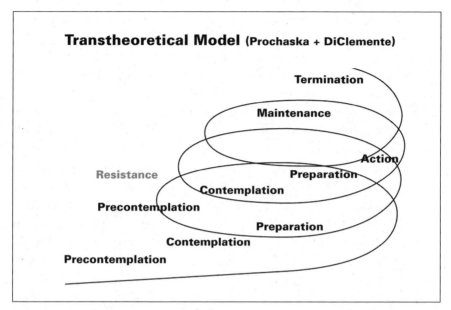

Figure 10.4

to be effective with clinical patients trying to stop smoking (Prochaska). In the early 1980s Prochaska and DiClemente began the work of matching theoretical concepts with strategies used by individuals who had successfully changed an addictive behavior, either in an intervention setting, or of their own volition (Prochaska and Velicer). This second insight led to an important reconceptualization of the nature of behavior change. Whereas prior theory had tended to frame behavior change as an event, such as "quitting," Prochaska and DiClemente described change as a process, and observed that people use different types of strategies to make changes in their lives at different stages of the change process (Prochaska, DiClemente, and Norcross).

The Transtheoretical Model (TTM) of behavior change (figure 10.4) that evolved from this work is grounded in three central constructs. These are: *stages of change, processes of change,* and *levels of change* (DiClemente and Prochaska; Prochaska and Velicer).

Stages of Change

The six stages of change in the TTM are defined as *precontemplation, contemplation, preparation, action, maintenance,* and *termination*. People in the *precontemplation stage* are either unaware of the health risks of a behavior, or choose to ignore the risk. People in this stage do not intend to change their behavior in the near future. People in the *contemplation stage* are aware of the dangers that a behavior poses to them and are considering taking action to change the behavior within the next six months. People in the *preparation stage* intend to take action in the near future and have made some sort of plan for how they will begin, such as enrolling in a fitness class or seeking professional help. People in the *action* stage have taken some kind of concrete, observable action to alter their lifestyle in the previous six months. People in the *maintenance* stage have already modified their lifestyle in some way to resist performing the behavior. They are actively working to avoid temptation and prevent relapse. The maintenance stage is thought to last from six months to a lifetime. People in the *termination stage* have ceased to engage in the behavior and experience zero temptation to return to it. They can be said to have 100 percent self-efficacy to refrain from it. (For some health behaviors such as exercise, weight control, or use of condoms, a lifetime of maintenance is the end goal, because for a majority of at-risk individuals the temptation to relapse with these behaviors never goes away.)

The stages of change are not conceived in TTM as occurring in a linear sequence, but rather in a spiral pattern, in which people who take action to modify a difficult behavior may progress through one stage and then relapse back to an earlier stage, in some cases a number of times, before achieving lasting change in their lives.

Processes of Change

The processes of change are ten psychological and behavioral processes (identified from the review of psychotherapeutic literature) that Prochaska and DiClemente found to be present in the efforts of individuals who had successfully changed their behavior. These processes were identified as: *consciousness raising* (increasing one's knowledge of the problem and its consequences); *dramatic relief* (emotional release, role-playing, sharing with others); *environmental reevaluation* (assessment of the role and impact of the behavior in one's life); *self-liberation* (a rise in self-efficacy, or belief in one's ability to effect change); *social liberation* (a rise in social opportunities to enact steps toward change); *counter-conditioning* (skill learning and substitution of safer behaviors for risky ones); *stimulus control* (avoidance of temptation or removal of temptations from one's lifestyle); *contingency management* (self-reinforcements for behavior); *helping relationships* (reaching out to others who support the change).

A key principle of the Transtheoretical Model is that different *processes of change* (psychological or concrete steps that individuals undertake to effect change) occur within different *stages of change*. This implies that particular intervention approaches will be appropriate for individuals at certain points in the process, but not for those in other stages (Prochaska, DiClemente, and Norcross). Relationships between stages and processes as they are generally thought to occur are shown the table below.

Table 10.1 Stages of change in which change processes are most emphasized.

Precontemplation	Contemplation	Preparation	Action	Maintenance
Consciousness raising Dramatic relief Environmental reevaluation				
	Self-reevaluation			
		Self liberation		
			Reinforcement management Helping relationships Counterconditioning Stimulus control	

(originally published in Prochazka, J. "In Search of How People Change" *American Psychologist*, Vol 47. No. 9, 1102–1114; p. 1104. Adapted with permission.)

A finding from the work of particular importance to intervention design is that approaches that have an action-oriented focus can produce impressive results in individuals who are in the *action stage* at the time they are given the intervention. However, action-oriented interventions are likely to have little effect, or even a negative impact, on individuals in the *precontemplation* or *contemplation stages* (Prochaska, DiClemente, and Norcross). William R. Miller and Steven Rollnick, developers of *Motivational Interviewing* (MI) (Miller and Rollnick), a patient counseling technique based, in part, on concepts from the TTM, have described the phenomenon of *resistance* that occurs in patients exposed to action-based change messages too early in the behavior change process (Rollnick, Mason, and Butler). When resistance occurs in an individual (defined as an internal ego-defense mechanism that arises in response to pressure to change), the intervention may actually set the patient back in his progress toward change. Further complicating this issue for designers of intervention messages are findings that suggest that most individuals in an at-risk population at any given time will be in the pre-contemplation stage (around 40 percent) or the contemplation stage (around 40 percent), rather than in the preparation stage or later (around 20 percent)—the stages in which traditional action-oriented messages can begin to be successful (Prochaska and Velicer).

Behavior Change Research and Visual Communication Design

If we assume that at least one function of visual communication design is to influence behaviors in people, then the literature discussed above should point to many concepts that are fertile for exploration by design researchers. However, it is important to note that this literature does not explicitly address factors of visual communication design, even in studies where it is used as a component of a behavioral intervention. Studies that use visual communication in an intervention may report that pamphlets were distributed to participants (Jammer, Wolitsky, and Corby), or that videos or computer programs were produced and shown (Fisher and Fisher 1992; Redding et al.), but images of these elements are typically not published, nor is discussion of the development of visual concepts or prototypes present in any detail. Such reporting would be of tremendous value for both designers and social scientists working in the area of health communication when outcomes from exposure to visual media are being evaluated.

Despite the lack of reporting on communication design within these studies, important directives for designers emerge from the work. For instance, the IMB model of Fisher and Fisher clearly outlines the types of information within a behavioral intervention that are necessary for the program to have a measurable effect on behavior. The TTM of Prochaska and DiClemente provides guidelines for understanding points in time that particular kinds of information might be expected to move individuals further along in a change process. The TTM also suggests when particular forms of communication might be expected to be ineffective, or counterproductive. (For a discussion of measurement of the effectiveness of public health campaigns see Hornik and Snyder.) For example, the TTM may provide insight into the longstanding controversy in communication research regarding the efficacy of fear messages.

During most of the twentieth century public health efforts by government agencies and non-profit organizations turned more often to advertising or marketing firms than to graphic design firms for development of communication to be used in health intervention. These agencies were more closely linked to radio and television production—media regarded as the most important for reaching mass audiences. Marketing and advertising groups have also traditionally shown greater concern for measuring behavioral outcomes from exposure to communication than have designers.

However, with the rise of interactive computer technologies, the promise of tailoring health interventions to the needs of high-risk individuals emerges as an especially promising area of new health behavior research (Redding et al.). Visual communication designers are now as likely to be involved with interactive media production as are advertising and marketing entities, and in some situations may even be regarded as the preferred source for visual interface design of interactive learning software and innovation for the Internet. This puts our discipline on a collision course with growing scientific interest in these media as vehicles for delivery of health behavior change interventions. We should begin preparing ourselves now for the opportunity this presents to increase the breadth of knowledge employed by our profession regarding human behavior and psychological processes, as well as to improve the effectiveness of the work we produce. This convergence also presents enormous opportunities to raise academic standards for research methods and conceptual processes employed in design research, and for eventual constructive influence of professional practice, as well.

References

Ajzen, I. and Fishbein, M. (1980). *Understanding Attitudes and Predicting Social Behavior.* Englewood Cliffs, NJ: Prentice Hall.

American Institute of Graphic Arts (2003). Flier and Web site for the AIGA National Conference entitled "The Power of Design," scheduled for October 23–26, 2003, in Vancouver, British Columbia, Canada. *www.aiga.org*; *http://powerofdesign.aiga.org*; *http://powerofdesign.aiga.org/content.cfm/topicscategory*

Bandura, A. (1997). *Self-efficacy: The exercise of control.* New York: WH Freeman.

Bandura, A. (1986). *Social Foundations of Thought and Action: A social cognitive theory.* Englewood Cliffs, NJ: Prentice Hall.

Byrne, D., Kelley, K., and Fisher, W. A. (1993). "Unwanted teenage pregnancies: Incidence, interpretation, intervention." *Applied and Preventive Psychology* 2: 101–113.

Brinberg, D. and McGrath, J. E. (1985). *Validity and Reliability in the Research Process.* Beverly Hills, CA: Sage.

DiClemente, C. C. and Prochaska, J. O. (1998). "Toward a comprehensive Transtheoretical Model of Change: Stages of change and addictive behaviors." In W. R. Miller and N. Heather (Eds.) *Treating Addictive Behaviors.* 2nd Ed. New York: Plenum Press.

Fishbein, M. and Ajzen, I. (1975). *Belief, Attitude, Intention and Behavior: An introduction to theory and research.* Reading, MA: Addison-Wesley.

Fisher, J. D. and Fisher, W. A. (1992). "Changing AIDS risk behavior." *Psychological Bulletin.* 111(3): 455–474.

Fisher, J. D. and Fisher, W. A. (2000). "Theoretical approaches to individual-level change in HIV risk behavior." In J. Peterson and R. DiClemente, (Eds.) *Handbook of HIV Prevention*. New York: Kluwer Academic/Plenum Publishers.

Fisher, J. D. and Fisher, W. A. (2002). "The Information—Motivation—Behavioral Skills Model." In R. DiClemente, R. Crosby, and M. Kegler (Eds.), *Emerging Theories in Health Promotion Practice and Research*. San Francisco, CA: Jossey Bass Publishers, 40–70.

Gerrard, M., Gibbons, F. X., and Bushman, B. J. (1996). "Relations between perceived vulnerability to HIV and precautionary sexual behavior." *Psychological Bulletin* 119, 390–409.

Heller, S. (Ed.), (2003). *Teaching Graphic Design: Course offerings and class projects from the leading undergraduate and graduate programs*. New York: Allworth Press.

Hiebert, K. (1998). *Graphic Design Sources*. New Haven, CT: Yale University Press.

Hornik, R. (2002). "'Public health communication: Making sense of contradictory evidence." In R. Hornik (Ed.), *Public Health Communication: Evidence for behavior change*. Mahwah, NJ: Lawrence Erlbaum Associates, 1–19.

Jammer, M. S., Wolitsky, R. J., and Corby, N. H. (1997). "Impact of a longitudinal community HIV intervention targeting injecting drug users' stage of change for condom and bleach use." *American Journal of Health Promotion* 12(1): 15–24.

Janz, N. K. and Becker, M. H. (1984). "The Health Belief Model: A decade later." *Health Education Quarterly* 11(1): 1–47.

Kirk, J. and Miller, M. L. (1986). *Reliability and Validity in Qualitative Research*. Beverly Hills, CA: Sage.

McGuire, W. J. (1985). "Attitudes and attitude change." In G. Lindzey and E. Aronson (Eds.), *The Handbook of Social Psychology*. Third Edition. New York: Random House.

Miller, W. R. and Rollnick, S. (1991). *Motivational Interviewing: Preparing people to change addictive behaviour*. New York: The Guildford Press.

Misovich, S. J., Martinez, T., Fisher, J. D., Bryan, A., and Catapano, N. (2003). "Predicting breast self-examination: A test of the Information—Motivation—Behavioral skills model." *Journal of Applied Social Psychology* 33(4): 775–790.

Murray-Johnson, L., Witte, K., Boulay, M., Figueroa, M. E., Storey, D., and Tweedie, E. (2001). "Using health education theories to explain behavior change: A cross-country analysis." *International Quarterly of Community Health Education* 20(4): 323–345.

Prochaska, J. O. (1979). *Systems of Psychotherapy: A transtheoretical analysis*. Homewood, IL: Dorsey.

Prochaska, J. O., DiClemente, C. C., and Norcross, J. C. (1992). "In search of how people change: Applications to addictive behaviors." *American Psychologist* 47(9): 1,102–1,114.

Prochaska, J. O., Velicer, W. F. (1997). "The transtheoretical model of health behavior change." *American Journal of Health Promotion* 12(1):38–48.

Rand, P. (1970). *Thoughts on Design*. (Second edition). New York: Van Nostrand Reinhold. (Original edition, 1947, New York: Wittenborn Schultz).

Redding, C. A., Prochaska, J. A., Pallonen, J. S., Velicer. W. F., Rossi, S. R., Greene, G. W., Meier, K. S., Evers, K. E., Plummer, B. A., and Maddock, J. E. (1999). "Transtheoretical individualized multimedia expert systems targeting adolescent's health behaviors." *Cognitive and Behavioral Practice* 6, 144–153. Association for Advancement of Behavior Therapy.

Rollnick, S., Mason, P., and Butler, C. (1999). *Health Behavior Change: A guide for practitioners*. New York: Churchill Livingstone.

Rosenstock, I. M., Strecher, V. J., Becker, M. H. (1994). "The Health Belief Model and HIV Risk Behavior Change." In R. J. DiClemente and J. L. Peterson (Eds.), *Preventing AIDS: Theories and Methods of Behavioral Interventions*. New York: Plenum Press.

Snyder, L. B. and Hamilton, M. A. (2002). "A Meta-analysis of U.S. health campaign effects on behavior: Emphasize enforcement, exposure and new information, and beware the secular trend." In R. Hornik (Ed.), *Public Health Communication: Evidence for behavior change*. Mahwah, NJ: Lawrence Erlbaum Associates 1–19.

Strecher, V. J., DeVellis, B. M., Becker, M. H., and Rosenstock, I. M. (1986). "The role of self-efficacy in achieving health behavior change." *Health Education Quarterly* 13(1): 73–91.

Wayment, H. A., Wyatt, G. E., Tucker, M. B., Romero, G. J., Carmona, J. V., Newcomb, M., Solis, B. M., Riederle, M. and Mitchell-Kernan, C. (2003). "Predictors of risky and precautionary sexual behaviors among single and married white women." *Journal of Applied Social Psychology* 33(4): 791–816.

PART FOUR

Living Spaces as Communication Spaces:
From the Home to the City

From the house to the city our life develops codifying and identifying the social meaning of physical structures. Our task began first in relation to natural spaces and to our very survival, assessing the possibilities and the risks associated with a given setting. Today, from the front page of a newspaper to the structure created by furniture in an interior space, to the signs in a city, our life is a life of identifications, recognitions, and taxonomies that allow us to travel through these spaces with efficiency and social grace. The task of the designer, from the micro to the macro level, is always connected to the understanding of existing codes, and to the extension of these existing codes. This is done in order to introduce the enlivening sense of novelty that to a greater or to a lesser extent, all of us enjoy. But the task is not easy, and understanding the needs, and producing an intelligent response is not enough: getting things done also requires mastery in the politics of interpersonal relations. The result is a space that is understandable, but that also adds to the culture of a place, and has a unique identity.

CHAPTER ELEVEN

Space as Process

Bernd Meurer
Hochschule Darmstadt, Germany

The space that we experience as living space is space of action, orientation, and communication. Space is not something finished, but something that develops in form and content always anew. It happens through action. Space is an endless series of events that take place in their respective present and are never completed. We are confronted by the problems associated with the space that we perceive, that we appropriate, that we exploit as a resource, and that we use for social interaction and communication. For us, space is urban space, landscape space, public and private space, and space that is constantly transformed by our use of it; space that we either overcome as distance or eliminate by means of communication; space that we imagine in our minds and that we simulate and generate as virtual space.

The sensory perception of space is physiologically limited. From this point of view, our living space appears to be a curved layer wrapped around the earth. If we include the atmosphere, aeronautics, and satellite technology, the height of this might amount to a few kilometers. If we take into consideration only what is directly connected to the earth's surface, namely our action space above and—to an extent—below ground, this layer is at most only a few hundred meters thick, and normally only ten to fifteen meters thick. The space of an individual's direct field of action and range of vision is usually limited in height to less than four meters and in depth to extremely short distances. Despite being such fundamental categories for the normal understanding of space or geometry, distance and size are scarcely of importance for the transmission of information today.

The microprocessing of everyday life (the daily products and processes affected by technology, computers, and automation) has changed the meaning of time, movement, and speed. It has changed almost all fields of space, especially of space in communication. Today, communication partners who are separated in space are brought together thanks to telecommunications. Through tele-presence, we can travel without ever leaving our original location. All locations can be potentially tele-present at one spot. The place that we perceive as tele-reality and the place where we do the perceiving are synchronous. Real proximity is replaced by the image of closeness. Real time prevails over real space. Space and time disconnect.

Accordingly, the status of the means of transportation is changing. As machines for reducing time, they have been rendered technologically obsolete by data transmissions, but they are gaining importance as machines for transportation. A fourfold increase in the volume of passengers is projected in air transportation for the next ten years, as well as a 50 percent decrease in flying time because of a new generation of airplanes. Clearly, this time saving has reached a new limit. The earth is simply too small to allow flight speeds any faster than this. The acceleration and braking phases would eat up any extra time gained. The decisive problem no longer lies in increasing the speed, but instead in factors that were considered until recently as a matter of peripheral importance. Secondary factors in the past have become major obstacles today.

Not only the speed of means of transportation but also the capacity of the routes is spatially limited. Computer-assisted traffic control does allow us to further increase the density of traffic up to a certain extent; however, road and railway traffic are treated unequally. Whereas the railway in certain countries has to bear all costs, including external costs, such as noise protection, etc., automobile traffic is required to pay only about 10 percent of the cost of road building and maintenance. With the development of "Just-in-Time-Production," not only the transport industry profits but also the manufacturing sector benefits. By Just-in-Time-Production, the traffic subsidy is directly converted into a production subsidy. This has changed public transportation space into private storage areas. Just-in-Time-Production converts the road space from public transport into private storage areas that are constantly in motion.

To respond to that situation by constructing new roads alone misses the crux of the problem, just as much as the goal of restricting mobility. Individual mobility and autonomy cannot be separated. We need to develop technological and social options rather than merely extrapolating principles from the past into the future.

New and better roads are definitely required, but the opportunity lies in a joint consideration of traffic and of the context from which it arises and which it influences. The decisive question is: How and according to which criteria can traffic and communication be socially organized?

In research and development of mobility, for instance, the mixture of people, processes, and things has already become an everyday event. Modern mobility development includes a whole string of processes and persons that intertwine with each other. There are product innovations (such as the development of new vehicles), infrastructural measures (such as in the fields of highways and railways), logistics (such as the link of forms of traffic and communication), development of processes (such as intensifying the product use by car renting and carpooling), and the development of new organizational structures (between transport, services, political authorities, and the users), up to new forms of communication. The decisive difference with ordinary product development is that various tasks are no longer handled separately but rather are thought of and designed as a mixture of people, things, and processes.

We change our environment by using it. Changing implies planning and design. The traditional notion of design is object oriented; however, a transformation of objects and events takes place when design is seen as a process. People and things come to share a common destiny. In his book, *We Never Had Been Modern*, Bruno Latour explains that people and things are crossed over with one another. Objects and spaces are conceivable as sensitive and interactive entities that are capable of reacting automatically to brightness, temperature, and moisture, and to the absence or presence of people with whom they are able to interact. Products acquire transformational qualities, and this marks the point where the manufacturing process begins to extend beyond what is generally understood by the production of finished goods. Karl Marx's idea that the production process becomes complete in consumption takes on a completely new perspective.

This relation, however, is mostly experienced as something different. The world appears for the designer as one of objects, one that is separated from the world of subjects. Things appear as a gigantic accumulation of artifacts, as an arsenal of buildings, of landscapes, of infrastructures, of means of traffic and communication, of technological aggregates, etc., and of all the other material as well as immaterial products that are part of life. In the traditional understanding of design, the development of civilization from this point of view is reduced to the material. The irreconcilable division between the world of objects and the world of subjects has its predecessor in pre-industrial design methods. The objects were thought of as if they did not have a self-dynamic momentum—with the possible exception of, say, wind and water mills. This static understanding of artifacts still continues to have a strong effect on design. Historically, the first decisive change in the concept of design happened during the course of mechanization. Starting from mechanical engineering and from transport and communication, thinking in terms of process- es began to enter design in the eighteenth and nineteenth centuries. The second step took place with the microprocessing of daily life. A new concept of processes characterized by developments in the electronic sector is condensed in the prod- ucts. With the Internet, the growing knowledge-orientation of the economy, and the scientific insight that inter-objectivity exists as well as inter-subjectivity, the ambivalent relation of subject and object is up for debate. People and things are involved in process-related associations; they form collectives, and they are transformational.

The economically densest region of Europe, the so-called "development banana," stretches from London across northern France, the Benelux countries, the Rhine- Main region, Strasbourg, Basel, and the Alps to Turin and Milan. All the signs indicate that this area will become a continuous polycentrically structured devel- opment corridor. Let us take the Rhine-Main region as an example. A sprawling agglomeration is developing between Frankfurt, Wiesbaden, Mainz, and Darmstadt. The space between the cities and villages recedes more and more. A city-like entity is emerging here, a prototype for areas increasing urban density, which defies description in terms of urban and rural areas and their transitional forms in the traditional sense of these concepts. What was once an unbroken expanse of landscape is being transformed into meandering park-like islands dot- ted about the increasingly dense architecture and infrastructure of the built areas that enclose them. The Gestalt pattern of the past, the city as figure with the landscape as background, turns upside down in the urban areas, where the land- scape becomes the figure and the city the background.

The use of open country conflicts with its preservation. This is just as true for the major city-landscape visions of the past: Ebenezer Howard's "Garden City," Frederick Lay Olmsted's "Suburb," Frank Lloyd Wright's "Broadacre City," Le Corbusier's "Ville Radieuse," Ernst May's "New Frankfurt," Lewis Mumford's "Culture of Cities," and Ludwig Hilbersheimer's "New Regional Pattern" all had the goal of making the landscape usable for everyday life. In all these schemes, landscape does not function as something autonomous, but instead—and also in today's concepts for new interurban development regions—as raw material to be transformed into urban landscape. Unlike agriculture, for example, which also changes the landscape beyond recognition in its own way, this type of use is not directly dependent upon its preservation. With the reshaping of landscape into urban greenery, industrial parks, etc., landscape is treated like an exploitable resource, hardly different from coal, oil, or water. It is consumed.

For industry and commerce, landscape that is not marketable for tourism or attractive as a living environment is a usable area whose value as a location depends primarily upon the available infrastructure. Landscape in the edges of cities has become a rare commodity; therefore, not only its use but also its preservation has become interesting for the exploitation process. In architecture, landscape has historically—if it was even taken into consideration in the first place—hardly ever been seen as anything other than a panoramic view. Here the appropriation of landscape space is reserved for the contemplation of the privileged or the vanity of architects and developers. The socially motivated concepts of the garden city in the late nineteenth century, the de-urbanization projects in the early twentieth century, and the socially engaged concepts of public housing of the thirties in the Weimar Republic were all social visions. Today, however, in the development of interurban agglomerations, such visions do not play any role. The new urban landscape is not a product of a specific design idea. Economic and infrastructural forces dominate its design process.

At the same time that these distinctions are disappearing, economic concentration of power is increasingly centered on the most important capitals of the world. Saskia Sassen of Columbia University speaks in this context of a new type of urbanization that she calls the "Global City." The global city, besides industrial production, can be characterized as the informational city, the knowledge city, and the science city. These are the three main fields of modern economy on which a city can exist. What these three fields have in common is their process-oriented character. But this character is not visible. The more invisible factors produce a change, the more this change is environmental, and the less it is easily visible.

This development can be clearly illustrated by the example of the city of Frankfurt and the Rhine-Main region. The role of Frankfurt as a "global city" is defined above all by its function as a financial center. Because of the decision to locate the European Central Bank in Frankfurt, what is already one of the most prominent financial markets in Europe will become one of the most powerful financial capitals of the world. The development of the city and the region, which is directed toward the global financial markets, coincides with the development of the Frankfurt airport as a global traffic junction. From a transnational planning standpoint, the Rhine-Main region serves as an economic hub of both Germany and the European Union, as a kind of complement to the Paris urban complex. The growth prospects for the entire region are rated significantly above average. In direct correlation to the extreme functional specialization of Frankfurt in the financial area, the economic and social needs of the region are changing. The mixture of uses, needs, and functions in other cities of the Rhine-Main region and the interurban areas lying in between has been completely transformed. The provision of sufficient housing, on the one hand, is urgently needed, but that of commercial space, on the other, conflicts with the preservation of the so-called soft location advantages of the region such as greenbelt recreational areas in proximity to the city. The open spaces and still unbroken stretches of forest are essential for the climate of the inner city and for the adjoining forest areas. Today, of course, the renaissance of the city is being discussed. Terms such as growth, stagnation, and shrinking lead the discussion, but one cannot really speak about shrinking in Germany. The situation is far from being satisfying, because the area for living and traffic is still growing around 105 hectares daily (2003 data). Turned into a more vivid picture, 147 soccer fields are sealed by concrete every day.

Nothing can replace the characteristic features that distinguish each individual living space from every other as a unique interactive space divided into units, each with a specific function: be it, for instance, high-tech-production, knowledge production, scientific development, management, administration, doctors' or lawyers' practices, or cultural institutions. In addition, and especially in the growth area, a lack of development land calls for new forms of architecture to be created. One answer to this question is to create hybrid forms of architecture. The first hybrid building with a multifunctional character was built in Chicago as early as the end of the nineteenth century. The prototype of multifunctional buildings, capable of adapting to changing requirements, was developed and realized there at that time. An exemplary demonstration of this was Adler and Sullivan's design of the Schiller Building (1892), with its successful combination of two theaters, a club, multi-sized shops and a vast office space all under one roof. Certainly the economic motivation of that time was foreign to the ecological and urban priorities of today.

When we speak of the functional overlapping or hybrid structures of today, we are also talking about emancipation from traditional spatial and architectural concepts. For example, Uwe Kiessler's Heliowatt-Project of Berlin Modell Industriekultur (1988), combined socially separated functions of housing, production, research, administrative offices, service facilities, planning offices, consumption areas, public space, and cultural activities with a new type of underground traffic freight system in an open structure. Conflicting functions and activities are placed physically, economically, and organizationally in relation to each other to induce confrontation. Such concepts of hybrid action spaces, trying to take into account the requirements of a mobile and reflective society, are in conflict with the traditional thinking of fragmented zoning places.

With the help of modern data processing, the differences between external space and internal space, as well as private and non-private space, are blurred. In the past, architectural space, urban space, and the relationship of urban areas to rural areas were defined by clear boundaries: within the buildings, by floor, ceiling and wall; in the city, by streets lined with buildings; and by open spaces between the city and its surrounding areas. The window opening between internal and external space, which was limited to immediate sight, preceded the microprocessing penetration of far and near space. The door permits the crossing from inner space to outer space or vice versa. The window allows television to a limited extent, and this kind of television is as old as mankind.

Probably the most decisive design breakthrough of its time in the architectural understanding of space came with the open-floor plan borrowed from industrial architecture. Anonymous succession of rooms dominated the bourgeois architecture for living in the nineteenth century. Shortly after the transition from the nineteenth to the twentieth century, Frank Lloyd Wright designed a house with an open-floor plan and free transitional areas between the various spaces and levels. This was presented as a new bourgeois form of living. The garden city and, later in the twenties, the ribbon development broke open the confines of street space. Arising from the open-floor plan and the principles of industrial construction, the first concepts of flexible living were created in the twenties. In the meantime, the additive principles have evolved into integrative ones.

Today, the borders of industrial design, communication design, and architecture disappear. In Norman Foster's design for the Stansted Airport (London), for example, the customary borders between building design and equipment design have already evaporated. Architecture becomes an aggregate and information medium. The roof of the building is supported by treelike structural towers that combine air conditioning, lighting, acoustic, and visual information, monitors, directional signs, and fire fighting equipment. Daylight and artificial light are arranged so that they intensify each other.

The beginning of artificial bright lighting came first with gas, and later with electricity toward the end of the nineteenth century. Night became day, and the side effects from night work up to nightlife grew at a dizzying pace. Within the twentieth century, electricity became a scientifically developed field, and its economic role is that of the most important energy deliverer. Light began to play a role almost as important as food.

In the media society, public space that has been lost as urban space, and selected according to the interests of the information industry, enters private space through computer and TV screens. This electronics-based development had its mechanical precursor in the shape of mass motorization. The automobile as private space on wheels occupied the public space and more or less destroyed it. Today, they penetrate each other reciprocally and cancel out each other's usual function and form. Urban space was originally conceived as public space. Some parts of it became criminalized, and others became high-security space if the police had already decriminalized it. More and more public space is privately planned, financed, supervised, managed, and integrated in the space that is controlled and built by private enterprise.

The private is no longer a stronghold against the public. The place of living has become a stage for the public, and the public has become a stage for the private. We do not know how and in what form individualization and socialization will unfold. And we hardly know to what forms of life the dissolution of the difference between object and subject will lead. Today, the disappearance of bipolar relationships between subject and object is up for debate. The things (the objects) and the people (the subjects) cannot be split because they are in a dynamic interrelation. The living is not exclusively a place of the private, nor is it a place in which the things that bring the public into the living, for instance, the telephone, the television, and the laptop, can be seen as isolated. Space has an endless transformational character. Subjects form with objects processing associations.

Note: This is a revised and summarized version of "Die Zukunft des Raums/The Future of Space," published in the book of the same title, edited by Bernd Meurer and published by Campus Verlag, Frankfurt, 1994.

CHAPTER TWELVE

The "Faces" of Space

Rosalind A. Sydie
University of Alberta, Edmonton, Canada

Places of public reception in houses, ought to be like squares and other open places in cities; not in a remote private corner, but in the center and most public place, where all other members may readily meet.

(ALBERTI, 84)

Children and maids, among whom there is an eternal chattering, should be entirely separated from the Master's apartment, and so should the dirtiness of the servants.

(ALBERTI, 85)

The two quotes from Alberti exemplify an ideal front stage/back stage arrangement of space in a private, fifteenth-century Italian house of a relatively wealthy man. The terms, front stage/back stage, are taken from Goffman's analysis of social interaction in *The Presentation of Self in Everyday Life*. Goffman's theatrical metaphor indicates that the front stage is the "place where the performance is given" (107) and the place where selected or "accentuated facts make their appearance," in contrast to "a 'back region' or 'back stage' where the suppressed facts make their appearance" (111–112). The distinction between the front and back stage is generally clear to members of the same culture or sub-culture because the front and back stage "characteristics of certain places is built into them in a material way" (124). The material markers are the façades or the "faces" that are presented to denote the significance and meaning of the space and place.

Physical space has meaning to the extent that it is "*appropriated*" and "is literally made social" (Soja, 93). Soja continues with the observation that "To be alive is to participate in the social production of space, to shape and be shaped by a constantly evolving spatiality which constitutes and concretises social action and relationship" (90). More specifically, social space always conveys a message about its use and significance—it tells a story about how the users or the inhabitants *should act* and interact as well as *how* they act and interact (and the normative *should* and the practical *how* can be quite different). The "face" presented is therefore saturated with social meaning and significance.

Alberti's architectural treatise covers everything to do with the built environment, whether in the city or the countryside. It is a detailed prescriptive manual on how the component parts of the built environment can work to present an appropriate "face" to the world. Alberti understood the essentially social nature of the manipulations of space and the focus of his attention is both normative and practical. The focus of Alberti's attention is on the way in which a particular built item, such as a door, window, or column, works to inhibit or facilitate ideal social interaction in a humanist society. In general, the face that interiors and exteriors present to the world should be designed to indicate the status and role played by its ideal inhabitants and these spaces with their particular "faces" are distinguished in terms of front and back stages. For example, Alberti recommended that rooms be "designed for Virgins and young ladies, fitted up in the neatest and most delicate manner, that their tender minds may pass their time in them with less regret and be as little weary of themselves as possible" (107). Whether the virgins and other young ladies who had such spaces set aside for their "delight" did in fact pass their time in passive, limited activity is probably doubtful, but the point was that such rooms were designed to promote particular ways of being predicated on specific cultural assumptions about the nature of women. In fifteenth century Italy we can confidently assert that for a family that can afford to set aside separate quarters for its virgins and young ladies, such spaces are likely to be "back stage" in contrast to the "front stage" of "places of public reception."

Goffman also points out that the front and back stage distinction is based on the character of the ideal user. He notes that in our society we generally "make a division between the front and back parts of residential exteriors. The front tends to be relatively well decorated, well repaired, and tidy; the rear tends to be relatively unprepossessing. Correspondingly, social adults enter through the front, and often the socially incomplete—domestics, delivery men, and children—enter through the rear" (123). The front/back binary is complemented by other binaries of pure/impure, clean/dirty. It is possible for front spaces to become back spaces, but it is rarely the case that back spaces are transformed into front spaces.

The designation of front and back space is culturally, and often class and gender, specific. For example, the bedroom is generally, in our culture, a back space. But the bedrooms of kings and queens of European societies in previous eras were front spaces in which the status or "majesty" of the monarch was affirmed by the intimate attendance to the body of the monarch by other members of the aristocracy. Elias (86) recounts the extremes to which the courtly etiquette of a front stage bedroom played out in pre-revolutionary France.

"The maid of honour had the right to pass the queen her chemise. The lady in waiting helped her put on her petticoat and dress. But if a princess of the royal family happened to be present, she had the right to put the chemise on the queen. On one occasion the queen had just been completely undressed by her ladies. Her chambermaid was holding the chemise and had just presented it to the maid of honour when the Duchess of Orleans came in. The maid of honour gave it back to the chambermaid who was about to pass it to the duchess when the higher-ranking Countess of Provence entered. The chemise now made its way back to the chambermaid, and the queen finally received it from the hands of the countess."

The intricacies of precedent and status that governed the royal bedchamber are replicated to a lesser extent in the management of social interactions that govern all of our lives in both the front and the back places, whether public or private space. An important part of the signals that indicate the front/back distinction are the behaviors or performances as well as the structural features—the artifacts and decorations—that produce the appropriate "face" of the space.

Space itself, and the artifacts with which it is filled, does not directly cause social action or interaction, rather it "inhibits or facilitates the development of processes originating in society as a whole" (Saunders, 84). However, there are certain fundamental forms or qualities of the space that affect "the structuring of communal life" (Frisby and Featherstone, 138). These fundamental forms are: the exclusivity of space in the sense that there is "a single general space, of which all individual spaces are parts, so every portion of space possesses a kind of uniqueness" (138); there are boundaries to space (141); and social forms are more or less "fixed" in space (146). Plus, the "liveliness of sociological interactions" is the result of the "sensory proximity or distance between people" (151), and the nature of spatial mobility such that different forms of social interaction "appear in the case of a wandering group in contrast to a spatially fixed one" (160). These fundamental social characteristics of space govern the production of front and back stage faces and spaces, in which the nature of social activity and the desired communications of their significance are conveyed. As Lefebvre pointed out, space and time are the concretisation of society.

I will examine the nature of spatial forms in relation to the communicative "performances" characteristics of front and back stages in the faces of domestic design. More specifically, I will discuss some of the changes in the design of domestic interiors in relation to changing presuppositions about family and gender in North America, especially as they appear in some of the new middle class, suburban homes.

Public/Private, Front/Back Stage

In looking at the front and back communicative nature of space, the public spaces of the city are more easily understood in these terms because the faces or façades are more readily identified and thus the performances or normative expectations with regard to behavior are fairly explicit and generally understood. There are front and back spaces in all cities—the front places are where the citizens communicate the positive features of themselves and their city in contrast to back places that are set apart and where the problems that are common to any urban environment are relegated and, hopefully, contained. Both front and back city spaces have their "appropriate" buildings, parks, and monuments that speak to the presentation of the political and cultural lives of its citizens. These buildings, parks, and monuments are carefully designed to present the appropriate face to the world to indicate the civic importance as well as the power relations that govern the city, and they impose certain normative expectations upon citizens when they traverse such spaces. For example, Alberti (82) pointed out that the "generality of particular buildings, and the city itself ought to be laid out differently for a Tyrant, from what they are for those who enjoy and protect a Government as if it were a Magistracy voluntarily put in their hands. A good King takes care to have his City strongly fortified in those parts which are most liable to be assaulted by a foreign enemy: a Tyrant, having no less danger to fear from his subjects than from strangers, must fortify his city no less against his own people, than against foreigners . . ." Given the historical political context of Alberti's treatise, the physical arrangement of space for the control over the behavior of the citizenry was a central preoccupation.

The design of public spaces and buildings is rarely haphazard, although the sub-sequent use or abuse may contradict the original architectural and civic inten-tions. Overall the intention is to construct "faces" in space that communicate to people "what they can and cannot be, which, in part, defines what people feel about who they are and how they feel about each other" (Walker, 829). However, Castells observes that although spatial forms "express and perform the interests of the dominant class according to a given mode of production and to a specific mode of development" there is always instability in the command of the dominant over spatial communication because "spatial forms will be ear-marked by the resistance from exploited classes, from oppressed subjects, and from dominated women" (4). For example, "street people" are often a visible reminder of the instability of the political and social ideals expressed in the design of the city. More specifically, it is often in structural as well as cosmetic modifications to domestic spaces that resistance is more clearly evident on the part of the disenfranchised, minorities, and the marginalized. For example, Jencks (111–112) maintained that "working class and middle class people don't like the humane and artistic solutions of modern architecture"; on the contrary, they find them "inhuman and inartistic . . . because they don't have the conven-tional signs of domesticity, protection, and identity and because they signify 'council housing,' 'social deprivation,' 'estate,' 'anonymity,' 'the wrong side of the tracks,' 'factory,' and so forth." It was not only the working class who found mod-ernist design a problem. Freidman points out that Edith Farnsworth, for whom Mies van der Rohe designed his famous Glass House, was profoundly unhappy with the result despite the fact that it was recognized as one of the "masterpieces of modern architecture" (147). Jencks includes an illustration of Le Corbusier's low cost Pessac Housing, which was "transformed" or, in the eyes of the archi-tect, "ruined, aged and articulated by a traditional language." In the photograph of the transformed houses, "The signs of personalisation and security have effec-tively distorted the purist language so that it sends out welcoming messages of domesticity and 'home' instead of factory, sugar cube and hospital" (112).

Space, especially domestic space, is manipulated and is "the medium and the out-come of social action and relationships" (Soja, 94) so that the "exterior façade and style along with the interior decoration, furniture, style and layout of hous-es" all compose a "semiotic system that signals status, class, and public display and creates meanings that observers, visitors, and the public may interpret and read . . . " (Mezei and Briganti, 840). Reading the interior faces of middle class homes as front and back stages is instructive in relation to assumptions about family relationships and gender roles. As a physically bounded, private space the middle class home has been predicated on gender role differentiation and idealizations of loving, secure, stable family relationships. The front/back spaces and faces of the "home" essentially refer to these idealized assumptions about family life and thus communicate the appropriate behaviors or performances to be expected in such a space.

Front Stage/Back Stage and Domestic Spaces

For most individuals the "home" (however that is understood or physically structured) is a theatre of domesticity with front and back places that call for different types of action and interaction according to indicators of family status, gender, and age, as well as indicators of race, ethnicity, and religious identification. In North America there is an important social value attached to a specific domestic space—the single family, private, detached home—the "American Dream." This "dream" is reinforced by the mass media's promotion of the required objects, artifacts, and decorations as the latest in style and comfort that will produce the appropriate face of this domestic ideal.

In the nineteenth and first half of the twentieth centuries the cultural coding of middle class domestic spaces in North America on the part of developers in particular, but also of professional architects, has been constantly elaborated by the addition of special spaces for particular actions and interactions and for particular individuals. These spaces are governed by social forms of uniqueness and relatively fixed boundary markers, that delimit who can be welcomed into the intimate domestic space and who will be held at bay or allowed only into specific back stage spaces. Key to the social forms of domestic space and the face it presents are the gender binaries and assumptions about the "normal" family that govern the front and back stage spaces and the decorative face of those spaces. For example, the study as the domain of the husband and sometimes the sewing room, but more likely the laundry room, as the domain of the wife were often common features of middle class homes. Interestingly in gender terms, the study was more front stage space in which particular forms of masculine "relaxation" were to be expected, in contrast to the definitive back stage space of a sewing room or a laundry room intended for women's work.

In more recent times the sewing room, as well as the study, are rarely included in the spatial design of domestic interiors. The re-configurations of domestic space are, however, still bounded by relatively fixed markers that are structural, functional, and decorative. In previous eras, an important marker of middle class status was the piano located in the parlor. This marker was an indication of the gentility and taste of the inhabitants, especially of the women of the house, and, in its reference to a more aristocratic lifestyle, spoke to the status pretensions of the family. The parlor was a front stage space that was set apart for visitors and special occasions and it was a space that was off-limits to some members of the family, notably children, unless under the strict eye of a parent. As Chapman (21) remarks, the parlor "in its 'ideal' form . . . is the repository of sentiment and has few other functions."

The television set is a more recent example of a marker that governs domestic interaction and use of space. Like the piano it presents a face of conspicuous consumption that communicates a desired status to the visitor. The elaborate cabinets of the early years have given way to the more sleek designs of today and, for the ultimate face of status, the home theatre. A more functional marker is the content and design of the kitchen, which in the past was definitively a back place for women's work. The markers in the kitchen were functional, in the sense of providing for the sustenance of the family, as well as being the means for the expression of the wife/mother commitment to the welfare of the family. The kitchen retains its functionality and connotations of the center of family happiness and well-being, but it can become a front stage arena when it is designed as an integral part of the entertainment patterns of the family. Structurally, however, kitchens are usually set apart and located, literally, at the back of the house. However, with the increasing use of open plan designs the division between this back stage and the front stage of the home became less definitive.

By mid-twentieth century open floor plans in middle-class North American homes had replaced the elaborate separation of rooms of the previous era, making the distinction between public and private, front and back spaces less clear-cut. Open floor plans often incorporated a "family room" although in some cases the formality of a traditional living room (the former parlor) space was retained. Grier (63) suggests that by the 1920s the parlor was increasingly replaced in North America with the "living room" and it was a space that was "intended to be less overtly and enthusiastically artificial than the parlor, both in the social life taking place there and in its mirroring décor." In fact the openness did not usually eliminate dividers or structural markers indicating the functions of different spaces and the performances to be expected in that space. The family room is based on the notion of a "normal" nuclear family and is designed as the back space for intimate, face-to-face relations for all members of the family. It also assumes that a family desires such spaces for comforting "togetherness" in the face of the problems and tensions of the outside world. Whether or not family harmony is actually evident, it is in the family room that the residents are supposed to perform as a "happy family."

More recently, the so-called Great Room seems to have displaced the family room. The so-called Great Room is a bit of a puzzle. Unlike the family room, which is set off from, although frequently adjacent to, the kitchen, which is traditionally a female back space, the Great Room often incorporates the kitchen space along with many other previously delimited front and back spaces of the home. The name itself seems misleading in the sense that it implies something of the figuration of the house of a much earlier era that Elias describes in his *The Court Society*, which quite explicitly set out the front and back stages of social intercourse. In the court society of the ancient regime houses contained different reception rooms and their use produced the "characteristic double face" of such society. "This double face finds expression in the differentiation of the reception rooms. In gatherings in the *appartement de société* amusement and conversation will be more prominent . . . " (53).

The ceremonial *appartement de parade* in which "the public character of the lord, the maintenance of the interests and prestige of his house, are in the foreground" would be a "Great Room" or hall, and a front stage in every sense of the word, in contrast to the smaller, more intimate (although not exactly back stage) space of the *appartement de société* (Elias, 53). However, the "Great" rooms of current housing stock bear no resemblance to the Great Rooms or Halls of the past. Here it would seem the analogy is more on the order of the relatively undifferentiated space of earlier peasant or working class housing in which there is no formal front stage and only a minimal boundary marking the definitive back stage of, for example, the privy. If the analogy is in fact in reference to the presumed *gemeinschaft* of peasant social life in contrast to, and as preferable to, the two-faced social relations of the bourgeoisie and aristocracy, then the Great Room may well represent a removal of the front/back stage figuration of social relations. Chapman (53) suggests that the "absence of resident domestic servants may partly account for the decline of formal behaviour in the middle-class home. The need to demonstrate social difference to inferiors in all matters of domestic life no longer exists."

The Great Room, like the family room, may represent an idealistic notion of family "togetherness" as well as encouragement of back stage informality in all social interactions that more traditional separation of spaces in the home discouraged. Certainly the gender binaries will be less evident as will the distinctions of adult/child, formal/intimate, guest/family in such spaces. Although the Great Room is "like" the family room in that it is a space of informality and relaxation, it is unlike to the extent that it presumes there is no need to present a different face or performance for friends and guests. Like "family" they are welcomed as a matter of course into this presumably "informal" back stage space.

The Great Room eliminates the distinctions between front and back domestic space and seems, therefore, to signal a different, new understanding of the boundaries of intimate, primary relations. It certainly seems to break down many of the traditional domestic binaries of, for example, female and child back spaces in contrast to male and adult front spaces. The Great Room seems to acknowledge the fact that the so-called "traditional family" now forms a minority of western households and that the design of domestic space needs to take into account the variability of family composition at any one time. However, to see this development as an indication of more equitable gender relations in the home or the widespread recognition of alternative family forms is a mistake. Domestic work remains largely women's work and single parents or same-sex parents remain a problem for suburban enclaves. Furthermore, the elimination of front/back stage tends to produce other rooms that can be devoted to necessary back stage activities. These added back stage spaces are usually spaces for women's traditional domestic maintenance work, such as the laundry. A recent feature on new home development suggested that the laundry room is becoming the room of the "new generation" which should be decorated with as much care as other spaces in the home and possibly reconfigured as also a "craft centre or playroom," certainly as more than "just a washer/dryer." It should be a space that will "put a smile on your face every time you go in" (*Edmonton Journal*).

The reconfigurations of space in more recently built suburban homes do not dislodge the heterosexual, nuclear family stereotype and this is signaled by the exterior faces of these homes. The homes that are constructed with Great Rooms may be internally undifferentiated in both design and performance expectations on the ground floors but they are often marked by difference in their external facades that speak to a presumed earlier time of family ease, harmony, and comfort. These homes usually display a variety of exteriors that seem to be deliberate attempts to overcome the homogeneity of older suburban housing. The exterior faces are, however, ironic in that they are usually modified transplants of older North American and European designs and, like the Chippendale cabinet that has been modified to contain a bar or a television set, they are the front stage face of nostalgia and status aspiration.

The Great Room appears to confound the traditional front/back stage domestic distinctions but in fact it produces more elaborate spatial distinctions in order to take account of the messy and necessary back stage domestic work. The laundry room of the "new generation" is described as a "home organization area" where "garment racks, storage shelves or cabinets . . . eliminate clutter." Consequently, although the presumption of informality and the elimination of traditional binaries is suggested by the designation "Great Room," it remains a front stage space. As a "lifestyle consultant" remarked, the key meaning communicated by the Great Room space should be not "complete comfort" but "casual elegance" (*Edmonton Journal*). What the Great Room suggests is that the line between the informality of the back stage must be closely monitored because the same space is front stage for visitors, guests, and non-family members.

Goffman recognized that spaces can serve as front as well as back stage spaces but the transitions between these spaces have to be handled with care because when "individuals witness a show that was not meant for them, they may, then, become disillusioned about this show as well as about the show that was meant for them" (136). One answer is to segregate the audiences so that individuals who witness one role will not be present to witness another role. Segregation is, however, difficult to maintain in some cases, and certainly in the space of the Great Room segregation could be an ever-present difficulty. The pitfalls of integrated front and back spaces are illustrated in Goffman's example of the visitor, happening on the back stage behavior of "a husband and wife in the midst of their daily bickering." This encounter will occasion confusion, which will require considerable impression management to defuse and "embarrassment is almost certain to result" (Goffman, 139–140).

The Great Room seems, therefore, to be a place in which the performance of family and self is potentially an anxiety producing situation. The informality of the domestic back stage, the "relaxing slovenliness in dress and civil endeavor" which is "usually restricted to the kitchen and bedrooms" must be controlled in the face of the simultaneous front stage nature of the space (Goffman, 127). The "casual elegance" of the space must not be compromised by the messiness of domestic necessities. Consequently, the housework is made more onerous unless other back stage spaces are built in that can take care of the needs and functions of everyday domestic, family life. Rather than a comfortable *gemeinschaft*, the Great Room is a deceptive arena that still demands the demonstration of front stage "Good Taste," appropriate style, and consumption patterns. In this sense the Great Room may well be compared with the Great halls of the *ancien regime* and the "double face" presented to the world in such rooms. In private life it is assumed that "relaxation, amusement, conversation" are appropriate faces in contrast to the "professional life" where behavior is instrumental with respect to "career, the medium of one's rise or fall, the fulfillment of social demands and pressures which are experienced as duties" (Elias, 53). Although "one face may be more strongly accentuated than the other; the former is more easily blocked out than the latter" and so it seems it would be the case in regard to the "face" of the space of the Great Room.

The comfort, familiarity and ease promoted by builders and interior designers for the single family dwelling in the designation of the Great Room is a contradiction. The room is a front stage *posing* as a back stage and the anxiety that this produces in the face the space presents is a key component of the ironic expansion of separate spaces, such as a laundry room, as comfortable back stages.

References

Alberti, Leone Battista (1955). *Ten Books on Architecture* (trans. by James Leoni). London: Alec Tiranti Ltd.

Castells, M. (1983). "Crisis, Planning and the Quality of Life: Managing the New Historical Relations between Space and Society," *Environment and Planning D: Society and space*, vol.1, 3–21.

Chapman, Dennis (1955). *The Home and Social Status*. London: Routledge and Kegan Paul.

Edmonton Journal, April 17, 2003, Section E1.

Elias, Norbert (1983). *The Court Society*. New York: Pantheon.

Friedman, Alice, T. (1998). *Women and the Making of the Modern House*. New York: Harry N. Abrams.

Frisby, D. and Featherstone, M. (Eds.) (1997). *Simmel on Culture*. London: Sage.

Goffman, Erving (1959). *The Presentation of Self in Everyday Life*. New York: Doubleday Anchor.

Grier, Katherine C. (1992). "The Decline of the Memory Palace: The Parlor after 1890." In Jessica H. Foy and Thomas J. Schlereth (Eds.), *American Home Life, 1880-1939*. Knoxville: University of Tennessee Press, 49–74.

Jencks, Charles (1980). "The Architectural Sign." In Geoffrey Broadbent, Richard Bunt and Charles Jencks (Eds.), *Signs, Symbols, and Architecture*. New York: John Wiley & Sons, 71–118.

Lefebvre, Henri (1974). *La Production de l'Espace*. Paris: Anthropos.

Mezei, Kathy and Briganti, Chiara (2002). "Reading the house: A Literary Perspective," *Signs*, 27/3, 837–846.

Soja, Edward (1985). "The Spatiality of Social Life: Towards a Transformative Retheorisation." In Derek Gregory and John Urry (Eds.), *Social Relations and Spatial Structures*, New York: St. Martin's Press, 90–127.

Walker, Lynne (2002). "Home Making: An Architectural Perspective," *Signs*, 27/3, 823–835.

CHAPTER THIRTEEN

Sign of Design:
Deciphering the Audience's Codes—Design in the Urban Landscape

Ronald Shakespear
Diseño Shakespear, Buenos Aires, Argentina

When James Ivory entrusted Anthony Hopkins with the construction of the servant, that fantastic character in the movie *The Remains of the Day*, Hopkins had at one point a problem of a conceptual nature and asked him for help. Ivory advised him to talk to an old Windsor butler, an expert on the subject. Hopkins invited him to tea, and they sat down and chatted for a while. But when the meeting came to an end, Hopkins had a feeling that this old servant had told him nothing. He walked him to the door, but as he was about to leave, and determined to extract something from the character, he blurted out: "Tell me; finally, what is a servant?" The old man turned, thought about it for a second, and then said, "A servant is someone who, when he walks into a room, makes it look emptier than it was before."

I have tardily found that this is exactly the role of our work. And as far as my own work is concerned, I have been involved for over forty years in what we, the inhabitants of the wet pampas, call the graphics of large spaces, universally known as an urban signage system, which basically involves making the city legible.

I met Jock Kinneir in the early 1970s, and the meeting was both charming and enlightening in terms of defining my own profession. I remember two fundamental things that Jock Kinneir told me: 1) "These urban scale design mega-projects are a

test sent by destiny for us to prove our ability to remain." 2) "Man speaks in small letters, he shouts in capital letters."

For many years since, and after becoming involved in works known around the world as man-eating because of interdependence, the involvement of various disciplines, interaction with various forces related to the work and its management, I have repeatedly thought about Jock Kinneir and the desire to remain. It has also been said that this perceptive nature of the design profession is somehow related to narcissism and self-centeredness, and I think this is partly true.

This strong urge to affix iron signs with letters and figures to cities' concrete walls, so that they live the lives of people beyond time, is related to the desire to remain present. In the course of the mega-projects that we have developed in Argentina since the 1970s—signage system for the city of Buenos Aires, signage system for the Buenos Aires subway, city hospitals, trains, highways, zoos, entertainment centers—we have realized that Kinneir's words were true: man-eating projects.

Generating spaces where signs are designed not only to give directions and to solve circulation problems, which are their primary purposes, but also to construct a landscape, to construct communication, in an effort to make the place legible, and to contribute to the "scenic" aspects, as Antonioni would say, presents some substantial management complexities.

I am not so sure about the real value of innovative forces. Jorge Frascara's students sent him a letter that he was kind enough to forward to me in Buenos Aires. And I want to tell you about this letter. These Canadian graduate students were given an assignment by the Canadian government to do some research work on the reason for the width of Canadian railway tracks. As you know, the width is four feet, eight inches. This is approximately one meter, sixty centimeters. The Canadian government wanted to establish exactly why this width had been chosen, taking into account its strong impact on the related basic support, that is, the wooden sleepers that have always been a concern in Canada.

The students conducted the research and found that Canadian railways had that width because it was the width of United States railroads: four feet, eight inches. And why was that? It was simply because U.S. railroads had been managed by English engineers who had used pre-existing English plans. And why did the English use this four feet, eight inches measurement? It was because it was the width of old English streetcars. And where did that come from? It was actually the width of the roads that existed before streetcars did. And why did these roads measure four feet, eight inches from one gutter to the other? It was because the old carriages that rode along them needed to match the gutters exactly so that they would not break. And where did these roads come from? These four feet, eight inches roads came from a project developed over two thousand years ago by the Romans for their legions. And why did those Roman roads measure four feet,

eight inches? It was because that was the standard width of all roads in the Roman Empire. And why was that? It was because the Romans had discovered that four feet, eight inches was the width of two horses' rumps.

It is interesting. The Canadian students ended by saying that they had actually discovered that the width of a turbogenerator for the Apollo capsule was constrained by those four feet, eight inches, since these turbogenerators were transported from Utah to Cape Canaveral by train, and railroad tunnels were built for tracks separated by four feet, eight inches. This led the students to arrive at the conclusion that humankind's ultimate state-of-the-art technology is based on two horses' asses. Where is innovation now?

We cling to our habits and customs much harder than we think. And, in fact, our earthly profession, design, is so closely related to people—the final beneficiaries of our work—that how could we possibly not respect their habits and customs.

I was told that, a few years ago, while architect Belaunde Terry was the President of Peru, the Pope visited that country. After he arrived in Peru, and because he was going to grant a number of interviews during his stay, some old Incas requested to see him. President Belaunde understood that Incas had a legitimate right to see the Pope, so three elders from the tribe—obviously the oldest of them—went to see him. They walked up to the Pope in the main room of the presidential palace, and the oldest of them carefully took out an old and battered little book: a 500-year-old Bible. He carefully handed it to the Pope, and said: "Look sir, our people want to give you back this little book you sent us. My people say it has not been useful to them."

I found this interesting in the sense that, to some people like me, who had grown up in cities and had never set foot in a cloister, empirical knowledge has a powerful significance. And I have to confess that most of the bibles that have reached my hands have not been vitally useful to me. Intuition is eventually proved right.

At times, we spent months in angst and stress, trying to solve problems that were often not solvable. I remember that we sometimes obsessed about the matter of signs sequence, that is, their proper placement to permit their cultural recognition, their previous decoding. This is basically linked to another factor in public signage systems: namely, their predictability. The public knows, they should know, and they think that they know where, how, and when they are going to find a sign, because that notion is already present in their minds. I find this notion of predictability to be extremely important in the construction of the public landscape, because it involves cultural factors and it is linked to the quality of the service finally rendered by the signals: a public contract.

Finally, I think that we should also consider another factor anticipated by Jock Kinneir. This was the third thing he told me about: the struggle for power and the designer. Tackling this type of project involves certain rare skills that are not inborn but obtained over time. This is a form of actual establishment of a relationship in the search to generate a project and especially to ensure that it survives. It has to do with the relationship between the designer and the client, the bureaucrat. You surely remember the agreement between Leonardo da Vinci and Ludovico Sforza. Ludovico il Moro was a sinister human being, but Leonardo's contract was just a piece of contractual organization, just an agreement between two parties, which I find particularly insightful. And the contract enabled Leonardo not only to prosper at what was his obsession at the time but also to satisfy his client who, in Borges's words, was a rustic man.

Ludovico Sforza wanted from Leonardo the cosmetics of nightly feasts, or as we would say, "the party stuff," streamers and confetti, the decoration of ephemeral stages that lasted for one night or as many nights as the party continued. In his contract, once the party was over and the prince no longer required his services, Leonardo fought to obtain what he would have access to every single night: the palace's mortuary chamber, the morgue, where corpses that were still warm, that is, human beings who had died that very day, could be used in his vivisection work. The time that Leonardo spent at Ludovico's house in Milan resulted in the Anatomy Codex, which is now, as you know, part of the Windsor Castle collection.

What was left of Ludovico Sforza? In fact, as you walk about Milan, apart from a few statues and the palace, which is now a museum, you find the testimony that, in his house, in his palace, in the basement of his palace, at the morgue, the Anatomy Codex was written and drawn 500 years ago. For the first time in the history of humankind, Leonardo took a pancreas, he took a bladder, he took a liver, and he drew what he saw. To me, this is an exemplary agreement, and I want to emphasize this, because generally we tend to regard our profession as an almost magical situation in which great projects are generated by the talent of those who carry them out. I find this to be relative and unreal in a number of aspects. Great projects are generated because someone was capable of establishing a relationship with the client that turned the project into a real, lasting product.

In actual terms, the connection between the designer and the client has a twofold meaning, because a number of assignments are actually made as such, whereas many others are generated by the intuition, the talent, the ability, the ambition, and the greed of those who wanted the project to exist on the face of the Earth. And this naturally involves an education that is not usually given at schools, is not to be found in manuals or in the Peruvian bible, and generally is not present in any design teaching model. It is like talking to the one who originates the design.

Sforza was mean, and Sforza was cruel, but he finally made it possible for humankind to benefit from the work of the great. I have to understand that the great made their part in this rare alchemy.

I have to say that this call to work systematically in public areas has given us our share of pain and frustration. When reading Nelson's work a few nights ago, I reread some pages that particularly interested me in his bare and skeptical vision of the world. I have always had an interest in Nelson, I read his work with delight, and I have learned from him. Nelson claims that the only serious interpretation about the creation of the universe—a task that apparently took six days of hard work—is that failure was part of the plan. And if we read the story carefully, it seems that this apple thing happened: the apple was bitten, then there came expulsion, and these two characters from Paradise landed on the face of the Earth—a hideous place—where unfortunately there was no further testimony of the Creator's work. All that happened after that, from expulsion from Paradise to this day, is the work of human beings. Could the Supreme Designer possibly ignore that humans can take anything but perfection?

I have a feeling that failure was part of the plan. I have been involved in a huge number of large scale projects where I had that feeling. And now, as I look back, I cannot but confirm it: failure was part of the plan. It could not go right.

Design has changed more over the last 20 years than it did over the previous 500 years. It has become an extremely dynamic discipline, primarily devoted to giving satisfactory answers to an increasingly dissatisfied audience. The search to make a profit is the fundamental reason behind every assignment. The existence of globalization naturally means that there is a "globalizer." And he is dissatisfied too.

It has been said that there are no more technological frontiers; yet, while special effects simulations generate jumping dinosaurs in movie screens for fascinated crowds, we annihilate forests and whales. An irrational, blind greed is destroying the planet, apart from the thousands of honest people who work for the welfare of all in the belief that design is an answer to a social need that originates it and makes its existence legitimate.

"Europe discovered America.

That is not true.

My father was already here."

M. Carmichel

CHAPTER FOURTEEN
Dialogue of Many

Zalma Jalluf
Fontana-Diseño, Buenos Aires, Argentina
(Translation into English: Peggy Jones and Martin Schmoller)

In Buenos Aires, as in most of the world, urban activity privileges the driver over the pedestrian. Even along secondary streets far from the main avenues, pedestrians must step off the sidewalk and slow down at each corner to obey the traffic signs. In areas where pedestrian traffic is heavier than that of vehicles, such as cities' centers, the system is still designed to favor vehicular traffic.

What is the Use of Design?
Are We Here to Question the Order of Things?

Human communication is made up of the sum of big and small inherited habits, such as the one we have just mentioned, or the alphabet, the direction in which we write, or our city planning, and all are based on a number of valid functional, social, and historical reasons. Habits became entrenched at some times because of repetition and at others because of adaptation, and as they were systematically accepted they gradually became codes: a street is designed for vehicular traffic, whose flow must be interrupted by traffic signals to allow pedestrians to cross. For a street to look like a street, therefore, it must have a good dose of the features dictated by this conventional code.

"A wine label should look like a wine label," declared the Greek designer and essayist Juan Andralis, thus summarizing the scope of our trade which, rather than creating languages, manipulates cultural conventions. Even though they might seem immutable, codes evolve, which is why they should be verified in time and place. In Argentina, there are still many small towns where a street is the space that divides two rows of houses or trees.

Fortunately there are many ways in which we recognize a street as such. Identity comes into play in every one of them, and this makes it possible not only to particularize them culturally but also to recognize them visually, that is, to identify them. Identity emerges naturally upon combining universal conventions with the needs of a specific time and place. Communication and design strategy is based on the delicate tension between code and identity: code as the synthesis of convention, identity as its adaptation, that is, as the motor of innovation.

And what happens on a street? Everybody emits and receives, everybody communicates, and everything occurs and concurs. If the street is part of a big city, this multiple concurrence is visually evident. Massive concurrence of information allows natural self-organization to give way to visual external organization.

More or less legible, verbal, iconic, or chromatic, imperative indications order the circulation of pedestrians and vehicles, drivers and non-drivers, the sighted and the blind, mobile and disabled individuals, literate and illiterate people, public and non-public passenger transport, light and heavy freight transport, adults and children, and cyclists. All this is superimposed on the greatest communicational scenario that we have ever generated and in which each language attempts to regulate or adapt the possibilities and capabilities of each of the players in the system.

Figures 14.4 (STOP) and 14.5: Views of the cities of Santiago, Chile, area of Las Condes. The pedestrian sidewalk continues visually and physically on the street, which feeds a fast avenue. Pedestrians do not need to interrupt their walk in each corner: it is the vehicles that cross the pedestrian area. The scene shows a change in the visual expression of powers meeting in the same context. This proposes a change in a universal code, a habit maintained in most Western cities.

As in a street, in a newspaper page, or in the instructions on how to use a tool, a number of interests merge in every communication process. The main task is to interpret, participate, and negotiate between the interests and capabilities of the many audiences that converge in the use of a same object, context or act of communication. And each of these audiences contributes a fundamental part of the information that we need.

Ideologies, as well as forms and functions, always participate in the articulation of this simultaneous concurrence of interests. Subordinating the actions of all players in the street to vehicular behavior is inherent in an ideology that generates a specific organization that affects all users; considering the pedestrian as the guiding factor of the system, however, corresponds to a different ideology. Discriminating the occasions when each point of view should be subordinated to another is the result of the systemic, alphabetic intelligence of design.

Does Communication Design Have Its Limits?

Every now and again, an important innovation is created, an identity pattern that modifies a historical code, substituting adaptation for repetition. Even if the conventional organization of a street is inverted, the pedestrian crossing still crosses over the car lanes without lowering its level or altering its material nature. From a physical viewpoint, a univocal visual sign is constituted that reorders the power of the players in the system. In communication, all innovation operates on the limits of the code, and hence this street will continue to be recognized as a street.

I believe that the definition of our work lies in this simple and unpretentious intelligence, in the extreme laterality of this scheme. It is my feeling that, rather than creating contexts for communication, design participates in the dynamics of adapting contexts, historical cultural codes, to make them more accessible to the reality of a particular society.

What Is the Meaning of Design?

Although the question could lead to an interminable debate, we can begin by asking ourselves what it is that we design. In this context, and in apparent contradiction with the academic profile of our days, we might well reflect on de-specialization.

Let us return to the street macro-scenario. Reasonably, the so-called fast lanes or motorways privilege vehicular traffic, excluding pedestrian traffic for volume and safety reasons. The design of the signage of many Latin American highways appears to be based on the supposition that the driver knows the road and route, as if the signs were there solely to recreate the visual stage of a motorway. Should the driver decide to change the routine of his trip, it is possible that he would get nowhere. The major causes of accidents on these roads, however, are indecision at forks or junctions, the weather (rain or fog), or the lack of timely viewing of the warnings or signs. The latter is usually a result of speeding, which is one of the main causes of traffic accident deaths in Argentina.

Figures 14.6 and 14.7: A poorly designed or poorly placed sign can lead to tragedy. The lack of regulation and planning leaves road managers total freedom to manipulate typography, disregarding users' needs and abilities, as well as legibility principles. Nevertheless, not even the most sophisticated signage can eliminate all risks that derive from many other factors, natural and cultural.

As specialists in communication design, expert in legibility and typography, we know just how much can be done to improve highway safety. But, at times, a certain kind of inertia with respect to graphic solutions prevents us from seeing the limitations of graphic action. As designers, we must be able to provide solutions that will have an intelligent bearing on other links in the system that we call context.

For example, from the perspective of the concept of legibility, it would be useful to have a hand in establishing maximum highway speeds, and then design signage compatible with such speed parameters. When designing a sign, the options are generally analyzed on the basis of vehicle speed in relation to the type of roads; however, this criterion leads to a dangerous question: To what extent can the shape and size of lettering on signs be adapted to faster and faster cars?

Common sense dictates that it should also be possible to design the speed of a vehicle on the basis of the limits of human legibility from a distance. Following this same line of reasoning, for a number of years the design of the Discman CD player has built-in limits to sound volume that respond to the need to protect the user's hearing and not to the technological possibilities of the object.

It is, therefore, not a question of beautifying objects on the basis of a code, nor of ordering them harmoniously within the landscape; what we should design are the consequences that the possibilities and characteristics of each object or communication have on the functioning of the whole. What we should design in time and space are the effects of each part on the survival of the whole.

Communication cannot be used to mitigate or mask the intrinsic dangers in the design of certain objects or contexts.

Following this line of thought, around 1980 the Fokker aircraft manufacturers asked Delft Technological University to redesign the instructions on how to use the emergency exits because the crew did not understand them. After a number of studies and trials, the university team recommended that, to make the communication of the mechanism comprehensible and efficient, it was necessary to redesign the doors (Mijksenaar). Sometimes it is not enough to meet functional criteria (doors that open or close as required) adequately (door mechanism). It is vital to envisage the communication possibilities when designing the object. Upon creating an object, what is designed is its communication. Regardless of the design specialization involved, what is designed is always communication.

But let us return once again to design and highways. In this case, design involves applying visual or non-visual knowledge to create a solution that will provide higher quality (safety) in personal transport. Design entails getting involved in each and every one of the elements that participate in the characterization of a context. Despite the much advocated interdisciplinary action between all areas of design and communication, in reality most of the time each area restricts itself to contributing, in superimposed or simultaneous layers, specific and partial solutions to matters rarely pertinent to its functioning as a system.

Is It Possible to Be a Specialized Designer? Is a Comprehensive Vision Necessary?

Typographer Rubén Fontana maintains that with each letter the typographer designs he designs the landscape of the page (Fontana). In the same way, with each building that an architect designs he redesigns the face of a city. Every brand affects the sight of a market, a home, or a street. Although our field of action might be limited, our vision must include the whole.

For many years, objects were designed in a more holistic manner. For example, the so-called building trades—a conglomerate of different bodies of knowledge articulated to design the most beautiful habitations—believed that the name or location of a building was part of its overall morphology, was part of the same provisions that generate proportion between surfaces and heights, between people and ventilation requirements. Structure, ornamentation, identification, and functionality defined the identity of every space. The parts did

 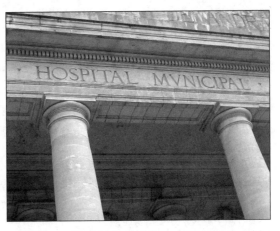

Figures 14.8 and 14.9: Just like many buildings, the old buses of Buenos Aires, designed by many contributing trades in harmony, were identifiable because of their patterns and colors. This was characteristic of the city and helped illiterate people recognize the bus they needed.

not betray the object, nor did the object betray the context. The personal view of the architect did not annul the context.

The same occurred with Renaissance publishing. Here, craftsmen were involved in all the stages of book-making, from proofreading to typographic design, from the manufacture of paper to printing and binding. They were not specialists in each of these crafts, but they were specialists in books, and as such could participate in all the steps involved in producing and selling a book. In this sense, our profession needs a comprehensive vision; in this sense, a certain degree of de-specialization is desirable.

How can we include this overall perception when teaching tomorrow's designers? Is it desirable and efficient to train specialized graphic designers, specialized industrial designers, specialized multimedia cartographers?

How should an academic program be designed to meet the reality of the design profession? And, vice versa, from what reality is it best to teach design?

Where Does the Designer Stand?

It is interesting to study communication scenarios and objects as contexts in which a multiplicity of audiences with different capabilities, possibilities, and interests converge and connect. Hence, the first step in any communication process is to identify the context, study it, analyze the origin of each of the codes that characterize it and weigh it all . . . but always putting oneself in the place of the other.

It is easy to imagine a house designed in complete accordance with the needs of a blind or handicapped person. But it is hard to imagine to what degree that person will be able to perform on common ground with the needs of a majority, that generally standardizes the limits and, hence, the reach of the communication.

Designing is always a matter of putting oneself in the place of the other to create communication from the right perspective. If I were asked to relate design to one of the branches of art, I would say that our profession is similar to that of an actor. We interpret roles so that, based on those roles, we can propose actions derived from our knowledge.

The alphabet was invented by people with no profession other than being merchants; nevertheless, over the centuries, specialists have developed forms, reproduction techniques, and methods of using this alphabet to optimize the qualities and quality of visual communication among people.

Teachers often have difficulty in transmitting this perception of design. In the Typography III course, which forms part of the Visual Communication career at the University of Buenos Aires, this concept has been the subject of a twofold experiment. The teachers requested one group of students to design a small users'

Figures 14.10 ("You can talk about it: avoid the misinformation media") and 14.11: Design contributes to enhance the legibility of texts and images, but readers also expect good information quality, and are often let down by the contents because good design is transparent, and allows one to see the lack of content of many journalistic materials.

guide to the university building to be used by new arrivals. This group had the best possible tool to make the guide understandable: actual daily experience. A second group worked on the design of a pension request form to be completed by the elderly to be eligible for pension and public health benefits. The complexity of each group's task did not lie in the handling of the appropriate techniques and resources. It lay in putting themselves in the place of the user. It was not a question of being a designer; they had to "be" the user.

When we redesign certain types of communication, we study the communication habits to determine which audience interests have been represented and which omitted. Within this framework, how can we broaden the usefulness of design? How can we place ourselves at the disposal of many other users with different capabilities? How many variables that are relevant to other users have been analyzed to create a standard perception of a group, such as legibility at a distance?

What Else Could Design Be Used for?

This is, in my opinion, design's major question. And to try to outline a conclusion, we have no alternative other than to study the needs and abilities of each link in all social strata so as to weave them into the general structure of communication. The task of design is to organize a system whereby each individual element makes its contribution to the overall characterization of the context.

Is it feasible, however, to talk about transmission? About a receiver? It is absurd to imagine an unequivocal linearity between one and the other. People interact with the context from the perspective of their lives. The only difference between their routines and our work is that, as designers, we must be able to consider all possibilities, thought, and actions from many other perspectives.

Design does not have readers, spectators or users, nor audience, patients, or receivers. It works for people immersed in an active social and cultural weave called reality. No one except a designer will buy a book solely to appreciate the marvelous subtlety of a Garamond typeface. But many people could well give a book up without understanding why they found the text so hard to read.

What Does Design Expect from People? What Do People Expect from Design?

A successful design is recognizable because it makes the transmission of content or the functionality of an object more accessible. And in that instant it ceases to exist visually. Expectations lie in the design of an object or the clarity of content, but do not relate to design, or, less still, the designer. In other words, design is part of an indissoluble structure of objects and contents that we relate to daily.

Only when facing a painting are people predisposed to appreciate the sensitivity of the artist, the energy of its colors, and the tension of its forms, and sometimes there is not even a need to interpret a message, because observers know that they are viewing a work of art. In other words, when facing a painting, the spectator can dissect the object and evaluate each of its production features independently.

But when faced with a newspaper page or when in a supermarket, people are not so inclined, because the context does not predispose them to analyze the quality of the lettering or the beauty of the colors. As users, their demands relate to matters that pertain to the functionality of the message. This does not make us less responsible, however, for either the graphic and aesthetic quality of our communications or for the visual culture that we build or destroy every time in every communication.

In December 2001, the Argentine economic crisis climaxed when the banks illegally seized their customers' savings. In Buenos Aires, an unprecedented popular demonstration demanded and achieved the president's resignation. During two days, there was horrifying police repression, and the press lost popularity for not transmitting—other than the more or less official description of the events—the magnitude of the public disapproval. The city spontaneously launched its opinions on the street. Some took advantage of the opportunity to participate in this dialogue of many, but to do so they used the anonymous language and the only independent resource available: the street. This strategy, intuitive and spontaneous, emerged from putting themselves in the place of the people. The news media received the same demand in relation to the invasion of Iraq. They were required to provide legibility, which in this case meant reliable content.

Dialogue of Many

As designers and users, we participate continually in a diverse social and cultural dialogue of many—a dialogue in which we participate after it has begun, which has to be listened to carefully. This dialogue includes intermingled informational, commercial, and ideological interests that reconstruct the status of public opinion and the communicational possibilities of the context. Do we situate content in context? Do we adapt context? Do we create communication context?

Context provides design with its best source of information, and it affords us the sense of the opportunity, or rather the parameters, that indicate how to say certain things at a certain time so as not to hinder the current of information. Mechanisms or languages from different contexts should never be used indiscriminately.

How then should we evaluate design? And how should we evaluate the responsibility of the designer? The scope and responsibility of our work is often defined as follows: "Certainly, with our work, we are never going to kill anyone." We know, however, that design is a manifestly premeditated, analytical, calculated activity, related to planning and not to improvisation. We know that it can be used to inform and misinform. There are areas where it can be difficult to measure the consequences of our participation, but there are innumerable cases of malpractice or of information designed to confuse, and that involve risks for society.

In 2001, a bridge collapsed and twenty-one schoolchildren fell into a swift river in the south of Argentina. Eight children died. The teachers who accompanied them did not see a danger sign that indicated that not more than three persons should cross at one time. The sign was on the opposite shore. It is an almost absurd example, constantly repeated in all corners of big cities, in the information leaflets accompanying medicinal products, in frequently used forms, and in product labels.

But let us use a more global, more brutal example. It would seem that the future of the world today depends on the will of a handful of men; it would also seem that this handful of men were chosen by another handful of men in the United States, who had trouble filling in the box of the candidate they wanted in the ballot.

Note

Juan Andralis (1928–1994) was a typographer, designer, painter, and printer. He was born in Greece and went to Argentina at an early age. He returned to Europe as a youth where he participated in the French surrealist movement with André Breton, and later worked with Cassandre and Frutiger. Upon his return to Argentina, he ran the El Archibrazo printing shop for almost thirty years, where he developed an intense activity, merging his multifaceted nature as printer, publisher, translator, and man of letters. He participated in the Graphic Department of the Di Tella Institute and was the curator of *tipoGráfica* magazine during its first seven years.

References

Fontana, Rubén (2004). "De signos y siglos. Breve historia conocida con final incierto" (On signs and centuries. A brief known history with an uncertain end). In *Ensayos sobre diseño, tipografía y lenguaje* (Essays on design, typography and language). Mexico: Editorial Designio.

Mijksenaar, Paul (2001). *An Introduction to Information Design*, Spanish translation. Mexico: Editorial Gustavo Gili.

This chapter was first published as an article in *tipoGráfica* 63, XVIII, October–November 2004, 34–40.

CHAPTER FIFTEEN

Centered on Society:
Exploring Public Knowledge of Design

Bonnie Sadler Takach
University of Alberta, Edmonton, Canada

Well-intentioned visual communication designers, guided by user-centered training and the disciplinary directives of responsible action, aim to serve society by crafting messages targeted to receptive audiences, and designing informational and educational products that perform appropriately—all while making design decisions based preferably on some sort of evidence, but sometimes on assumptions alone.

Designers have been taught that effective communication results from the meaningful interpretation of well-designed artifacts, and we have learned, among other things, that context, purpose, and individual experiences affect that interpretation. Despite numerous research methods and design strategies at our disposal, to claim that we know with certainty how every message will be interpreted would be overstating our abilities as designers. To produce effective results, we must work continually with members of the public to assess and calibrate our actions.

This requires an ongoing negotiation of the roles that both designers and non-designers play in creating, affecting, and interpreting the communicational spaces in which the products of design are situated and used. No matter who initiates design action, vital working relationships are likely to be built on trust, knowledge, empathy, and respect for points of view other than our own, with a view to empowerment rather than control.

In this reflection, questions about the working relationships between visual communication designers and the society we serve are considered broadly within the context of design practice, research, and education.

How Can We Gauge the Public's Awareness, Perception, or Knowledge of the Benefits of Visual Communication Design?

Approaches to design thinking and action vary widely. They range from striving for relative certainty using linear design methods and engineered solutions—where people are considered in terms of generalized behaviors and average measures—to the just-in-time response of systems such as customizable Web portals, in which individual needs are addressed and individual differences are celebrated. Prevailing notions have shaped these approaches across related disciplines about the nature of people's interaction with design and their role in creating and influencing communicational spaces.

We may perceive that our role is serving citizens and clients with varying degrees of awareness and knowledge about what we believe are the benefits of "good" design. Arrogance surrounds the commonplace notion of the need to "educate" the public about design, as if perhaps people might not comprehend, for example, information in a public service message or interpret the imagery in a poster. If a product of design is not performing well, then it is not the user who is in error, but the design.

In practice, building relationships between designers and the people we serve is central to the real work of responsible design. Yet this is difficult when we are not always clear about public knowledge of design, including the impact of design on people's lives. No longer only commissioned problem-solvers, many designers are trained to identify problems and develop interventions. These can influence the nature of the communicational spaces we share. No matter who initiates design action, we are not always certain about how our work is perceived, or even if it is welcome. In designing interventions, it would be important to know whether we are improving or invading public spaces and private lives.

Visual communication design in public spaces may be connected to marketing concerns, public service, or community building, such as signs in parks that commemorate special people. Public awareness, perception, and knowledge of the benefits of design might be reflected in the kind of design products that fill communicational spaces, and whether they have been created by, with, or without designers.

Re-branding exercises, overtly manipulative imagery in social campaigns, fear-arousing information design telling us how to survive terrorist attacks, and "improvements" to telephone bills for no apparent reason may trivialize what we do in the public's view. People can adapt to using even poorly designed products, find humor in altering preachy anti-smoking billboards, and improvise their own solutions for warning signs.

A realistic measure of public knowledge of effective design might be gained from observing the types of improvisation that people do, with positive results, in the face of real communicational needs. At the University of Alberta, a cumbersome on-line registration system was redesigned by a frustrated student user, who then made it available to others. This act of design desperation was as functional as it was generous, as it not only enabled the student to register more easily, but saved hours of time for others.

But people without design training improvise design solutions, or choose to collaborate with designers, not because designers have not done the job well, but because they have relevant knowledge and experience to contribute to the design process. There are cases where a collaborative client-designer relationship throughout the design process has been written into the contract. Some clients observe how their employees successfully solve problems, such as creating "cheat sheets" for procedures, and then hire professional designers to develop the work for mass production.

In developing safety materials for employees of a small drilling company, the owner noted what his employees themselves had produced, and adopted their practices in creating both an updatable warning poster, and individual, laminated pocket-size check cards for safety procedures. This was more than an informal type of usability testing, and the results showed it. To build morale within different drill crews, the same client had employee drawings incorporated into embroidered, "designer" crew badges. Clearly, he knew how to use visual communication design, not only to improve job safety, but also to build good working relationships through collaboration.

Participatory or collaborative design is misused when it is merely an exercise through which participants' views, concerns, and experiences are disregarded. Such was the case with a group of usability designers who, having enlisted a class of elementary school children to help develop an interactive learning game, treated them disrespectfully, ignored what they said, and did not appreciate the children's interest in doing meaningful work.

Good design is not really invisible, as we are sometimes told; otherwise people would not be aware of it at all. It is the result of meaningful relationships between designers and the society we serve, in which we are bound to share with the public evidence for how design contributes integrally to effective communication.

Should We Be Making a Greater Effort to Share Our Design Research with the People Whose Lives We Are Committed to Improve?

We have a professional responsibility to make our research visible to the public, because we all share the responsibility for the quality of our communicational spaces. When effective communication can be recognized by its fitness to purpose, context, and audience, different types of design research have likely been employed. Designers can help share the means to critically evaluate research-based design solutions.

But we must examine carefully methods that offer generalized or predictive ways to understand people's responses to products of design, as this may result in a glossing over of individual differences, and an over-simplification of actual concerns. We should guard against guaranteed, off-the-shelf solutions, and the use of out-of-context, sound-bite evidence, which hinder the development of our field. A few years ago, a surprise teleconference resulted when a group of provincial court judges called a designer, expecting to be given, on the spot, cited evidence supporting the use of a particular type font at a particular size for the design of statutes. Although the judges should be commended for an attempt to make evidence-based decisions about design, a nine-minute phone call right before an imminent printing deadline was hardly sufficient to make a sound decision. In fact, this type of situation can result in a negative perception of design research as a tool to satisfy clients, and one that does not necessarily result in improving the effectiveness of information.

If they knew of the possibilities, would citizens demand a more functional communication space, especially in terms of critical situations, more pleasurable experiences, or more satisfying interactions with the products of design? Many non-designers become involved in design research through necessity, interest or with the understanding that public participation in research will improve communicational spaces for everyone.

Much can be learned from talking to people of all ages who can challenge our assumptions about designed solutions. Children involved as research partners in evaluating a CD-ROM encyclopedia were concerned less with media effects than they were with efficiency of use, using inclusive, comprehensible language, and ensuring that there was no offensive material. In researching possibilities for designing effective communications for the lifespan, the idea of a different type of sustainable design emerges, where we would likely discover, for example, that well-designed signage is legible for both children and their grandparents as well.

Design research involving public participation is a type of advocacy. As citizens, we are all responsible for helping to create communicational spaces that are functional, appealing, and inclusive. As visual communication designers, we can act as advocates for responsible communication, by actively challenging zealous media coverage, for example, to limit children's exposure to images of 9/11, or by improving the performance of information such as health notices, student loan forms, voter ballots, traffic signage, insurance policies, and medicine labels. Working with people, we can help develop more holistic solutions that support the need to challenge legislation about medicine labeling, for example.

Research originating from members of different communities affords additional opportunities for sharing knowledge and learning new practices that enrich our ability to contribute to society. Recently, members of a northern Canadian aboriginal community approached an interdisciplinary team of researchers, including a visual communication design researcher, to collaborate with them to develop interactive media to teach youth about their own culture. This participatory design research used a consensus model that, while time-consuming, helped people consider all concerns and viewpoints. This is a valuable approach where effective communicational spaces are considered essential to the well-being of the community.

We also have a professional responsibility to share our work, both theoretical and practical, with other designers, making visible our design and research processes, to continue to strengthen our discipline and to allow for the exchange of ideas. This responsibility extends to training new designers.

As part of a research methods course, graduate visual communication design students developed an interactive communicational space, called Design Spaces, in the form of a blog, where people who would attend the Communicational Spaces conference at the University of Alberta in 2003 could connect in advance. During the conference, an actual space was created as part of the "Moving Through Meaning" exhibition, where conference attendees and members of the public could interact through ongoing written dialogues on large panels. This type of explorative research extends opportunities for designers and the public to interact in both virtual and physical communicational spaces.

As We Socialize Students Into the Visual Culture of Design, Do We Strip Away the Consciousness of Individual Choices and Reactions, and the Authenticity of Vernacular Expression?

When we teach design students, we may share our core beliefs about how we are developing our discipline and designing our own lives. We need to consider how to enable new designers to maintain authentic voices in shared communicational spaces.

Undergraduate visual communication design students eventually develop a level of visual literacy that differs from that of their friends and family. A frequent complaint from design students is that people don't know what they do. One set of supportive, but confused, parents kept a description of what their child was studying by the phone in case they had to explain it. Part of the curriculum that seems forgotten is equipping students with knowledge to tell people about what they do.

If students disconnect from how they viewed the world, with what made them part of the society that they serve, it may be difficult to empathize with views of design held by the public. Being aware of this shift helps us to relate to the public, as we cannot erase what we have learned of the language of images, typographic systems, and graphic symbols. People are now being encouraged to develop visual literacy and design-based skills, even beginning in primary school, to support the development of higher-order thinking such as analysis, synthesis, and evaluation; this helps them become critical users of design in communicational spaces.

Design educators have been engaging students in experiential, problem-based, community-based, design-based, and discovery learning long before these became trends in education. At the University of Alberta, our visual communication design curriculum includes working on real-life projects. In one senior undergraduate design course, students participate in "design jams," involving collaborative brainstorming sessions, to work with clients to improvise initial concepts that will be developed into final solutions. This is one way we can help students develop skills to work with the public in ways that are empowering for everyone.

We must be careful about promoting or imposing a "change-the-world" outlook not grounded in real possibilities. While pro-bono work can be very satisfying, students need to know that designers have a right to make a living. We can recognize that although involving people in improving their lives can be powerful, change may only come from empowering people when they are ready to push for change.

Many design students understand that design goes beyond style to action, and have made efforts to design their lives and work toward community-building. When renovations physically split a learning and design community at the University of Alberta, undergraduate design students initiated a virtual and actual social network to help not only each other, but also non-profit groups that could benefit from design action. They coordinated connecting events, the first of which attracted 150 students and professional designers. This design action had an ongoing effect. Students fully recognized the efforts of international groups like Design for the World, but wanted to stay connected to society through local action.

Centered on Society?

As visual communication designers, we need to balance core beliefs about responsible action with design training and creative ability. We should design for the lifespan, developing solutions that enable everyone to use design products effectively at different ages, and in consideration of different challenges. We are really advocating on behalf of people, having been invited to enter their lives, and to work with them to design effective communicational, informational, and educational products that will be part of their everyday lives. Rather than setting our sights on narrow demographic segments, we need to honor individual experience, helping people maintain their own, authentic voices, and empowering them to become critical users of design in our shared communicational spaces.

Acknowledgment

Jorge Frascara told me that he believed in the power of things to create their own vitality, and that vitality was connected with empowering without controlling. I thank him for the gift of this idea, which I carry with me, and for providing so many opportunities to create and share vital communicational spaces.

PART FIVE

The Space of Language and Graphics

Text has a very deceiving apparent transparency. Culture is embedded in every bit of it, from the kind of code used for the notation to the equivalent sound that silently works in the mind, to the visual appearance of the letter, the word, and the text. Visual and cognitive nuances are exploited in the hands of the perceptive designer. A wide range of possible shifts in the positioning of a text offers possibilities for both enjoyment and precision of aim.

CHAPTER SIXTEEN

On Signs and Centuries

Rubén Fontana
Fontana-Diseño, Buenos Aires, Argentina
(Translation into English: Peggy Jones and Martin Schmoller)

Culture has distinctive features and has the capacity to condense human experience. The slightest glance at our behavior, our intellectual and social environment, our relationships, and our systems of production and exchange, confirms that complex networks of signs, many of which have yet to be translated, traverse our entire lives.

Lettering Today

The task of a typeface designer is, above all, to generate spaces for communication, context, or structure, and when designing a font, the typographer is partly anticipating future communication conditions. Typographers build the contexts and part of the circumstances surrounding the reading of a message that does not yet exist. They work from their knowledge and, at the same time, influence a historical convention and its projection into the future, that is to say, in a cultural and temporal context. They develop systems of abstract forms to represent abstract sounds.

Rhythm, structure, color, legibility, proportion, and harmony are designed and recombined for each new communication purpose, recreating the most conventional forms capable of manipulation. When analyzing the form of each letter, the thought behind the shape of its counter, the force of its black and white rhythm, the course of its strokes, the space that will envelop it, joining or separating it, a

Figure 16.1: Sumerian pictographic tablet (3100 BC). The information is presented in vertical and horizontal form.

typographer is not anticipating the beauty of a shape, but foreseeing the future of an as yet unknown word.

A font conveys conditions beyond the limits of time and message. Type styles developed in the sixteenth century continue to be reference models and provide the context for contents and forms of reading in the twenty-first century. Although the meaning of a text transmitted by a typeface might be ephemeral, the cultural framework in which the design of the font was generated can be timeless.

Type can be a good or bad interpreter of the word it represents. In its inevitable relationship, type and content either act harmoniously or disallow each other dramatically, obstructing communication. Typography starts with the interpretation of a style, the relevant one for the message, and thereafter its mission is to become transparent. Its behavior on a page is similar to that of paper; in other words, it should act as a medium, a background for the content, which will make the message more accessible and legible.

This brief summary leads to a series of questions, some of which have been answered by history in one way or another, whereas others have not yet been wholly formulated: When creating a font, how can we take into account this vast number of references? Can we predict to what extent the effectiveness of a message will be conditioned by its vehicle—letters? In the design of a page layout, can letters lead to varying subtleties of interpretation? What makes a typeface design timeless?

In Days of Yore

The Tower of Babel, the hanging gardens of Babylon, the epic poem of the legendary hero Gilgamesh, the Hammurabi Code, the walls of Ur and the ancient Nineveh are some of the milestones that have defined the cradle of western civilization for more than five thousand years. It is no coincidence that the alphabet was born in this region. In these territories, that witnessed the passing of Sumerians, Akkadians, Babylonians, Assyrians, Hittites, Arameans, Chaldeans, Persians, Greeks, and Romans, the myth of the universal flood was born and one of the first forms of writing emerged: the most important step in the creation of the conventions of communication until our times.

Why precisely in Lower Mesopotamia? It is because those arid lands saw the development of one of the most prosperous political and economic systems in history. The use of irrigation generated significant agricultural expansion and vigorous commercial activity with other cultures. The need to control trade between peoples with different, hard-to-transmit languages generated an urgent need for a more universal and less figurative form of writing, one that would be independent from the visual objects of each culture and that would express an idea by means of its sounds. On the day that they decomposed language into sounds and created abstract forms to represent these independent sounds and not objects, the Phoenicians endowed humanity with the most formidable cultural instrument and the most fervent promise of communication between cultures. Since then, writing has been the graphic system for recording speech.

It was between the shores of the Tigris and Euphrates rivers, the present invaded Iraqi territory, that, together with the letters of the alphabet, the notion of a system was born: a program that consisted of basic combinable, understandable and easily learned symbols that reduced the complexity of writing and reading. This was the first great step in the process of the standardization of communication, and thus was one of the most important agreements among mankind.

Many neighboring cultures had prefigured the phonetic alphabet that the Phoenicians eventually created. Sumerian cuneiform writing had left its mark in the East, and Egyptian hieroglyphics in the South. The Sumerians had an agglutinative language: monosyllables followed by prefixes and suffixes; these symbols became separated from pictography and ideography to be identified with syllabic sounds. Contrary to the Sumerians, whose writing evolved from pictography to an abstract cuneiform style, the Egyptians preserved a combined system of writing and drawing. The first examples go back as far as 3100 BC.

Their system of writing was different. Trade with Mesopotamian cultures brought the news that the Sumerians used writing. This opened new vistas for the Egyptian people, who promptly developed an original method of writing. Since then, and until the evolution of the present alphabetic system, from East to West, hundreds of cultures channeled their need for communication through the medium of letters and left their mark in its development.

Thus the processes of identification and flexibility that enabled the representation of the different languages emerged. The Greeks, as an example, upon adopting the alphabet, did what they had done with art, sculpture, literature and philosophy; they greatly enhanced its usefulness and beauty.

In the seventh century BC, the Greeks added vowels to the original twenty-two consonants of the earliest Phoenician alphabet, which includes a number of letters that have preserved their identity over thirty-five centuries, and this enabled them to pronounce the sounds of their language and incorporate ideas relative to their culture to the universe of words. The Greeks anticipated the system of capital letters in their inscriptions on stone, and used lowercase letters for their writing on papyrus or wax-coated tablets. In this, like the Egyptians, they were also original, because several centuries passed before the Roman alphabet adopted lowercase letters through a slow process of search for greater speed in handwriting.

The Greeks, in their inscriptions, were the first to build and systematize letters in straight, curved and diagonal lines. Pure geometric forms were incorporated, and this, among other aspects, made it possible to regulate and simplify writing; thus, the E, H, N and M were based on the square, the A on the triangle and the O on the circle. In this way, the definitive form of conceiving the structure of the characters was born.

Time and Materials

As widespread travel added structure to the alphabet, the aesthetic features of the characters were also influenced by the tools used and the medium on which they were drawn: the stroke of quill on papyrus is different from that of stylus on wax. Clay, stone, and brush all made successive contributions to the alphabet. Both medium and tool led to a rapid simplification and stylization of primitive pictography. The similarity between the symbol and the represented object tended to disappear, and characters capable of being drawn fluently with the quill became common. These tools began to progressively reduce the realism of primitive drawings, separating them from their association with their original reference models.

Figure 16.2: Clay tablet containing the Sumerian symbols for star, head, and water, showing the evolution toward a cuneiform style of writing (2500 BC).

The medium used helps us to understand why certain languages and systems of writing disappeared without leaving a trace, whereas others, protected from the rigors of time or favored by the climate and produced with resistant materials, have survived intact. The history of writing is the history of an exceptionally slow metamorphosis; born six thousand years ago, for reckoning and book-keeping purposes, it became a way of thinking, of conceiving, of creating, of being.

Today, we can state that, aside from cultures and techniques, the evolution of the alphabet was influenced by two phenomena in constant fluctuation: the need to ratify conventions to preserve the communication and the learning of the conventions; and the need to make it flexible, adapting it to the multitude of languages that adopted it and to their evolution.

The geographic distribution of writing is no longer as complex as that of languages. The cultures that use the Latin alphabet comprise around one billion individuals, and it is the alphabet used by the most numerous communities in the world.

Backs and Forths

Over time and the course of its travels from one language to another, the set of characters gained sophistication in expressing the particular sounds of each culture. The frequency of use of different characters in different languages gave rise to additions such as the Latin ligatures æ, œ and &, followed four centuries later by the X and Y in Greek.

The Romans assimilated the Greek alphabet. Twelve characters were left unchanged, seven were modifications of other Greek letters, and three in disuse were reinstated. After the Romans adopted the alphabet in 250 BC, the G was created to replace the Z. Each letter was designed as a specific form, rather than the sum of its parts, and special attention was paid to its counters and to the spacing between letters and lines in text composition. The Roman inscriptions represent the apogee of epigraphic writing and the starting point for typographic design as we know it today. Lapidary lettering, a model of sobriety and purity, rests on simple principles: geometry, light, and shadow.

Writing was originally one continuous progression, where the words followed each other without pauses, imitating the flow of speech. In those times, the reader had to be cultured and qualified, and reading was only conceived of aloud. The reader was responsible for punctuation. The concept of words as it is known today emerged in Ireland in the fifth century; the Irish used Latin as a second language and, therefore, were not totally familiar with it. Latin was, for them, a symbolic graphic language.

The turn of the eighth century saw the beginning of a general renaissance in culture and education in Europe led by King Charlemagne that, in AD 789, established by edict the formal characteristics of writing based on the work and counsel of Alcuin of York.

Charlemagne commissioned Alcuin to perform an important task: to revise and unify script writing variations in the production of books. The result of his work was a small, round and highly legible letter, the Carolingian minuscule: a new step in the process of standardization to preserve conventions. This script was the precursor of the contemporary alphabet, from which the concept of "one sound, one shape" emerged, obviating a quantity of ligatures and abbreviations that obstructed interpretation. In terms of legibility, the development of this minuscule was the most important step in the history of writing after the establishment of the Roman alphabet.

During the Middle Ages (fifth to fifteenth centuries), the J and the U were added to the alphabet, the latter being a smoother vowel than the V. Question marks and parentheses were not added until the eleventh and twelfth centuries, and the exclamation mark appeared in the fourteenth century. From around 1150, the Romanesque era evolved into the Gothic and, although it emerged in the north of France and in Great Britain, it expanded rapidly. The main characteristic of its form is an angular letter with marked profiles, generically called gothic. One of the reasons for its existence, apart from relating to the culture and architecture of the period, had to do with the substitution of the blunt writing stylus by the feather quill. The rapid handwriting that this quill enabled tended to eliminate the broad curves. Letters became narrower and taller, with the subsequent greater economy of space, materials, and time.

Where did all these incorporations and modifications lead us? Does the alphabet, in spite of so many years of existence, continue to be open, flexible, and dynamic?

Writing and Typography

The history of typography begins with Gutenberg. After the creation of the alphabet and Charlemagne's standardization, a new period of ratification of conventional forms began, but this time in relation with a new technology for the production of letters. Until then, the basic idea was writing; however, the mechanization of reproduction determined a new concept to define lettering: typography. The new technology absorbed the forms developed by innumerable scribes who progressively defined the graphic expression of sounds in their daily tasks throughout the centuries.

Profound transformations took place in the sixteenth and seventeenth centuries. In those days, the Italian Humanists began to replace Gothic lettering with characters rediscovered in the Roman inscriptions. Thus, Roman capitals were combined with Carolingian minuscules, producing a double alphabet that, henceforth, functioned simultaneously.

Around that time, another series of adjustments took place in relation to the need for the typographic system to harmonize the size of uppercase and lowercase

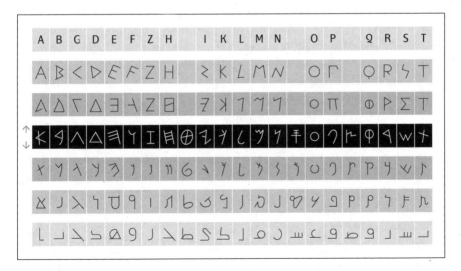

Figure 16.3: Diagram showing the evolution of European and Arabic writing from their common Phoenician source (centre row). From top to bottom: Modern Latin, Ancient Latin, Ancient Greek, Phoenician, Ancient Aramean, Nabatean, Ancient Arabic.

characters and the system of round with that of italic lettering. The Aldus italics, produced by Griffo under commission, are characterized by capitals with a height lower than the ascenders of the minuscules and also by long descenders. The semi-colon [;] was contributed by Aldus Manutius, and Geoffrey Tory introduced the apostrophe, the accent and the cedilla. The abbreviations survived until the period of the incunabula, but gradually gave way to the more standardized configuration of the words.

In the seventeenth century, the use of the V was still undefined, and the U was sometimes used to express it. A century later, a long s, more like the character currently representing the f, was still used together with the current s. Around the 1800s, the English added the sound of the double u, the W, and used it frequently in their language.

Historically, the letter ñ has been resisted by font producers. Possibly because it only exists in the Spanish language, European and North American type foundries were slow to accept it. More recently, those that market predominantly English-language software attempted to obviate it. Among Latin Americans, it is an everyday sound that differs substantially from the preceding nh, ny, nj, nn and gn digraphs. The ñ is a typical case of the union of two symbols to express a mixed sound.

After the Industrial Revolution, it was no longer enough for typography to function solely as a phonetic symbol. Increasing demands, as well as the evolution of the repertoire and context of communications, generated specific needs. The times required a transformation of the structures into visual forms, and that letters should cease to serve for reading only and incorporate visual components to adapt to the new circumstances. Over and above the progressive inclusion of the characters in use today, other attempts at typographic development were made, based in many cases on a return to previous eras. A case in point is that of the formal simplifications studied during the first half of the twentieth century with the purpose of expressing the characters in pure geometrical forms; a way of returning to the basic forms of the Greek characters and other constructive developments experienced during the Renaissance.

Systems of phonetic symbols created with combinations of letters to represent syllables were also tested: the possibility of an evolved simplification of the alphabet, by means of the union of parts or ligatures representing sounds. Attempts were also made to rationalize the form of writing by eliminating the capitals and speculating with the use of just one form instead of the uppercase and lowercase lettering employed to represent each sound. Similarly, the possibility of a linguistic evolution of the phonetic alphabet by means of the invention of ligatures capable of representing sounds created by combinations of letters was analyzed. More recently, and as if the above aspects were insufficient reason for continuous change, toward the end of the twentieth century, the Spanish Academy of Letters eliminated the *Ch* and *Ll* as independent letters.

From this perspective, can the alphabet be considered a consummate structure that transcends generations toward the future, or are we living in a world of small and constant adjustments that do not enable us to determine the future of the system? Is it possible to think in terms of a typographic system that will express sounds better than the present one?

Symbols of Identity

The way in which typography builds its framework of perception is directly related to the objectives established in font design, based on not necessarily written but undoubtedly inherited social conventions that transcend the present day. Typography, at times, acts as a frame of reference for the development of content and, because of its characteristics, determines contexts and usage. Thus, typographic forms, even as abstract symbols, are reference models for cultures, countries, and even languages.

Elzevirian, gothic, transition, Didot or sans serif styles, to name just a few, refer to message contexts that are, in their turn, recontextualized because of their use in specific communication formats. The formal characteristics of certain typefaces have become synonymous with language, culture, and nations.

Having mentioned no more than four of many examples, gothic lettering defines the historical period between the twelfth and sixteenth centuries, yet long after that period its formal characteristics frequently take us back to Germany and Austria. Garamond developed some exceptional matrices that have survived the passage of time because of their proportions and quality for editorial purposes; however, their forms are also synonymous with French culture. For some reason, possibly related to their spiritual culture or their identification with the nationality of their authors, the English identify better with the Baskerville, Gill, and Times typefaces, considering them highly legible. Last, the form of the characters created by Giambattista Bodoni was an anticipation of

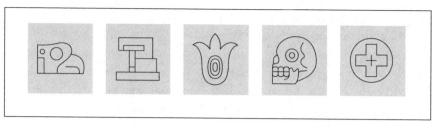

Figure 16.4: From left to right: Bird (Tiwanaku, Bolivia). House (Aztec, Mexico); Maize (Olmec, Mexico); Death (Aztec, Mexico). Earth (Argentina).

modernism. Because of their classic elegance, his characters are used worldwide, and it is said that, although many letters might reflect the Italian language, none sings like this typeface.

Tomorrow Is Today!

In both time and space, we are witnessing a historic evolution in writing and typography. Without professing futurology insofar as typography is concerned, it is the moment to ask ourselves certain questions regarding the future of the alphabet. Writing is a cultural fact, and its origins concern a limited number of civilizations. Many spoken languages have never been written down, and it is considered that, of more than two thousand languages, approximately four-fifths of them still lack proper written form. There are many regions where the graphic sounds of speech have not been developed. Only one out of every two human beings is thoroughly conversant with writing.

In the great majority of cases, these languages have no visual existence; they have not found the symbols that represent them, that record their history and their present, and that inform and set down the laws, habits, and customs that gave rise to them. Even in those cases where they have written expression, the language has not always been deciphered, and the sounds have been reinterpreted based on other written languages.

In other words, the invader decoded the sounds of these languages and adapted them to other sounds, to those with which he was acquainted in his own language. Hence, the invader imposed writing on the conquered people, reinterpreting or translating according to the circumstances, and not always in a respectful manner. Technology and the conquerors have had a lot to do with the delay in writing previously unwritten languages because for almost five hundred years technology was controlled by just a handful of countries. This determined that the evolution of letters was circumscribed to the needs and developments of a few central European languages.

New design, production, and font reproduction technologies have not only equalled the perspectives for the formal development of characters but also spawned a number of alternatives that involve accepting new responsibilities, and will, undoubtedly, in the near future resolve a number of needs that have not been addressed for over 500 years. The possibility for designers throughout the world to digitize alphabets opens an immense field that, in theory, would enable the formal writing of relegated cultures. And this leads to certain questions: In what way will the emergence of written versions of what have until now been solely oral languages modify current alphabets? Will specific situations modify the present overall circumstances?

Even if the formal codes of the current alphabetic system continue to be used to record the so far unwritten languages, it is possible that an unpredictable number of ligatures, diacritics, and digraphs might determine at least an extension of the present system. Will this extension be applicable to all in general, or will it be circumscribed to a particular language? Will one character with one diacritic interpret the same sound in different languages?

The big doubt is to what extent will predictable evolution continue to strictly ratify the inherited conventions and, if so, will it occur within a context of contention? Therefore, will the system, in its attempt to encompass and reach out to other cultures, follow a road of dispersion?

Part of the evolution of typography will continue within its formal sphere, which is no small matter if we consider the quality of some interpretations, but the new reality tells us that situations of another type will arise shortly because all cultures and their languages do not have the same needs, nor are they all contained within the current system. It is feasible that new formal expressions might proliferate to express frequent sounds in Latin American languages, such as those spoken by the Aztecs, Mayas, Quechuas, Mapuches, Guaranis, etc. Apart from the original 22 characters, today almost 600 are required to write all the Latin-based languages; in other words, the diversity of languages that adopted the primitive structure and its development over time has caused the system to grow approximately twenty-seven times.

Will the new systems of writing continue to increase the set of characters? And how far—as many as one thousand, two thousand, something similar to Chinese writing, although in this case it would encompass a number of languages and not just one? Because it is impossible today to think of a personality such as Charlemagne, who in his era regulated the system of writing spoken sounds, who will accept responsibility for the success of the development of the forms of writing?

During this next stage, it might be necessary for the designer to interact with disciplines that study the structure of new characters for cultures with unwritten languages.

Typeface design today requires a stronger relationship with anthropology and linguistics; because typography will no longer work solely on the basis of form it will again come closer to language. We have already seen that typography is not independent of the changes of society and that it evolves together with technical or cultural events, not only of language but also of everything concerning humanity. This dilemma has occurred over the years and in different cycles. Where are we today? What is the next cycle that we will live through? Will we find ourselves at a crossroads similar to that of the last six thousand years?

The new forms of writing and the specifics of the reinterpretation of existing ones indicate that we might possibly be facing a new stage in the development of typography that must respond to the needs and awareness of the sounds of the spoken word, and as before the work of the typographers must be intimately related to the circumstances of their time.

Note: This text is a revised version of lectures given at the Recoleta Cultural Centre in Buenos Aires, at the University of Alberta, Edmonton, Canada, and at the Intercontinental University of Mexico City in April and October 2003, respectively. The text was first published in *tipoGráfica* 60: Year XVIII, April–May, 2004, 12–17.

References

Bain, Peter, and Shaw, Paul (2001). *La letra gótica tipo e identidad nacional* (Blackletter: Type and National Identity). Valencia: Campgrafic.

Berry, John D. (2002). *Language, Culture, Type*. New York: ATypI/Graphis.

Calvino, Italo (1987). *Antes del alfabeto* (Before the Alphabet). Madrid: Alianza Editorial.

Carter, Sebastian (2000). *Twentieth Century Type Designers*. Veenendaal : Gaade Uitgevers.

De Buen, Jorge (2000). *Manual de diseño editorial* (Publishing Design Manual). Mexico DF: Ediciones Santillana.

La Nación. (2003) Editorial, Buenos Aires, March–April.

Fontana, Rubén (Ed.) (1996). *Pensamiento tipográfico, Cátedra Fontana/Typographic thought, Fontana Chair*. Buenos Aires: Edicial.

Frutiger, Adrian (1981). *Signos, símbolos, marcas y señales* (Signs and Symbols). Barcelona: Gustavo Gili.

Jean, Georges (1998). *La escritura, memoria de la humanidad* (Writing, Humanity's Memory). Barcelona: Biblioteca de Bolsillo.

Meggs, Philip. B. (1991). *Historia del Diseño Gráfico* (A History of Graphic Design). Mexico DF: Trillas.

Spencer, Herbert (1969). *The Visible Word*. London: Lund Humphries.

Stamm, Philipp, and Gürtler, André (1997). *Typografische Monatsblätter/TM RSI 1*. Edition of the Trade Union for book and paper for professional education, Switzerland.

CHAPTER SEVENTEEN

Paul Rand:
Using Context to Create Meaning

Barbara Sudick
California State University, Chico, USA

Communicational spaces can be viewed as a medium for processing informational transactions; like a conversation—always adjusting, changing direction and focus with stops, starts, and surprises—between individuals or groups with different cultural backgrounds, life experiences, thinking, or cognitive styles. Each individual shapes the dialog and forms his own unique understanding of a message that is influenced simultaneously by intercultural, cultural, social, and personal contexts. According to information architect Richard Saul Wurman, meaning is formed by a process of activating the communicational space through context, "through what surrounds, informs, and opposes an idea" (Wurman, 9). The application of any one or combination of these three elements will affect the meaning and an individual's understanding of a message. As context becomes increasingly personal, the message becomes more meaningful.

Gestalt psychologists examining the interaction of figure and ground have demonstrated how the dynamic character of the perception of simultaneous stimuli can change a message. The primary stimulus or figure, which normally attracts our attention, opposes the usually subliminal ground, which is a less complete stimulus. The combined perception of figure and ground forms a synergetic contextual message, which is much more than the sum of its individual parts. Over-stimulation of our senses by too many simultaneous stimuli (noise), without separation of distinct elements or interactions within a communicational space, causes the meaning of the resulting message to be diminished. Josef Albers experimented with context and the interaction of color—the dynamic relationship between figure and ground colors. He observed that "Colors present themselves in continuous flux, constantly related to changing neighbors and changing conditions" (Albers, 5). Like color, the meaning of all visual information (images, symbols, typography, etc.) is formative, influenced by distinct context—the content of the surrounding space.

We comprehend things through their opposites; we cannot understand black without white. In *A Primer of Visual Literacy*, educator/author Donis Dondis says that "All meaning exists in the context of polarities" (Dondis, 85). Media theorist Marshall McLuhan used a sensory metaphor of opposites to understand the power and effect of media. In his book *Understanding Media*, McLuhan employed the polarity of hot and cold to describe the contribution of context and the role of our physical senses and perceptions in creating meaning.

D. K. Holland, a contributing editor at *Communication Arts*, recently observed that, "We see with our brains, not with our eyes" (Holland). Beyond the perceptual influences of physical structure (opposing and surrounding visual information), context is affected by the cognitive process of informing (imparting information or knowledge). Participants in communicational spaces use personal experiences, knowledge and personalized information to inform their understanding of an idea. Although a designer can enable a viewer to participate in the creation of meaning by using ambiguity and abstraction, individuals must interpret information and create understanding for themselves. Context and meaning depend on an individual's ability "to interact with information in a way that helps us build personal context and integrate the information into our previous understandings" (Shedroff, 49).

American graphic designer Paul Rand was a master at using context to create meaning. He understood the power of abstract symbols—their potential as a universal visual language and, at the same time, to convey individualized meaning. With a thorough understanding of both design and communication theories, he also recognized the power of transforming passive viewers into active participants by engaging them in the discovery of meaning and understanding. The legendary designer George Lois once said that Rand's concern was "to create images that snared people's eyes, penetrated their minds, warmed their hearts and made them act" (Heller, 9).

Rand's work attracts the attention of its audience by using the language of visual arts to create contrast. Opposites reveal the unexpected. Interrupting the balance or harmony of visual elements, he breaks our focus, grabs our attention, and changes our thinking patterns. He often uses the element of surprise—juxtaposing objects from unexpected sources or making dramatic changes in scale, color, or arrangement to get our attention. Describing his juxtaposition of images on a magazine cover, he explained, "the form is intensified by dramatic narrative association. The literal meaning changes according to context; the formal quality remains unchanged" (Rand 1985, 13).

According to Adrian Frutiger, "a symbol with reduced form is more memorable than an ordinary picture" (Frutiger, 239). To make a message more accessible, Rand simplifies form and condenses complex information and concepts into highly informed and understandable visual communications. He said, "The historical process is (or should be) a process of distillation and not accumulation" (Rand 1992).

Rand constructs context with familiar symbols that bring meaning from everyday expressions, such as idioms, axioms, and clichés. These expressions represent a shared understanding, based on a common language and cultural experience, which begin a collaborative process of building meaning. They welcome the viewer and start a dialog. A visual pun is a familiar symbol that has different levels of meaning, depending on its context. Viewers are engaged in a process of revealing multiple meanings. Rand had a great acumen for creating simultaneous contexts and meaning—helping the viewer to understand new ideas and concepts by comparison with familiar images.

As McLuhan once said, "there's no participation in just telling" (Benedetti, 45). Knowing that we are moved more by suggestion than statement, Rand deliberately chose to engage viewers in a visual and conceptual dialog to discover meaning. Using ambiguity and abstraction to leave the message incomplete, he requires individuals to take an active role in the communication process. Rand understood that personal experience and involvement are necessary for an individual to transform information into knowledge.

Rand also understood the role of play, which encourages lateral thinking, multiple viewpoints, and interpretations. Without fear of judgment, play can help a viewer to restructure thinking patterns and create insight, which makes new connections and builds meaning. Understanding the importance of the interaction of play, Rand said, "There can be design without play, but that's design without ideas" (Heller and Anderson, 122).

Rand made visual problems more creative, dramatic, and engaging with mnemonics: picture puzzles and memory games that require participation and challenge viewers to discover solutions. "An idea that happens in the mind, stays in the mind," argue Beryl McAlhone and David Stuart (23) in their book on witty thinking in graphic design. Cognitive challenges make ideas more memorable—as do messages that elicit an emotional response, such as humor and surprise.

Humor is a consequence of play; it enhances meaning and helps make things more memorable. Play often follows the least likely path, deliberately trying the unexpected. Rand invites viewer interaction by re-contextualizing information to create humorous or playful messages. In an interview with Steven Heller, Rand said, "The notion of taking things out of context and giving them new meanings is inherently funny" (Heller and Anderson, 122). "Humor," Wurman suggested, "is a passageway to understanding" (Wurman, 113).

Although technology has made some ideas of past generations obsolete, it has made others more relevant. The work of designer Paul Rand is an important model for understanding visual communication as an interactive process, which creates meaning by constructing a number of simultaneous contexts. Like conversation, his method requires the viewer to become an active participant. With a utility of purpose, he makes the message accessible through simplification of form and engages his audience with ambiguity and play. Surrounding and opposing ideas with objects and thoughts from unexpected sources, he also utilizes the emotional response connected with surprise and humor to make ideas more memorable. Informing ideas with history, personal experiences, and knowledge, individuals are empowered to participate in interactive communicational spaces by constructing the context and meaning necessary for understanding.

References

Albers, Josef (1975). *Interaction of Color*. New Haven, CT: Yale University Press.

Benedetti, Paul and DeHart, Nancy (1996). *Forward Through the Rearview Mirror: Reflections on and by Marshall McLuhan*. Toronto, ON: Prentice Hall Canada.

Dondis, Donis A. (1973). *Primer of Visual Literacy*. Cambridge, MA: MIT Press.

Frutiger, Adrian (1998). *Signs and Symbols: Their Design and Meaning*. New York: Watson-Guptill.

Heller, Steven and Anderson, Gail (1991). *Graphic Wit*. New York: Watson-Guptill.

Heller, Steven (1999). *Paul Rand*. London: Phaidon Press.

Holland, DK. Editor's note to "Inkblot Test." *Communication Arts*, September/October 2002. <www.commarts.com/ca/coldesign/cech_160.html>

McAlhone, Beryl and Stuart, David (1998). *Smile in the Mind*. London: Phaidon Press.

Rand, Paul (1985). *Paul Rand: A Designer's Art*. New Haven, CT: Yale University Press.

Rand, Paul (1992). "Confusion and Chaos: The Seduction of Contemporary Graphic Design." *AIGA Journal of Graphic Design*. Volume 10, Number 1. <www.mkgraphic.com/chaos.html>

Shedroff, Nathan (2001). *Experience Design*. Indianapolis, IN: New Riders.

Wurman, Richard Saul (1989). *Information Anxiety*. New York: Doubleday.

PART SIX

The Space of Identity

The task of identifying is a central part of our cognitive system: we do not perceive because we have eyes, we perceive because we want to understand. Understanding is an active task and one of its main aims is to recognize identities. Identities are not only a design territory; practically everything that pertains to a given setting contributes to the identity of that setting. Identities make some people feel comfortable and others out of place and can become political statements. Social groups, business concerns, and even open spaces have identities, and, being human constructs, they can sometimes reveal and sometimes deceive. Identity can be spontaneous expression or planned information, but it can also be discussed as an ethical and moral issue in the design of communications.

CHAPTER EIGHTEEN

Representing the "Dutch Woman" at the 1898 National Exhibition for Women's Labour:
Avoiding Visual Miscommunication in the Public Sphere

Joan E. Greer
University of Alberta, Edmonton, Canada

In the year **1898** the Dutch National Exhibition for Women's Labour opened in The Hague. Inspired by the "Woman's Building" at the World's Fair in Chicago in 1893 and the Danish National Exhibition for Women's Labour in Copenhagen in 1895, the exhibition celebrated the inauguration of Queen Wilhelmina as the first woman in Holland to hold the position of head of state. Its more fundamental purpose, however, was to highlight the position and contributions of Dutch women, both at home and within the Dutch colonies.

A century later, in 1998, this remarkable exhibition was the subject of a centenary conference and exhibition held in Amsterdam by the Association of Women's History. It was also the subject of an important study by Maria Grever and Berteke Waaldijk, *Feministische Openbaarheid: De Nationale Tentoonstelling van*

Vrouwenarbeid in 1898 (translated as *Transforming the Public Sphere: the Dutch National Exhibition of Women's Labor in 1898*). An aspect of the exhibition of relevance to the larger thematic focus of the essays published in this volume is the very significant role played by visual imagery on the one hand and by exhibition design on the other in creating communicational spaces in which the agendas of the numerous groups involved could operate. The need to communicate clearly and appropriately felt by one of the groups, the Association for Women's Suffrage (Vereeniging voor Vrouwenkiesrecht: VvVK), is particularly noteworthy. This group commissioned a painting depicting "the situation of the Dutch Woman" for the exhibition from the male artist/designer Johan Thorn Prikker (Grever and Waaldijk, 107).

The design proposed by Thorn Prikker (figure 18.1), which I have discussed elsewhere in a different context (Greer 2003a), was one of a crucified woman. This drawing of a naked, splay-legged woman, bound to a cross, was rejected outright.

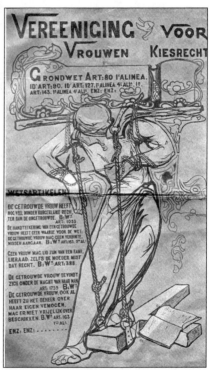

Figure 18.1. Image and permission courtesy of the Kröller-Müller Museum, Otterlo, The Netherlands

Figure 18.2: The author thanks the IIAV (International Information Centre and Archives for the Women's Movement, Amsterdam, The Netherlands) for having provided this figure. Efforts made to locate the copyright owner were without success.

It was replaced by another image by the same artist—this time of a clothed woman bowed under a heavy yoke (figure 18.2)—an image that, in contrast to the earlier one, was accepted by the Association for Women's Suffrage and displayed prominently at the 1898 exhibition.

In this essay I will investigate the rejected drawing, examining it in relation to the goals of the Association for Women's Suffrage. I will examine how the topos of a crucified figure, as well as the secondary figures in the composition, communicated to various constituencies in different ways. Such an examination leads to inevitable questions concerning the communication of meaning. Here, then, in what is part of a larger project in progress, how questions of gender, religion, and radical politics converge in this commission will be investigated and related to the communication of meaning in visual language at this exhibition.

The Context for (Mis)communication

It is useful to first briefly consider the background of the exhibition before turning to the commission itself. From about 1860, the Dutch had been openly debating what came to be known as the "vrouwen-quaestie" or, in English, the "women's question," an umbrella term that addressed women's problematic position in modern society. It included issues related to women's education, work, sexuality, and legal position within and outside of marriage. In the summer of 1898 (July 9–September 21) these questions were given broad public exposure through the use of this large-scale multi-disciplinary exhibition—the National Exhibition for Women's Labour. As Grever and Waaldijk have shown (Grever and Waaldijk), the focus of this exhibition made it unusual. Exhibitions in Holland were typically devoted to agriculture, trade and industry, to the fine and applied arts, but not to political questions. However, as Grever and Waaldijk also point out, the women's movement was no ordinary political movement. It brought together a diverse group of individuals and associations of women that crossed all class and educational boundaries. There was, therefore, no single, dominant approach to the "women's question," nor one aspect of the subject that took precedence. An exhibition, therefore, was seen as an ideal means of allowing the diverse voices of the women's movement to speak out, each in its own way. While the stated theme of the exhibition was "women's labour," loosely defined as "work undertaken by women," the question of emancipation became an integral, although not focal, part of the program. Ways in which this issue was present included some that were explicit (for example, this work; the lecture/presentation by the VvVK in Conference room;

VvVK material for sale) and some that were somewhat less direct in which the need for change was implied (exhibits highlighting poor labour conditions, educational/professional opportunities, and other problems related to women's issues).

The visitor, upon arriving at the exhibition, was confronted with a vast array of displays and of live demonstrations ranging thematically from the fine arts and photography to industry and trade; from work in the agricultural and fishing industries to work in the public health sector. An Indonesian village or *Kampong* was set up and included women demonstrating batik. The humanities and sciences were represented as were culinary and household education. There was a vegetarian restaurant. Lectures, discussions, and presentations were held in a large congress area. In short, all conceivable aspects of women's work were presented (Grever and Waaldijk).

One of the rooms, considered by many to be the heart of the exhibition (Grever and Waaldijk, 103), was entitled "Maatschappelijke Werk" or "Social Work." It is important to note that it was in this location that the painting representing "the situation of the Dutch Woman" from Thorn Prikker was to be hung, although it appears from the minutes of the exhibition's organizational committee that the Association may not have originally felt this to be the most appropriate location (Grever and Waaldijk, 202, 301). "Social Work" was represented in this room by organizations in which women worked that were in the interests of society in general including health care organizations and philanthropical institutions but also by organizations that worked specifically to address the position of women in society. All nature of women's problems were highlighted in this room, as were women's attempts to deal with these problems (Grever and Waaldijk).

Crucified Woman

It is against this backdrop that Thorn Prikker's design needs to be considered. According to archival records, the Association for Women's Suffrage decided in October of 1897 to be represented at the exhibition with "a surprise" (IIAV). The surprise afforded by Thorn Prikker's original conception, however, was obviously not what members of the Association had in mind.

What was it, then, that Thorn Prikker's imagery did communicate? The drawing, at its most basic level, refers back to the most familiar example of crucifixion, the crucified Christ. Such imagery, when done in a more traditional form, could be expected to function positively within traditional Christian frameworks. Less obvious from a twenty-first-century point of view, however, is that during the late nineteenth century, images of crucifixion were also functioning in very specific ways outside traditional religious frameworks, including within radical circles. Radical literary, fine, and applied artists, for example, turned to the image of a crucified Christ to communicate ideas of self—both in a personal sense and as related to their role and position as artist/designer in a broader framework (Greer 2003a, b). So, too, did political activists in anarchist circles (Greer 2000). The two, it is important to note, artist and anarchist, were by no means mutually exclusive categories. Thorn Prikker, himself, for example, was representative of a considerable number in avant-garde circles at this time who positioned themselves within both. The interest among artists and political radicals in using the crucified Christ figure in this way lends some coherence to Thorn Prikker's choice of a crucified figure to represent the modern Dutch woman—given that the commission was done for a group that represented a fairly radical side of the feminist political spectrum. To the feminists who commissioned this work, however, what this crucifixion undoubtedly communicated was an unacceptable, disempowered figure of vulnerability and victimization. Although the gender had been altered, through the image's association with traditional Christ imagery, it must have represented a masculinist, Christian tradition and one that, in their eyes, reinforced rather than broke with the hegemonic patriarchal discourses this group was attempting to challenge. This, however, I would like to suggest, although more than adequate in itself to lead to the rejection of the image, was only one part of the problematic signification.

An Accepted Alternative

The image that was accepted to replace the original drawing is informative in determining in what further ways the original design communicated information that led to its rejection. At the top of the work are the words *Vereeniging voor Vrouwenkiesrecht* (Association for Women's Suffrage), beneath which is the stylized figure of a woman, bound with a rope and weighed down by a yoke on her shoulders. The burden pressing down on the yoke from above is a block containing text that clearly outlines the offending articles within the constitution that kept woman in her oppressed position. Tied to the yoke, and weighing it down further, is a cross at the woman's feet with an open book of laws (Bremmer). These laws, then, are literally the cross this figure must bear. On the left of the composition a list of five of these laws are identified explicitly with references to where in the constitution they may be found. The list, however, does not end with the fifth entry. Rather, it ends with the words "etc., etc." (enz: enz:), indicating that just a few of many statutes are cited here.

The woman, although bowed under her load, is not completely incapacitated or resigned to her fate. She appears to be in the process of untying the bindings on her right hand. A strong foot, exaggerated in size, adds solidity to the figure and suggests that she may be taking a step forward. While the language of form was radical in its simplified linearity, and puzzled many (Grever and Waaldijk, 107), the image itself was accepted and served to represent "the situation of the Dutch woman" for the Association of Women's Suffrage. What it clearly communicated to the members was an image that pointed to what they saw as the source of women's problems—the legal system—and, just as importantly, one they likely felt could communicate this idea in an acceptable and constructive way to the wider public who would visit the exhibition. The image, then, communicated the group's own perspective, that is, the need for legislative change, and added an important optimistic note in that the woman is beginning to untie her bonds. That the design was received warmly by the Association members themselves is further confirmed by the fact that they chose not only to have it hang in the form of a painting at the exhibition, but also to be published as a print and distributed with the 1898 publication of their journal. H. P. Bremmer, an art critic and husband of Association member A. Bremmer, who commented on this work within the Association's publication *Maandblaadje*, described the image as representing "in the first place, a movement, a growing force" and "in the second place, a woman" (Bremmer). According to him, what the figure communicated foremost was a swelling socio-political movement and, only additionally, one related to gender.

The Rejected Image

The rejected drawing, it is clear, represents "the position of Dutch woman" in quite a different manner. The crucified woman is depicted naked, arms and legs bound to a cross which changes into a growing tree near the ground. The woman's legs are bound behind the cross in a way that is not unusual in traditional Christian images of crucifixion. It has the effect, however, of taking the image to heightened levels of implied sexual violence when the one crucified is a woman. From the arms of the cross are suspended the offending articles of law, here in the form of tombstones. The woman is additionally bound to/by these laws by means of a rope around her waist. This rope, like the cross, seems to give way to organic form—turning into plant tendrils with flowers. The most obvious reason for the rejection of this image, as stated, was the fact that woman was represented as 1) a vulnerable, helpless victim, and 2) in the guise of a borrowed traditional, masculinist emblem of the dominant patriarchal belief system. The image of crucifixion, then, was not gender neutral and could not be adopted as readily within a radical community of women as it could within avant-garde art and design circles—which, as statistics compiled by Chris Stolwijk for an article on the economic position of artists from the Hague indicate (Stolwijk, 17), were at this time almost exclusively masculine in their make-up.

Ironically, this appropriation of a Christian image may have led to the rejection of the drawing in quite another way as well. While it communicated an inappropriate message to the feminists who commissioned it, it would have been equally offensive to the numerous Christian religious groups in charge of exhibits of their charitable works in the same room. To them it may not only have been distasteful in its open nudity but also in its subversion of the traditional Christian image of a crucifixion. Given that it was not the intention of the organizers of the exhibition to present controversial political agendas (Grever), the image would not have met the wider expectations of the exhibition's organizational committee. The members of the Association of Women's Suffrage were, in fact, likely walking a fine line themselves in terms of what was deemed too radical given their agenda of obtaining equal rights for women. In other words, an image that communicated legislative reform was desirable to the Association members, but one that openly presented other radical agendas was likely not deemed appropriate for this venue and, indeed, may have been perceived as counterproductive vis-à-vis the overall communication of the Association's aims which, after all, included the important element of persuasion. And there are indeed further radical agendas present within the rejected work.

An Anarchist Call to Arms

The image of the crucified woman is the focus of the composition. Other details, however, surround this image. At the top are the heads of three men in top hats with what appear to be owls between and on either side of them. One man is holding up one of the articles of law. While owls traditionally communicate both wisdom and reason, they are also birds of the night, and can suggest the darker or more mysterious side of humanity. The presence of the three men is clearer: these are the men who possess the power and authority (backed by the law) to keep woman in the state in which she appears below. It is the area at the bottom, however, that likely presented the most problems. Directly at the foot of the "cross" or "tree," presented literally as the root of the matter, are two Biblical quotations in Latin. First, the words from Genesis 3, verse 16. This is the well-known passage after the "Fall" in the Garden of Eden in which the voice of God is heard: "Unto woman he said, I will greatly multiply thy sorrow and thy conception; in sorrow thou shalt bring forth children; and thy desire shall be to thy husband, and he shall rule over thee." It is the last part, including the words "and he shall rule over thee," that appears here. Second, from Corinthians I, chapter 14, verse 34, is written in full: "Let your women keep silence in the churches: for it is not permitted unto them to speak; but they are commanded to be under obedience, as also saith the law." Placing blame for women's plight on the Church in this manner was undoubtedly seen as too strong and too direct an attack on the Christian belief system. This aspect of the work was further complicated— or, if one looks at it from another perspective, was further strengthened and politicized—by the figures below.

In the lower section of the composition are three figures. They are, from left to right, a bishop with mitre and staff; a king, with crown, scepter and world orb; and a capitalist, each of his outstretched palms holding a coin. The three come together to represent the system that implicitly, but nonetheless quite clearly, must be overthrown in order to improve the position of woman. That this message was felt to be far too subversive for the intended public display of the painting was likely only heightened by the anarchist symbology present here. The gallows with hanging figures between the king and capitalist, along with the sword-like object running along the left side of the composition between the articles of law and the bayonets visible in the upper right corner of the composition, were all, at this time in the history of visual culture, recognizable anarchist calls to revolution. There was a radical visual language at work within this image that was widely recognized at this time as it was found in popular form on posters and in magazine and broadsheet illustrations as well as in fine art prints and in paintings (Greer 2000).

There is one last point that needs to be raised in respect to the three figures at the bottom. The anti-clerical, anti-capitalist stance represented by the figures was undoubtedly problematic. But the anti-monarchist position, in particular, given the fact that the exhibition was commemorating the inauguration of Queen Wilhelmina, was certainly adding an unwelcome republican note at this particular historical moment.

Conclusion

The drawing discussed here deals with a form of visual communication that has to do with a well developed language of form, one that is specific to a particular period in time (the late nineteenth and early twentieth centuries) and place (Holland, but the language is largely transferable within northern Europe). Although widely recognizable as radical, it is a form of visual communication that, stylistically and iconographically, is best understood by members of specific social and political communities who communicated with these visual codes. The commission indicates how the reception of visual language is not monosemous or universally coherent. This reception, in the case of the specific works examined here, is informed by issues of gender, religion, state, and radical politics—all of which function in differing ways depending on who is doing the looking. What was clearly the problem in the case of the rejected drawing by Thorn Prikker, however, was not that it did not communicate clearly but rather that what it did communicate was deemed inappropriate by those who had commissioned it—inappropriate in terms of their own conceptions of self-identity but, more importantly, in terms of their goals vis-à-vis how their ideas were communicated to the larger viewing audience.

References

Bremmer, H. P. (1898). "Bij de Plaat," *Maandblaadje*, special issue, no page.

Greer, Joan (2000). *The Artist as Christ: the image of the artist in The Netherlands, 1885–1902, with a focus on the christological imagery of Vincent van Gogh and Johan Thorn Prikker*. Dissertation, Free University, Amsterdam.

Greer, Joan (2003a). "Drie Christusschilderijen uit 1892 van Johan Thorn Prikker: `Een kunst van hun eigen bloed en vleesch,'" part I, "Christus aan het kruis." *Jong Holland* 19 (1): 18–26.

Greer, Joan (2003b). "Drie Christusschilderijen uit 1892 van Johan Thorn Prikker: `Een kunst van hun eigen bloed en vleesch,'" part II, "Een Liefde en De Bruid." *Jong Holland*, 19 (2): 28–36.

Grever, Maria (1999). "Vorstin van heel het vaderland? Orangisme en feminisme in het laatste kwart van de negentiende eeuw", *De Negentiende Eeuw*, 23 (1): 76–87.

Grever, Maria and Waaldijk, Berteke (1998). *Feministische Openbaarheid: De Nationale Tentoonstelling van Vrouwenarbeid in 1898*. Amsterdam: Stichting Beheer IISG, 1998, 67-160. (translated as Transforming the Public Sphere: the Dutch National Exhibition of Women's Labor in 1898. Durham, NC: Duke University Press, 2004).

IIAV (1998). Exhibition documentation from International Information Center and Archives for the Women's Movement.

Stolwijk, Chris (1994). "'Benden van rampzaligen?' De economische positie van Haagse kunstschilders in de tweed helft van de negentiende eeuw." *Kunstlicht*, 15(34), 16–21.

CHAPTER NINETEEN

Cross-Cultural Comparison on Attributing Meaning to Corporate Logos

Barbara Martinson and Sauman Chu
University of Minnesota, St. Paul, USA

Symbols are a basic component of human communication. They have appeared in all cultures during all periods of history and they illustrate the development of civilization. Symbols contain powerful messages, and at the same time, they stimulate people's emotions, intellect, and spirit. Particular meanings for specific symbols may vary. This is especially true between cultures or over time.

Numerous studies have examined the meaning of symbols and subjects' differing perceptions of symbols dependent upon age, gender, and cultural differences. However, there are few studies that look specifically at business logos. Logos are visual identities that represent companies, corporations, businesses, and institutions. The purpose of a logo is to allow audiences to identify a company upon the perceived logo. A logo is used to represent the overall essence, philosophy, or feeling of a company (Crow). Although the role of a logo is essential to the image of a company, little research has been done to examine how logos are perceived and how they come to represent the values of a business or service.

Related Research

Numerous studies have been done to investigate the perception of symbols and how subjects from different cultures might perceive symbols differently. A study done by Cochenour, Rezabek, and Westhoff indicated that people have different interpretations of perceived symbols. In their study, subjects were asked to interpret the meaning of twelve different abstract graphic symbols. The results were grouped into categories of meaning. For example, "love" and "affection" were grouped into one category of meaning. The outcome showed that there were widespread interpretations by the subjects. The minimum number of categories of meaning for a symbol was twenty-six and the maximum was fifty-six, indicating a high degree of variability. Star and cross shapes had the least number of categories of meaning.

Moriarty and Sayre used advertising to examine the relationship between subjects' perceptions of messages and the intended messages. Results indicated that more than half of the perceptions were different from the intended messages. Griffin's cross-cultural study suggested that there are cultural differences in the interpretation and meaning of symbols. The meanings of abstract symbols were the most difficult for subjects to comprehend.

In contrast to these findings, a cross-cultural study by Messaris provided a different perspective. According to Messaris, certain basic elements of design, such as straight versus curved lines or symmetry versus asymmetry, carry the same implied meanings across different cultures. In other words, human beings share common responses and interpretations to basic visual elements.

These contrasting outcomes imply that basic design elements may be perceived as symbols—their form carries meaning. Messaris's study used basic design elements that are non-representational images in any culture. Conversely, representational symbols are more frequently culture-oriented images. For instance, an owl represents wisdom in American culture, but people from other cultures might interpret it differently. According to Jung, cultural symbols are collective images accepted by individual societies and these symbols have gone through a long process of transformation and conscious development. Therefore, representational symbols tend to be culture-specific.

Meaning and Symbols

A symbol is used to represent an abstract, metaphysical concept. Symbols stand for something else by relationship, suggestion, interpretation, resemblance, or association. The purpose of symbols is to convey and simplify particular ideas and concepts. The meanings of symbols are accumulated slowly from generation to generation. Connotations vary based on the cultural context, as well as the influence that symbols have on one another. In terms of cultural perception, the meanings of objects are interpreted differently because of their diverse frames of reference. For example, a fat belly represents gluttony in the Western culture while in Chinese culture it represents the wealth of god. Yellow signifies the imperial in China, whereas in northern Europe it stands for deceit and timidity.

The perception of an image is rapid—almost instantaneous. According to Pettersson, three assumptions for the perception of symbols can be made. First, several different symbols may convey a similar meaning and a specific message. Second, a particular symbol may be able to carry different messages. Third, as an audience, we have to learn the intended meaning of symbols.

Symbols play an important role in human life because they are essential for the perception of reality. Their importance is reinforced by Charles Peirce's explanation that symbolism is the nature of human beings because we are symbol-using and sign-using organisms (Nowak-Fabrykowski). Additionally, the major objective of symbols is to facilitate communication beyond the limitation of words. The formulation of things, events, and natural ordering of the world are all symbolic expression or symbolization. Symbols signify aspiration, broader abstract or philosophical cultural principles, and belief systems that go beyond specific contextual meanings. Especially with belief systems, symbolic representation plays an essential role in the construction and reinforcement of concepts. Symbols take on a critical role in connecting individuals, cultures (through ideologies) and holding entire communities together (Page).

Perception of Basic Design Elements

A new dimension of human communication began when the first graphic images were scratched into rock walls. The images included animals that people saw or hunted. In an important sense, this was the beginning of a new generation of awareness that there are images that people within a particular community perceive in a similar way. Since prehistoric time, symbols have been constructed and formed by basic fundamental elements: lines and dots. These elements contribute to the forms of most design symbols.

Human vision is most extensive in the horizontal plane because people move in it. The dominant plane of experience for people is horizontal and this is reinforced by the natural and constant appearance of the parallel planes of land and sea. Only sporadic natural phenomena such as rainfall and lightning follow a vertical line of movement. Consequently, humans have adapted to the constancy and stability of the horizontal plane and line in their natural environment (Frutiger).

Oblique lines create a sense of uncertainty and they are always judged in relation to the horizontal and vertical planes. How close an oblique line is to either of these planes will create a different feeling. A close proximity to the horizontal plane creates a feeling of rising upward, whereas a close proximity to the vertical plane creates a feeling of falling. A curve leads to the formation of circles or circular forms and this creates a sense of infinity, as well as a feeling of precision and an invisible center (Frutiger).

Project Goals

The primary focus of this study is to examine the perception of corporate logos in order to determine what visual variables contribute to the perceived attributes of a business, service, or corporation. Our goal is to measure possible cross-cultural differences in the perception of attributes among United States and Hong Kong students. Our long-term objective is to improve the design of visual identities so that audiences from diverse cultures will better perceive the intended meaning of logos.

Research Questions

The focus of this study is to examine differences, if any, in the perception of logos between students in Hong Kong and the United States. Additionally, the focus is to identify specific visual elements that contribute to the selection of a textual attribute for each logo. Therefore, the research questions are:

• Will United States and Hong Kong subjects interpret visual forms similarly?

• Can distinct differences be detected between the two cultures based on the relationship of form to business attribute?

• What specific formal elements elicit certain responses from subjects?

Method

A list of eighteen positive business attributes were derived from the literature (Lavin). These attributes are: cooperative, democratic, diverse, dynamic, efficient, endurance, expansive, focus, hierarchical, homogeneous, individual, innovative, omniscience, quality, stability, strength, tradition, and value. These terms reflect attributes that corporations would like their visual identity system to convey.

Six non-representational abstract logos were used in this study. These logos contained basic geometric shapes and other elements such as lines and dots. Each logo was presented along with a word list of eighteen textual attributes and subjects were asked to identify which attribute best described the logo. The instrument was presented in a booklet format and consisted of six pages. The logos were arranged in a random order.

The study was conducted in the U.S. and Hong Kong. The same booklet, written in English, was used in both countries. As one of the researchers was born and completed high school in Hong Kong, the assumption was made that University students in Hong Kong are well-educated in comprehending and reading English. Therefore, the booklet was not translated into Chinese.

Participants in the United States were college students at the University of Minnesota. The majority of the participants in the survey were majoring in graphic design. Approximately 70 percent were female and 99 percent were in their freshman year. Age of the subjects ranged from eighteen to thirty-five years old. Participants in the focus group were all graphic design students in their junior or senior year of study and approximately 80 percent were female. Age of the subjects ranged from twenty-one to thirty years old.

Participants in Hong Kong were college students at the Hong Kong Polytechnic University. All participants in the survey and focus group were majoring in graphic design and were in their senior year of study. Gender distribution was quite even among the subjects with 55 percent being female. Age of subjects ranged from twenty-one to twenty-four years old.

Procedure

The study was conducted in the United States and Hong Kong during a period of two years. Two methods were used to complete the study in each country. One was a survey and the second was a focus group discussion. The survey was intended to gather information from a large group of subjects. The survey attempted to answer the first research question that examined the relationship of form to business attribute. The focus group discussions were designed to examine which specific visual variables influenced the selection of a specific attribute to be paired with a logo.

This study reflects the idea of a two-phase design process as described by Creswell. In this type of study both a quantitative phase and a qualitative phase are completed. This combined process helps us to better understand the different aspects of a problem being studied. When the results are compared or integrated, the researcher has a more complete set of data with which to address the research questions.

Both of the researchers conducted a survey and a focus group discussion in the United States. One of the researchers conducted a survey and a focus group discussion in Hong Kong. A faculty member from the Swire School of Design of Hong Kong Polytechnic University helped to recruit the subjects for that focus group discussion.

Survey

The survey was presented to a combined total of 170 subjects: 110 subjects at the University of Minnesota in the United States and 60 subjects at the Hong Kong Polytechnic University. The same procedure was used in conducting the survey with both Hong Kong and U.S. subjects. Students received a brief introduction to the project and were told that the focus of the study was on corporate logos and positive business attributes. This inclusion of context helped to frame the students' criteria for selection and could have influenced their decisions. Subjects were then asked to complete the survey by circling the term (from the list of positive business attributes) which they perceived to be the best visual description of each logo. No discussion or verbal communication was allowed while subjects were working on the survey. All booklets were collected at the same time. The results from both cultures were reported using descriptive statistics that were then analyzed by using a paired sample T-test. Due to the unequal sample sizes, data was entered using the proportion of responses. The null hypothesis was that there would be no difference between the two cultures' responses to the logos.

Focus Group Discussions

An identical procedure was used to conduct the focus group discussion in Hong Kong and the United States. Thirty subjects in Hong Kong were recruited by a faculty member from Swire School of Design of Hong Kong Polytechnic. The discussion was held in a classroom and the researcher conducted and completed the discussion in an hour. Thirty subjects from the University of Minnesota were students from one of the upper division graphic design courses. All subjects were asked to complete the same tasks, and each subject was required to complete the survey booklet individually without discussion. Later (using an overhead projector), each focus group was shown the same logos and word lists contained in the booklet and was asked to come to an agreement on selecting the three most appropriate textual attributes for each logo. Agreement was obtained by voting or discussion. When the three textual attributes were selected, subjects were then asked to identify specific visual attributes that influenced their word choices. The same procedure was applied to the discussion of all six logos.

Results

Survey

The completed surveys for both Hong Kong and the United States were tabulated in percentages and the top three responses for each logo are represented in Figures 19.1–19.6.

Figure 19.1. Logo 1.

HONG KONG		USA	
Value	20%	Focus	19%
Focus	15%	Hierarchical	15%
Expansive	12%	Quality	10%

Figure 19.2. Logo 2.

HONG KONG		USA	
Innovative	18%	Innovative	29%
Dynamic	16%	Dynamic	14%
Diverse	16%	Expansive	11%

Figure 19.3. Logo 3.

HONG KONG		USA	
Cooperative	26%	Cooperative	41%
Traditional	22%	Dynamic	15%
Dynamic	15%	Homogeneous	10%

Figure 19.4. Logo 4.

HONG KONG		USA	
Hierarchical	17%	Dynamic	20%
Stability	13%	Diverse	14%
Dynamic	12%	Innovative	12%

Figure 19.5. Logo 5.

HONG KONG		USA	
Diverse	12%	Dynamic	20%
Cooperative	12%	Cooperative	15%
Hierarchical	10%	Diverse	12%

Figure 19.6. Logo 6.

HONG KONG		USA	
Cooperative	20%	Expansive	20%
Traditional	15%	Focus	12%
Expansive	8%	Cooperative	10%

With the paired sample T-test, all of the results are not significant (p value> 0.05). There are no significant differences between how subjects, grouped by nationality, responded to the logos. Since the research question focuses on measuring the perceptual differences between subjects from two countries, these results suggest interesting implications.

Focus Group Results

The three words that were selected by each cultural group and the visual variables that affected their decision to choose those three textual attributes are described in Table 1.

Table 19.1. Results of focus group discussions

	HONG KONG	USA
Logo 1	**Quality**	**Focus**
	• the three triangular shapes pointing down form a diamond shape	• the largest shape, pointing down, depicts the action of focusing in on something
	• the diamond shape depicts the concept of high quality	• there is a focal point in the center
	Stability	**Hierarchical**
	• horizontal lines create the perception of steps and stabilize the overall symbol	• horizontal lines create the perception of steps
	• symmetrical balance	• lines create a platform
	Democratic	**Expansive**
	• shapes look like a podium	• shapes go both inward and outward
	• looks like a royal image	• base has expanding movement like stair steps

	HONG KONG	USA
Logo 2	**Innovative**	**Innovative**
	• perceived as technology-related	• implied direction
	• implied direction	• movement of similar shapes
	• gradation of shapes creates depth perception	• a willingness to cross over boundaries of larger shape
	Dynamic	• shapes change as they cross the line
	• gradation of sizes	**Diverse**
	• black and white shapes create movement	• different sizes of the same shape
	• repetition of shapes create rhythm	• black and white shapes
	Focus	• small shapes cut through larger shape
	• the black oval shape draws attention to the center	**Expansive**
		• position of shapes and alignment
		• sense of perspective
		• ovals seem to go back into space
Logo 3	**Cooperative**	**Cooperative**
	• same shape repeats and goes around in same direction	• same shape repeats and goes around in same direction
	• three similar shapes merge together	• proximity of shapes; each shape just barely touches another
	Dynamic	• shape is familiar, looks like the yin/yang or the recycle symbol
	• movement in a circular form	**Dynamic**
	• positive/negative space relationship	• movement in a circular form
	• sense of continuation	• positive/negative space relationship
	Efficient	• sense of fluidity of weaving, curving line
	• shapes are actively moving	• inner shape is also dynamic
	• implied speed, and speed depicts efficiency	**Focus**
		• shape is similar to a camera lens turning
Logo 4	**Efficient**	**Hierarchical**
	• sequence of shapes suggest efficiency and professionalism	• sequence of shapes suggest stacked blocks
	• even figure/ground relationship suggests a sense of order	• shapes suggest going up and layering
	• figure/ground relationship suggests the direction of moving upward	• figure/ground relationship suggests a direction, left to right or low to high
	Expansive	**Strength**
	• the lines create movement going up	• unity of shape
		• linked blocks emphasize strength

	HONG KONG	**USA**
	• the overall shape looks expandable	• repetition of a strong shape
	Homogeneous	**Stability**
	• symmetrical	• reads as blocks stacked up
	• all parts are the same	• 3D quality of blocks provides depth and feeling of stability
	• rigid shape	• man-made shape, not organic, mechanized
Logo 5	**Diverse**	**Dynamic**
	• interlacing of lines	• looks like it is growing
	• lines expand in different directions	• there is an outward motion
	Quality	• suggests that lines will go on
	• looks like it is growing	**Cooperative**
	• shapes interact	• all the lines are linked together
	Hierarchical	• interlacing of lines
	• the lines create movement going up	**Expansive**
	• looks like an emblem	• lines all start at the same point and expand outward
		• the two triangles point upward and downward
		• the overall shape looks expandable in any direction
Logo 6	**Traditional**	**Omniscience**
	• looks outdated	• whole ball contained by white space
	• not much movement	• eyeball shape
	Focus	• communication: the globe brings the world and people together
	• circle implies focus	**Focus**
	• intersection made by two white lines	• circle implies focus
	Cooperative	• four points of black shapes all meet at white cross
	• the circular form implies cooperation	• intersection made by two white lines
	• the two white lines intersect	**Cooperative**
		• the two white lines keep the shape together
		• four black pieces create the whole

Discussion

Survey: Results for Hong Kong

The highest percentage of agreement for each logo ranged from 12 percent to 26 percent. Logo 3 received the highest agreement with 26 percent of the subjects choosing "cooperative" as its textual attribute. Logo 5 received the lowest percentage of agreement with 12 percent of the subjects choosing the terms "diverse" and "cooperative." The breadth of responses was quite large for this logo and several others as well.

Survey: Results for the United States

The highest percentage of agreement for each logo ranged from 19 percent to 41 percent. Again, Logo 3 received the highest agreement with 41 percent of the subjects selecting the term "cooperative" (which was the same attribute selected by Hong Kong subjects). For logos 1, 4, 5, and 6, the ranked first.

Survey: Cross-Cultural Comparison

Based upon these survey results, several conclusions can be drawn. First, the non-significant outcome of the paired sample T-test for all of the logos suggests that subjects from both cultures have similar perceptions of the visual attributes of each logo. This, in fact, implies that people from these two cultures have similar interpretations of certain visual elements. Second, based upon the results of the top three responses from each culture, two of the three selected attributes for four of the logos (2, 3, 5, and 6) were the same for both cultures. Third, for logos 2 and 3, the most popular selected attributes ("innovative" for logo 2 and "cooperative" for logo 3) were the same for both cultures.

Focus Group: Results for Hong Kong

Participants tended to come to an agreement very quickly. Based upon descriptions, subjects focused on analyzing the design elements of each logo, particularly shape, line, and figure/ground relationships. For instance, to describe logo 3, subjects indicated that the logo was perceived as "cooperative" because the "same shape repeats and goes around in same direction" and "three similar shapes merge together." Subjects also tended to relate a logo to a particular object. For instance, in logo 1, subjects said that the logo "looks like a podium" and "the three shapes form a diamond shape." These explanations are consistent to the meaning of symbols as described earlier, namely, that "symbols stand for something else by relationship, suggestion, interpretation, resemblance, or association." People tend to associate a visual icon with something that they already know and that is familiar to them.

Focus Group: Results for the United States

Participants tended to describe a logo in one of two ways: (1) by examining the visual elements that contribute to a particular attribute, and (2) by associating a logo with an object. These outcomes were similar for subjects in Hong Kong's focus group.

Focus Group: Cross-Cultural Comparison

The responses for four out of the six logos were quite different between the two focus groups. There were two logos (3 and 6) for which two of the three selected textual attributes were the same. Although the selected attributes were quite different between the two groups, it is interesting to note that the descriptions for some of the logos were quite similar. For instance, in logo 1, Hong Kong subjects described the "shapes pointing down" as forming a diamond shape that speaks of "quality." United States' subjects also described the "shapes pointing down" but said that those shapes depicted "focus." Additionally, the horizontal lines in logo 1 conveyed the perception of steps to both groups; however, subjects in Hong Kong perceived this as "stability" whereas subjects in the United States perceived it as "hierarchical."

Cross-Method Comparisons of Data

Results from the U.S. and Hong Kong focus groups suggest that there was more variation in the selected attributes than those found in the survey. For logos 2 and 3, the most popularly selected attributes ("innovative" for logo 2 and "cooperative" for logo 3) were the same for both cultures. In fact, the selected attributes matched the responses to the survey.

For logo 1, the attribute "focus" was selected by three out of the four focus groups. For logo 2, "innovative" was the first choice for all groups. For logo 3, "cooperative" was the first choice for all groups. For logo 4, the attribute "dynamic" was chosen in surveys by two groups. The outcome contained widespread interpretations for this logo. For logo 5, both the attributes "diverse" and "cooperative" were chosen by three groups. And for logo 6, "cooperative" was selected by all four groups.

Conclusion

This study uses non-representational logos to force subjects to focus on basic design elements and how those elements contribute to a particular perception. The non-significant outcome from the survey T-test indicated that subjects from both cultures had similar perceptions of the logos.

Our study indicates that there is an association between the logo and a word demonstrating some degree of consensus in interpretation across both cultural groups. Some visual aspects of certain logos resulted in the codification of the word/sign and demonstrated a definite relationship between form and attributed meaning.

These outcomes suggest that the arrangement of design elements contributes to a certain "expression" and that people from different cultures may interpret those design elements in a similar way. This outcome is similar to Messaris' study that found that basic design elements such as shape and line carry the same implied meaning across different cultures. The findings from this study may help designers to better understand basic design elements and suggest that the arrangement of those elements carries similar meaning across different cultures. Understanding how basic design elements contribute to a particular meaning (such as "focus" and "diverse") will help designers to create more effective logos.

References

Cochenour, J. J., Rezabek, L. L., and Westhoff, G. (1999). "Interpreting symbols: The spread of visual meaning." In Griffin, R. E., Gribbs, W. J., and Williams, V. S. (Eds.), *Natural Vistas: Visual Literacy and the World around Us*. Texas: The International Visual Literacy Association, 65–71.

Creswell, J. W. (1994). *Research Design*. Thousand Oaks, CA: Sage Publications.

Crow, W. (1986). *Communication Graphics*. New York: Prentice-Hall.

Frutiger, A. (1989). *Signs and Symbols: Their Design and Meaning*. New York: Van Nostrand Reinhold.

Griffin, R., Pettersson, R., Semali, L., and Takakuwa, Y. (1995). "Using symbols in international business presentations: How well are they understood?" In Griffen, R. E., Braden, R. A., and Beauchamp, D. G. (Eds.) *Imagery and Visual Literacy*. Texas: The International Visual Literacy Association.

Lavin, M. (1989). "Design in the service of commerce." In Friedman, M., *Graphic Design in America*. New York: Harry Abrams, 126–143.

Messaris, P. (1993). "Analog, not digital: Roots of visual literacy and visual intelligence." In Beauchamp, D. G., Braden, R. A., and Baca, J. C. (Eds.). *Visual Literacy in the Digital Age*. Texas: The International Visual Literacy Association.

Moriarty, S. E., and Sayre, S. (1992). "Technology and art: A postmodern reading of Orwell as advertising." In Braden, R. A., Clark-Baca, J., and Beauchamp, D. G. (Eds.), *Art, Science, and Visual Literacy*. Texas: The International Visual Literacy Association, 22–34.

Nowak-Fabrykowski, K. (1992). "Symbolism, learning, and creativity." *Journal of Creative Behavior*, 26 (4), 268–272.

Page, J. (1992). "Symbolizing the future—Towards a futures' iconography." *Futures*, 24 (10), 1,056–1,063.

Pettersson, R. (1999). "Graphic symbols—Design and meaning." In Griffin, R. E., Gribbs, W. J., and Williams, V. S. (Eds.), *Natural Vistas: Visual Literacy and the World around Us*. 27–35. Texas: The International Visual Literacy Association.

CHAPTER TWENTY

Identity in Sheep's Clothing

Dietmar R. Winkler
University of Massachusetts, Dartmouth, USA

Americans may have no identity, but they do have wonderful teeth.

JEAN BAUDRILLARD, PARAPHRASED

Behind the concept of "identity," hidden, lies a much more powerful human trait, namely the sense and extreme need for ownership, control, and territoriality. Through physical, social, and cultural territoriality, humanity is animated by nature to compete aggressively for emotional space, rewards, and attention. This activity is aggravated further by a continuous change in the population aggregate—shifting or increasing competition for all resources—and the consequential physical (as well as emotional) stress, with a continuous emancipation of citizens, distancing themselves from control by others; embodied in the state, business, and church.

Identity as Territorial Marker

The concept of territoriality is part of the sociology of the "survival of the fittest," as well as the foundation of capitalism, and in fact, of all human competitive institutions—from commerce and education to sports and church. In this sense, even charitable Mother Theresa was a serious territorial contender and competitor. Very few persons could give away as much as she did, owning nothing and wanting little more than salvation. She emerges as one of the fittest in the contest for supremacy over the field of benevolence, equally admired or despised as if she had been a political or sports figure in their respective realm.

Language as Identity

Claude Levi-Strauss, Belgian-French anthropologist and structuralist, a contributor to structural anthropology, argues that kinship and identity contain fundamental aspects of culture that are made up of specific kinds of structures, including the structures of myths of a clan or tribe. These highly structured myths facilitate understanding of cultural relations and relationships. He placed concepts of myth into opposite differentials of extremes, juxtaposing semantic concepts, and because the language structures of the narrative supplied the syntactic glue, he sees his anthropological research as part of the Language domain.

Myths, being everywhere, not bound by rules of accuracy or probability, nevertheless follow the same language structures no matter where they are found. Levi-Strauss argues that myth is language, because in order to exist myths have to be placed into narratives and their structures belong to language. Social and cultural myths live in the paradox of timelessness and in time. He also argues that myths are not just subsets of Language, but are language themselves. Language is also the holding tank for the valuation process. Without language metaphors it is difficult to establish norms, standards, and values.

The Loss of Language is the Loss of Identity

Linguists agree, when a language, the most important individual element identifying a culture and its people, dies, the unique and special knowledge of the culture, which is embedded in the language representation of customs, ceremonies, myth, and lore, is lost. Of 7,202 languages spoken worldwide today, 440 will be extinct within two decades, while the total aggregate will be cut in half within this century. At this point in time, fewer than 10,000 or 0.3 percent of the world population speak one of the 3,340 rarest languages (Example: The only 185 people who speak Karitiana live in a Brazilian village with not more than 191 inhabitants). Today, 52 percent of the world population are speaking one of just twenty languages. The reasons that half of the languages presently still in use will be silenced within this century are mostly global/economical and plainly self-survival. Hundreds of aboriginal and native tribal languages will be forgotten, having the unfortunate fallout, that anthropologists will be unable to construct migration patterns or a more appropriate taxonomy and timeline of the evolution of languages.

In the U.S., the concept of the "melting pot," a gradual, often unconscious process of assimilation, tries through a mildly coercive process to assimilate minority groups into a national mainstream. The pressure to meld individual ethnic, cultural and social differences into a national standard is pernicious. It is in complete contradiction to the concepts of individuality, diversity, and choice. It favors the dominating cultures and subverts the minority cultures.

Seen from a single standard society, this sometimes heavy handed approach is necessary, because the more room is given to individual identity, language, or tradition of a minority, the greater the increase of separation and distance from the mainstream.

According to Professor James A. Hijiya, History Department, University of Massachusetts Dartmouth, Northerners think that American identity starts at Plymouth Rock, Massachusetts; Southerners at Jamestown, Virginia. Even Westerners seem to agree that their national identity begins when English men and women alight from their boats and plant their boots along the seaboard of the East. Massachusetts and Virginia, according to the consensus, are gradually joined by eleven other colonies touching the Atlantic; and from there westward the course of history takes its way. The colonies pull apart from England, rush to the Mississippi, purchase Louisiana, annex Texas, steal California, and foil a plot to drag history southward through secession. As commonly thought and taught, early American history moves steadily across the map from right to left.

The defining event is either the Revolution or the Constitution: "colonial" history is limited almost exclusively to those people in those colonies, which in 1776 (or 1787) will create a new nation. Because the configuration of individual states provides the basic structure for American history, and therefore the American identity, it is inevitable that people belonging to different states will be neglected. The Native Americans, the Spanish (and, later, the Mexicans), and the French are relegated to serving as backdrops, not actors. Thus, the typical schoolbook hurriedly introduces the Aztecs, Columbus, and Samuel de Chaplain, but then forgets them as it settles down to describe in chapter after chapter the minutiae of Anglo-American life, without reference to the rise and fall of a Native American empire. As now conceived identity occurs only in close proximity to Anglo-Americans.

Hijiya's history includes the immigrants from Asia whose descendants will trek east as the true "pioneers," the actual first "settlers," of America. His history places the Spanish and the French not along the English border but in the centers of their own empires in America; a story not merely of "territorial expansion" but of expansion for some and contraction for others; of conquest and defeat. He proposes to show that "America" does not start as a colonial seedling along the Atlantic seaboard that naturally grows across the continent but is instead a land mass occupied in different places by different people with different identities, at different times.

It is a fact, in the Massachusetts land trials, as recently as a decade ago, that the collision between two language worlds, the written and oral, was not properly refereed, when claims of ownership by Native Americans were denied on the basis that they could not show archival proof of their identity and therefore of their existence.

Place as Part of Identity

Even if a geographical location has ramifications, "Place" is not just an intersection on a map, a point between two railroad destinations or where one resides or stops for the night. It is an amalgam of diverse physical, emotional, and perceptual elements—real and imagined. "Place" is football field, factory, neighborhood, garden, park, and childhood hiding place, house and home, school, church, and hospital (see figure 20.1).

The individuality of "Place" is forged by the people that inhabit it over time and the evolution of their sense of personal success, failure, alienation, or belonging.

1.000 Identity through the mythology of place	1.010 Identity through the history of place	1.020 Altruistic concepts of place	1.030 Religious identity and place	1.040 Values: freedoms and legal protection
	1.011 Identity through ethnicity of inhabitants of place: immigrants, settlers, and native people	1.021 Freedoms of expression, movement (newspaper, radio, tv)	1.031 Viversity/singularity of religions of place	1.041 The right of habeas corpus
	1.012 Identity through the dynamics of place: Growth/decline, and development	1.022 Freedom of the assembly	1.032 Identity through religious segregation	1.042 Protection against unlawful entry
	1.013 Identity through the quality of governance of place: town counsels, mayors, forms of assembly	1.023 Freedom from censorship	1.033 Identity through religious freedom (choice)	1.043 Rights of trial by jury
	1.014 Roots of place: geographical locations (coast, mountain, planes, etc.)	1.024 The bill of rights (to be innocent until guilty or guilty until proven innocent)	1.034 Identity through separation of religion and	1.044 Prevention from seizure
	1.015 Identity through the historical events that shape place (internal/external)	1.025 Rights of ownership (pysical/intellectual property, etc.)	1.035 Perception of hierarchy in comparison of types of religion of place	1.045 Innocence until proven otherwise
	1.016 etc.	1.026 Professional/vocational opportunities of place	1.036 etc.	1.046 Prevention of double jeopardy
		1.027 etc.		1.047 Equality: Prevention of social, racial, economic, educational segregation
				1.048 etc.

2.000 The physical identity/face of place	2.010 Natural resources	2.0200 Quality of urbanization	2.0300 Agriculture	2.0400 Commerce
	2.011 Recreation, scenic protection 2.012 Wildlife (birds, fish, mammals) 2.013 Water (pollution, desalinization, irrigation) 2.014 Minerals (iron, copper, aluminum, etc.) 2.015 Parks, reservations 2.016 Conservation/ depletion of land (problems with nsecticides, fungicides, herbicides) 2.017 Energy, resources: oil, gas, coal, wind, solar, atomic, hydro-electric 2.018 Landscaping, architectural quality of styles 2.019 etc.	2.0201 Village, town, city, metropolis 2.0202 Demographics ethnic diversity 2.0203 Population density/ explosion 2.0204 Suburbia/country 2.0205 Slums 2.0206 Centers for shopping, business, entertainment 2.0207 Transportation 2.0208 etc.	2.0301 Farms 2.0302 Price supports 2.0303 Mechanization of farming 2.0304 Labor problems 2.0305 Surplus 2.0406 etc.	2.0401 Airlines 2.0402 Automobiles and roads 2.0403 Shipping and waterways 2.0404 Steamships 2.0405 Railroads 2.0406 Businesses/shops 2.0407 Industries 2.0408 Professions 2.0409 etc.

3.0000 The people, the community of place	3.0101 Education identity	3.0200 Health care	3.0300 Culture of Place	3.0400 Politics of Place	3.0500 The social identity of Place	3.0600 Leisure
	3.0102 Personal school experience: high, medium, low 3.0103 Belief/disbelief in educational television 3.0104 Belief/disbelief in teaching machines 3.0105 Belief/disbelief in testing techniques 3.0106 Quality of primary, secondary schools, colleges 3.0107 Accreditation 3.0108 Segregation, diversity 3.0109 Drop out rate 3.0110 Open education (for everybody) 3.0111 Continuous education (adult, vocational, professional) 3.0112 etc.	3.0201 Fears/comfort with forms of available care 3.0202 Experience of child-birth, convalescence, Hospice 3.0203 Quality of training for physicians/staff 3.0204 Systems of social care: Medicare 3.0205 Insurance costs 3.0206 Mental health (psychiatry, tranquilizers) 3.0207 Care for health calamities (cancer, Aids) 3.0208 Heart diseases 3.0209 Accidents 3.0210 Smoking, alcohol 3.0211 etc.	3.0301 Identity through art, literature, music 3.0302 Identity through the selection of entertainment 3.0303 Identity through music (folk, jazz, fine arts, opera etc.) 3.0304 Identity through theater 3.0305 Identity through literature 3.0306 etc.	3.0401 Political identity: communists, fascists, libertarians, etc. 3.0402 One, two, multi-party system 3.0403 Foreign relations 3.0404 Common market 3.0405 Belief/disbelief in the need for legal structures (congress, states, cities, etc.) 3.0406 World consciousness 3.0407 etc.	3.0501 Crime: detection, prosecution, penal system, rehabilitation 3.0502 Children, adolescents, aged: Delinquency, social support for various age groupings, social security) 3.0503 Commitment to the poor 3.0504 Commitment to desegregation 3.0505 Support for native Americans 3.0506 White/blue collar support, education 3.0507 Labor/management relations: employment, unemployment, job loss, job gain, minimum wage scales 3.0508 Youth (4-h, scouts, jr. achievement, etc.) 3.0509 Financial and social depression 3.0510 etc.	3.0601 Travel 3.0602 Entertainment 3.0603 Sports 3.0604 etc.

Figure 20.1. Example of Complexity: Identity Based on the Identity of Place. Researchers into identity have looked at an amalgam of dynamic, situational, and contextual forms of identity, each with its own enormous complexity, trying to sort out the various delineations.

J. A. Holstein and J. F. Gubrium, in *Identity in a Postmodern World: Narrative Identity in a Postmodern World,* organize a taxonomy of self through the following filters (not necessarily in the same order or with the same emphasis): the self that is actualized through everyday activities and work; the self that is active, interactive, and socially situated (knowing when it is necessary to conform, to assert, to be aggressive or passive); the self that can be observed and is what it is; and the self that transcends into man's mythological world of potentials.

This example was chosen to illustrate the complex web of interrelationships between the identity of an individual relying on "place" as the primary source. Like in the stock market, the power of variables is infinite.

They invent "Place" and in return, "Place" gives them certain identifiable characteristics. "Place" is the heartbeat of a community that offers over a lifetime security, fulfillment, and contentment but also tragedy, pain, and despair. It is a valued refuge, home of origin, the center where things are discovered, ideas set in motion, relationships found, and plans developed.

"Place" is deeply imprinted on the soul. When removed from "Place" one's memories activate and bring bittersweet longing for the personal, cherished quality of things, persons, and experiences connected with it. Acts of recall—activating all senses through mementos, keepsakes, and correspondence—generate deliberate, sentimental, and pleasurable nostalgia, comprised of fact and fiction. They also provide the plans for new futures.

Natural Corollaries

Bauer Birds build nests of amazing complexities from reeds and grasses and fill them with glittering assortments of objects just to attract their mates, as well as signal to other birds an identity marked through territorial boundaries. It seems that inherited natural identity, a combination of color arrangement and feather formation, posture, and agile motion, is not enough to signal to others the outstanding and singular qualities of an identity. In this case, to become distinguishable from the species, even the environment has to be incorporated and rearranged in considerable ways to achieve the goal.

Maybe humans are not much different. In their sphere, identity is also not natural and organic, but artificially constructed in relationship to a complex system of values that are permanent or in constant state of change, self-selected or selected and imposed by others. Ordered into a biological and ethnic taxonomy of language communities and placed in fecund or less fertile environments with a variety of geological and climactic conditions, each micro system, in addition to the characteristics of shared features, has its own variables— which are manifested in the construction of cheekbones, eyelids, eyebrows, hair, skin color, and other features. Within each major ethnic segment of the human social culture there are shared proportions of the human skeleton, muscles, skin tone, and hair, spawning standards of perceived ideal proportions, which change over time and lead to judgments of too big, too small, not the norm, or perfect.

There are good reasons why a person (who in relationship to the norm is too tiny or emaciated) would want to project characteristics of strength and power and offset reality to impress others. Samurai and most tribal warriors understand the necessity to project and intimidate through an illusion of larger or taller body size in the form of broad-shouldered battle dress, larger headgear, and feathers that extend the dimensions and the volume of the figure.

The Social Construction of Identity

Social anthropologists suggest that the human species has evolved to such an extent that members are actually capable of creating individual biotopes—niches in which physical, social, and cultural environments become suitable for certain kinds of stereotypical personality projections—namely, the ideal business man or woman, the politician, the lawyer, or the clergyman.

From childhood on, the culture learns to deal with levels of integrity perceived in individuals or groups. Examples abound of hidden, masked, and changed identities in literature. In Gottfried Keller's *Kleider Machen Leute* (Clothing Makes the Man), charlatans living by their assumed identity become socially acceptable for a moment by merely changing their outer appearance.

Children are introduced to fables like "the wolf in sheep's clothing." Even in traditional mythology, embedded in the success-story of the nineteenth century German sea merchant Ballin, is the concept of a fake identity—Ballin, without any financial backing or social standing, worked from a tattered shack on the pier in Hamburg. But by corresponding with smartly engraved stationery, he worked himself up the social and financial ladder so that today one can find boulevards in Hamburg named after him. This mythology contextualizes the fact that one of the very first typography courses was not taught within an art or design school, but at the Harvard Business School. It helped to shape the identities of early corporations, at a time before the dawn of marketing.

Mythology fast forward: at some business schools applicants have to choose a metaphoric animal identity and describe themselves in terms of the characteristics of the animal of their choice they feel will represent all of the qualities and traits of their character. In the admissions process, carnivores like wolves, lions, cheetahs, and tigers, or animals of cunning like the fox and coyote, usually win out over animal identities like stallions, gazelles, and zebras. In a competitive world of survival, the paper-scissors-stone game is real.

The Fear of Not Having a Specific Identity

In our own historical backyard, Lazar Lissitzky becomes El Lissitzky, Ludwig Mies changes into Ludwig Mies van der Rohe, Charles-Edouard Jeanneret takes the name of Le Corbusier, and Marcel Villon turns into Marcel Duchamp. Do these changes represent dissatisfaction with family heritage and social and middle class standings? A wish to drop all former identifiers? (Thus immerging incognito while cutting bait from tradition and shedding former histories.) The name Mies, for example, translated from German is not very flattering. "Mies" is a term mostly used to describe conditions of weather and negative qualities of experiences, like "a miserable dinner party" or "the wretched weather." By adding his mother's maiden name with the specific prefix "van der," which is very common in family names of landowning farmers and their offspring in the northern regions of Holland and Germany, he anoints himself aristocrat. In Germany the same prefix of "van der" is also attached to a lower rank but well recognized level of nobility. Through this name change, consciously or unconsciously, Mies van der Rohe is escaping the specter of middle class standing and the trauma of having his work called miese or wretched—even *woeful* architecture.

Designers and the Field of Language

When designers enter into the field of identity they are hardly equipped to deal with the obvious and hidden complexities of social language, its development and acquisition. They rarely step out off their one-way visual language platform, which is connected to formal image and icon making. They avoid the communications aspects that involve the meaning maker—namely the reader of images and icons—who has to make sense of a very stilted and abbreviated language. The interpreter is asked to traverse an enormously deep social and cultural crevasse, mostly through instinct, but without much guidance.

Internationalism, from which stem the doctrines of standardization, streamlining, and the military-like process of designing institutional and corporate images, believed that there is universality in the experience of all peoples. This may be true for the most basic survival needs, like provisions for food, shelter, procreation, and even for emotional security, freedom of thought, expression, and movement. But not for much more, because people from different cultures belong to different language communities and their language systems represent and encode completely different sensory worlds and value systems. Even the concept of death has multiple positive and negative interpretations. From anthropological sources, one can ascertain that certain Native American tribes hold little vocabulary, with none for ownership of objects and space or time. Their experiential filter would not translate to European or Asian sensibilities, and vice versa.

The Corporate Struggle with Marketing Identities

There are too many examples that epitomize the reality and conflict with identities or what identities can or cannot deliver. Identity is critical in the hierarchical struggle for dominance of a market as in the "Cola Wars." It separates and connects at the same time. One could question the reality of Generation X. Did it really exist or was it artificially concocted or contrived? Did individual youths find their identity in the value descriptions presented by the media or did the media clearly see a social phenomenon in action?

The late Jay Doblin, weaned on Raymond Loewy's streamlined marketing methodologies, at one of the rare occasions that allowed him to let down his hair, mused about identity design and corporate images as the most lucrative aspect of design service. At the same time, he suggested that identities are without any kind of proven functional reality or proven communication benefits. "Identities may be good for clients, but they are great for design businesses" (Doblin).

Maybe the most difficult task for an identity is to be more than what the whole of an entity can be. There are some negative after-effects when the book's cover is more exciting than the contents or where negative behavioral attitudes of personnel belie the concepts of helpfulness, responsibility, openness, or selfless service.

An identity can exude moral or ethical attitudes. But during a time in the last century, while the Container Corporation of America ran an outstanding advertising campaign of humanistic themes of duty, morality, and ethics (Great Ideas of Western Man), its CEO was driven in a chauffeured limousine to prison—where he was interred nightly for unethical price fixing. No matter how wonderful the external image may have been, it could only rub off some (but not enough) of the tarnished truth.

There are corporate identities that function well. They are mostly bound to a single person or family who over long periods have delivered quality and dependable goods or services. However, in these times of runaway and rollover mergers, restructuring, and reengineering, there is no time to really assess the real characteristics that make up these newly emerging companies. What are they? Who is behind them, corporate wolves or sheep in Gucci clothing? Who knows? Time will tell and reveal their true identity. You are what you are, not what you want others to believe.

References

Baudrillard, J. (1986). *Amérique.* Paris: B. Grasset.

Doblin, J. (1978). *Icograda 1978 World Congress*, Chicago. Planning meeting at RVI Corporation, Chicago, Fall 1978.

Gottfried Keller (1874). *Kleider machen Leute. Mit sieben Bildern nach Holzschnitten von Karl Mahr.* Leipzig: P. Reclam, junior, 1940.

PART SEVEN

The Learning Space

From the teaching of typography, that is, from instruction in a tradition, to the teaching of strategies for design thinking, the learning space requires conscious planning of the frames within which the instructor-student relation operates. It has been proven that knowing the objective of a task improves the performance of the learner. Rather than teaching content, helping people understand the tools, the territories of activity, and the rules of the game, users can interact with sources and build their own learning in more meaningful, varied, and effective ways.

CHAPTER TWENTY-ONE

Reading Minds:
The Book as a Communicational Space

Susan Colberg
University of Alberta, Edmonton, Canada

There is a book design adage that if a book is a success, it is because of the writing and if it is a failure, it is the cover design (Smith). This puts a considerable amount of pressure on the book designer charged with creating the conditions necessary for the potential reader to make contact with the content of a book. Practical limitations, agendas of the various stakeholders in the functional, aesthetic, commercial, and critical success of the book, and sensitivities and expectations of the readership all help delineate the parameters of the visual codes, selected by the designer, which frame the communicational space with which the public interacts.

Book designers research, compile, and interpret information that helps them to determine the various formal attributes of the book. What size should it be? What format should it have? What should be the approach to the cover design, the typography, and the structure of the layout? The selected attributes may make certain impressions on the potential reader about the nature of the content. These impressions are interpretations of meaning, which may create expectations about the character of the book, its content, and style of writing. In other words, the formal attributes give the book a certain visual identity that is intended to represent to the reading public, in a carefully selected visual language, the essence of the author's work.

The interesting thing about books as communicational spaces is that they are, at the same time, repositories of ideas, vehicles for culture, and cultural artifacts. They function as holders, preservers, and disseminators of knowledge and information. Books, if they are substantial in content, visually arresting, persuasive, or aesthetically beautiful in form, have a chance of living a long life and contributing to the knowledge and enjoyment of people. Jan Tschichold wrote, with respect to book design and typography, that it is not style, old or new, that matters—quality is what matters. If the books endure, they can communicate the quality, or the lack thereof, in aspects of the culture, particularly the visual culture, of the time period in which they were designed and produced.

The creation of the book as a communicational space could be considered a two-step process. Meaning and expectations are created first, when the designer, responding to intrinsic and extrinsic demands, assigns certain formal attributes to the book, and second, when members of the reading public interpret those attributes and, as a result, are compelled or not, to examine the book or to purchase it.

What are the intrinsic and extrinsic demands of the book design process that cause the designer to select some components of visual language over others? Many of the decisions concerning the formal attributes of the book are made on the basis of practical limitations such as budget—in my own work for scholarly publishers this often means using a six-by-nine inch vertical format, two-color cover, paper pre-selected on the basis of price and availability, and black ink for the interior. The remaining formal attributes are determined by reading minds.

Reading Your Own Mind

An inevitable part of the design process is the effect of intrinsic demands—the designer's own cognitive styles and abilities, motivations, personal interests, value systems and ethical standards. These vary considerably. The primary concern of some designers is that their cover designs command attention in bookstore windows or that they "jump off the shelves" and say "buy me"—others are concerned with representing the author's work, and some with creating beauty, balance, and harmony, while some aim to provide an easy and pleasurable reading experience. In the process of designing, the task is filtered through these wants, needs, and ways of knowing, and is interpreted accordingly.

When designing and when teaching design, I often begin and ask my students to begin with a statement of the communication need or goal that can lead to generative ideas which are often, at least initially, intuitive responses to the design task. Even in devising a statement of need, we filter information through our internal systems. It is often difficult to frame the task verbally at the beginning of the design process—the subconscious brings up multiple possible directions that may be pursued and developed. The initial idea may come from within, but always in response to, or framed by, demands that come from without.

In the process of teaching book design and typography, I intentionally and unintentionally color the students' understanding of and approaches to their work through my choices and areas of interest. They learn from Jan Tschichold, for example, that care and attention to detail in the production of a book are as vital as thorough and incisive editing (McLean).

If designers develop the ability to read and understand their own minds, they may gain insights into their own intuitive, associative, and creative processes—their own agendas. Awareness of these processes, through introspection, may make them better able to continue the design work while simultaneously carrying on a focused search in their own worlds of associative connection and responding to extrinsic demands.

Reading the Client's Mind

The design of a book begins when the publisher or editor briefs the art director or designer about the content. The author may have expressed expectations or opinions about certain aspects of the design. The marketing manager will also likely have contributed ideas, but for entirely different reasons.

In the process of developing a concept, book designers act on behalf of many people: the author, the publisher, the marketing manager, the editor, the production manager, and, near the end of the line, the bookseller. Becoming familiar with and being respectful of the content of a book, designers must also take into consideration the interests, expectations, desires, interpretations—the agendas of these stakeholders in the outcome of the design process, while responding to and being in tune with the prevailing trends and visual culture of the time.

"Will this book put the author's work 'on the map'?" "Will it win a design award?" "Will it cause the reading public to 'shell out' $39.95 plus tax?" If designers can communicate with the other stakeholders, verbally and visually in a kind of cross-cultural communication, about their research-based and intuitive responses to the design task, they can negotiate and eventually articulate shared visual codes—codes where a high degree of consensus exists concerning their interpretation.

On the path that leads to the creation of the physical communicational space (the book), an astonishing number of intellectual, emotional, and psychological communicational spaces are created. These shared ideas and revelations are complex.

"The type is good, very 'hip,' but could you make it a bit 'edgier'?" "No pink. It's written from a feminist perspective. It will give the wrong impression. And no brown. . . the author hates brown."

"I like it. I really do, but it doesn't say 'sociology' to me." These negotiations, for better or for worse, help shape the designed product. After much description, interrogation, and deliberation with the other stockholders, and equipped with various insights, it is possible for designers to approach the "appropriate" and the other stakeholders become aware that, in their version of the process, the designer's personal agenda is included with the extrinsic demands.

Several approaches may frame and take the communication concept in several directions at once. In an iterative design process, the approach that is selected may be determined mainly by the manner in which clients can reconcile it with extrinsic demands, including the motivations of the designer.

It is difficult to articulate the process through which verbal communications are translated into visual ones. There are no precise answers—the designers' interpretations, attitudes, and beliefs along with the communication context will help to determine them. Designers should be aware of the signs, associations, images, thoughts, and metaphors that are put in place during the iterative process and how they are related to the communication task at hand (Lakoff and Johnson).

Teaching the skills involved in this process is also difficult since it involves "reading" the reactions of people to information and also their interpretations of that information. It is an asset to be a skillful interviewer, listener, and observer. I encourage students to scrutinize and analyze the client's written and verbal remarks and to consider the notion that clues, yielding more or less appropriate approaches, can be found in them. Approaches with a strongly subjective or expressive character are invariably more difficult to translate into a form that can be shared with and interpreted by the readers of the book.

When there is a consensus about particular approaches to a design, the concepts selected—the ones that seem to communicate especially well—tend to provide a strong and direct link between the designers' or design students' motivations and the extrinsic demands of the task. Upon seeing the finished designs for the first time, clients have been known to say, "It's just right. It's exactly what I wanted. How did you know?" We explain to them that we read minds.

Reading the Reader's Mind

The designer explores the communicational terrain, taking various routes, and routes suggested by the stakeholders, until a shared terrain is discovered and an understanding of the task emerges. Only then is an approach chosen and carried out.

Along come the members of the reading public, with all their biases and sensitivities. The book has been designed. The book exists. The possibility for a communicational space to be created between book and reader exists. Do the potential readers share the established communicational terrain? Do they meet the message? How do they see, understand, and interpret the book?

The first point of contact between book and reader is generally the front cover. In his book *Front Cover: Great Jacket and Cover Designs*, British writer Alan Powers says, "The book cover is the marriage broker, continually driven to seduce and deceive, even if in the most charming and learned ways" (Powers). This gives the potential reader little credit and fails to take into account that, when scanning book covers on bookstore shelves or in window displays, the average glance time is one-quarter of a second—not a great deal of time for seduction and deception, let alone interpretation of meaning (Smith). In that quarter of a second, possibly in a six-by-nine-inch space and in two colors, potential readers expect, knowingly or unknowingly, to see something that is visually arresting, meaningful, and in tune with the trends of the time, to get enough of an impression about the content of the book, to enable them to decide whether or not to investigate further and perhaps to "shell out" $39.95 plus tax. Who needs a marriage broker? It is decidedly a "love at first sight" situation.

Although it is possible to delineate approaches aimed at a specific segment of a reading audience and to deal with the notion of fitness to public through research, many share the perspective of Scott Richardson, Art Director of Knopf Canada, Doubleday Canada, and Random House, who says, ". . . There is no science to this. There's nowhere I can go and find out that if I use this colour, or this image or this type I will sell X number of books. It's not like the advertising business, where they focus-group to death. In the book business, it's guesswork" (Smith, 14).

Is it guesswork? Or is it considered work by a designer, in collaboration with a group of experts, all of whom have a broad general knowledge and detailed and specific knowledge of the issues involved in the production of a book.

The design of a book can be the result of exploration, interaction, and negotiation with the objective of creating a communicational space where the resulting visual attributes of the book ". . . favour the interpretation of a message in a certain (approximate) predictable direction" (Frascara) and allow for interpretation by the audience.

Conclusion

Author P. L. Travers once said, "A writer is, after all, only half his book. The other half is the reader and from the reader the writer learns" (Simpson). The book designer learns from both reader and writer and is, perhaps, the glue that binds those two halves together.

Under the best conditions the designer designs a book that assists the author in putting his or her ideas in contact with readers. The design adds dimensions to the book as a cultural object of value, as determined by the various stakeholders, and delights the readers along the way. Under the best conditions, the designer has created the book as a communicational space.

References

Bringhurst, Robert (1992). *The Elements of Typographic Style*. Vancouver, BC: Hartley and Marks.

Frascara, Jorge (2003). *Creating Communicational Spaces: Conference Outline*. Conference Prospectus, University of Alberta, Edmonton, conference held 1–4 May 2003.

Lakoff, G., and M. Johnson (1980). *Metaphors We Live By*. Chicago, IL: University of Chicago Press.

McLean, Ruari (1975). *Jan Tschichold: Typographer*. Boston, MA: Godine.

Powers, Alan (2001). *Great Book Jacket and Cover Design*. London: Mitchell Beazley.

Simpson, James B. (1988). *Simpson's Contemporary Quotations*. Boston, MA: Houghton Mifflin.

Smith, Stephen (2002). "Covering Up: The Importance of Canadian Book Jacket Design." *Amphora* (129), The Alcuin Society, December 2002, 12–17.

Tschichold, Jan (1975). *Ausgewählte Aufsätze uber Fragen der Gestalt des Buches und der Typographie*. Basel: Birkhäuser Verlag.

CHAPTER TWENTY-TWO

Ec(h)o:
Ecologies for Designing Playful Interaction

Ron Wakkary, Marek Hatala, Kenneth Newby
Simon Fraser University, Surrey, BC, Canada

Do **we play in museums?** Anthropologist Genevieve Bell identifies the notion of play together with learning in museums. She describes museums as different *cultural ecologies* in which the museum visit has the qualities of *liminality* (a space and time set apart from everyday life) and *engagement* (where visitors interact to both learn and play) (Bell). Guided by the notion of play in a museum experience we have considered playfulness equally with functionality and learning in the design of an adaptive museum guide. Our approach includes a tangible user interface (TUI), spatial audio, and an integrated user modeling technique combined with semantic technologies that support exploration and discovery. We understood our interface as playful action along the lines of aesthetic interaction. By this we do not mean the type of structured play that is found in a software game on a mobile device, rather we refer to the less structured and open play that is always possible and often can be subtle and implicit like toying with a ball.

Here, we will describe our case study of an augmented reality museum guide, known as *ec(h)o*, which we installed and tested at the Canadian Museum of Nature in Ottawa. We discuss our use of a set of ecological approaches from the domains of acoustics, ethnography, and information technology. Acoustically, we based much of our work on the ideas of sound ecologies. We also adopted the idea of museums as ecology informed by Bell's *cultural ecologies* and Nardi and O'Day's *information ecology*. This approach led to us being inspired by simple physical displays and puzzles we observed in our ethnographic sessions. These observations encouraged the playful tangible object and use of puzzles in our audio content. We were also motivated by the storytelling of the museum staff and researchers that was often humorous as well as informative. In this project, we found that learning effectiveness and functionality can be balanced productively with playful interaction through an adaptive audio and tangible user interface approach and that diverse ecology models help define the imaginative space and contextual aspects of play.

Previous Work

Ec(h)o shares many characteristics with the adaptive systems of HyperAudio, HIPS, and Hippie (Petrelli et al.; Benelli et al.; Oppermann and Specht). Similar to ec(h)o, the systems respond to user location and explicit user actions. All systems adapt content to the user model, location, and interaction history. Among the key differences with ec(h)o is that these systems depend on a personal digital assistant (PDA) and graphical user interface (GUI); ec(h)o uses audio display as the only delivery channel and a tangible object as an input device. In addition, ec(h)o uses inference at the level of semantic descriptions of independent audio objects and exhibit, and ec(h)o treats user interests as dynamic.

Prior to the evolution of adaptive and user modeling approaches in museum guide systems, there has been a strong trajectory of use of the PDA graphical user interface. Typically, hypertext is combined with images, video, and audio (Semper and Spasojevic; Proctor and Tellis). Yet, a PDA is essentially a productivity tool for business, not a device that lends itself easily to playful interaction. Given that PDAs use miniaturized desktop-based GUIs, we wondered if we should metaphorically carry around our desks in order to experience such things as museums—in what might be described as a *world-behind-a-desk* approach to mobile computing. Museum systems have mostly maintained the PDA graphical user interface approach despite the shifts in other domains to other approaches that better address the experience design issues most prominent in social, cultural, and leisure activities. The play constraints of these devices are too great for the level of interaction that goes beyond playing a software game on a mobile device. For example, in the area of games and ubiquitous computing, Björk and his colleagues have identified the need to develop past end-user devices such as mobile phones, personal digital assistants, and game consoles (Björk et al.). They argue that we need to better understand how "computational services" augment games situated in real environments. The same can be said for museum visits.

Audio is seen as an immersive display that can enrich the physical world and human activity while being more integrated with the surrounding environment (Brewster et al., Pirhonen et al.). In addition, audio tends to create interpretive space or *room for imagination* as many have claimed radio affords over television. In the HIPS project, different voices and delivery styles were used to create an "empathetic effect" between the user and the artifacts they engaged (Marti). We have adopted a similar approach to our use of audio content.

Description of Ec(h)o

Our approach includes a tangible user interface (TUI) for its inherent playfulness, spatial audio display for its imaginative qualities, and an integrated user modeling technique combined with semantic technologies that supported exploration. Our aim is to improve the visitor engagement by considering playfulness equally with functionality and learning.

The implementation went as follows: visitors are given a pair of headphones connected to a small, light pouch to be slung over their shoulder. The pouch contains a wireless receiver for audio, and a digital tag for position tracking. When in front of an exhibition display, *ec(h)o* offers the visitor three short audio pieces as *prefaces* that are acoustically to the visitor's left, center, and right respectively. This spatial structure allows the three *prefaces* to be distinguishable. The spatialization is mapped to the TUI, a wooden cube (see figure 22.1), for selection. The visitor *responds* by rotating the wooden cube in his hand and thus selecting a *preface*. The system delivers the audio object related to the *preface*. After the delivery of the object, the system again offers three *prefaces*. The visitor's response is expressed through the gesture selection with the wooden cube. Additionally, the system may be met by no response, because the visitor does not wish to engage the system. The system will then enter into a silent mode. The visitor may also have moved away and the system will then initiate a soundscape that continuously plays while the visitor is in the spaces between exhibition displays.

The audio objects are semantically tagged to a range of topics for possible integration with networks of information across the Internet. At the beginning of each interaction cycle, three audio objects are selected based on ranking, using

Figure 22.1: The *ec(h)o* cube

several criteria such as current levels of user interest, location, and interaction history reasoned through our user model (Hatala and Wakkary). The topics of objects are not explicit to the visitor; rather, the content logic is kept in the background.

In regard to the design process, many of the design choices were made through a series of participatory design workshops and scenarios (Wakkary). For example, the tangible user interface and its implementation as an asymmetrically shaped wooden cube resulted from these workshops, as did the use of the conversation metaphor, navigation, and audio interface. In addition, we prototyped the exhibition environment and system in our labs in order to design the interactive zones, audio display, and interaction with the exhibit displays.

Tangible Object

The tangible user interface is an asymmetrically shaped wooden cube with three adjacent colored sides (see figure 22.1). The cube was carefully designed to ensure proper orientation and ease of use. The "bottom" of the cube has a convex curve to fit comfortably in the palm of the visitor's hand and a wrist leash is attached to an adjacent side to the curved bottom, suggesting the default position of being upright in the palm and at a specified orientation to the visitor's body. The leash allows visitors to dangle the cube when not in use and frees the use of their hand. The opposite side of the bottom of the cube is colored and shows an icon denoting a pair of headphones with both channels active. The sides to the left and right are each uniquely colored and display icons showing active left and right channels of the headphones, respectively. The cube is made of balsa wood in order to mitigate tiredness from carrying the object and is therefore very light (approximately 100 grams or 3.5 ounces).

The input of the selection is done through video sensing. The ergonomic design of the cube and biomechanics of arm and wrist movement form a physical constraint that ensures the selected cube face is almost always held up parallel to the camera lens above and so highly readable. We experienced no difficulties with this approach.

Audio Display

The audio display has two components, a soundscape and paired prefaces and audio objects. In the latter component, we used a simple spatial audio structure to cognitively differentiate the objects. Switching between the stereo channels created localization: we used the left channel audio for the left, right channel audio for the right, and both channels for the center. In addition, we provided simple chimes to confirm that a selection had been made.

The *prefaces* were written to create a sense of surprise, discovery, and above all play, especially in contrast to the informational audio objects. In order to create this sense we used diverse forms of puns, riddles, and word play, such as *ambiguous word play* used in the preface "Sea urchins for sand dollars"; *turn of phrase* like the preface "An inch or two give or take a foot"; and *riddles* like "What is always naked and thinks on its feet?" In addition, the audio recordings of the *prefaces* and *audio objects* used a diverse set of voices that were informal in tonality and style. This added to the conversational feel and created an imaginary scene of a virtual cocktail party of natural historians and scientists that followed you through the museum.

Visitors' movements through the exhibition space in between artifact displays generated the soundscape. Visitor movement was tracked using a combined Radio Frequency Identification (RFID) and optical position tracking system developed by Precision Systems (www.precision-sys.com). We divided the exhibition space into interactive zones and mapped concepts of interest to each zone and display.

Figure 22.2: Still frames depicting the dynamic soundscape based on visitor movement.

The concepts are translated into environmental sounds such as the sound of an animal habitat, and sounds of animals such as the flapping of cranes' wings. The visitor navigates the exhibit exploring it on a thematic level through the ambient sounds that are dynamically created. If a set of concepts strongly matches the visitor's interest the related audio is acoustically more prominent (see figure 22.2).

Ecological Approaches

We endeavored to consider how our design both *intervenes* and *integrates* within a complex museum experience. The ecological models of *cultural ecologies* and *information ecologies* provided us with frameworks for contextual analysis (Bell, Nardi, and O'Day). This approach allowed us to look further into the design process, past the interface for guidance, into how our design decisions were integral to the ecology or its inhabitants, thus supporting us in developing more appropriate design responses. Bell's *cultural ecologies* formally linked different actions and attributes of the museum visitor into a coherent description. As a descriptive tool it validated our assumptions and provided a clearer link between what we observed and the design implications. It was therefore generative, much like Nardi and O'Day's *information ecologies* framework. Both guided us in specific design decisions, namely the high degree of physical interaction that suggested a tangible user interface; the wide use of puzzles, riddles, and games as modes of learning which led to our use of a riddle-like approach to our audio content; and the localized and informal storytelling on behalf of the museum staff and researchers that inspired us to structure our audio experience like a virtual cocktail party. (For further discussion of the role of ecologies in museums we refer readers to Wakkary and Evernden.)

The auditory interface is another form of ecology. It provides the basic mechanisms of navigation and orientation within the information space. This entails investigations of mechanisms for mediating space-time modulations within the narrative information space. These mechanisms form the key components of a modeled acoustic ecology that takes into account the variety, complexity, and balance of the informational soundscape. The research takes into account both psychoacoustic and cognitive characteristics of the ecology as well as compositional problems in the construction of a meaningful and engaging interactive audible display. Psychoacoustic characteristics of the ecological balance include spectral balancing of audible layers. Cognitive aspects of listening contribute to the design and effective use of streaming mechanisms allowing segmentation, selection, and switching among audible semantic objects within the soundscape. Compositional problems were addressed in the form of the orchestration of an informational soundscape of immersion and flow that allowed for the interactive involvement of the visitor. Techniques were drawn from sound design for cinema in developing relationships among soundscape, speech, and musical elements of the audible scene. The interface display takes into account transitions, beginnings, endings, and, perhaps most importantly, interruptions in the narrative audio-informational flow situating the awareness of the visitor.

Summary of User Evaluation

User experience was evaluated through observation, a questionnaire, and a semi-structured interview. The evaluation group included two men and four women, from twenty-five to fifty-three years old. We also performed expert reviews by a senior researcher and senior interaction designer from the museum. Participants found the system enjoyable and stimulating, perhaps in part due to its novelty. The results were quite clear that play was a critical experiential factor in using the system. It was often remarked how the experience was similar to a game:

"The whole system to me felt a lot like a game. I mean I got lost in it, I found myself spending a lot more time in a particular area than I normally would. And just the challenge of waiting to hear what was next, what the little choice of three was going to be. Yeah. . . . So I found it overall engaging, it was fun, and it was very game-like." (Participant 5)

The playfulness did in most instances suggest a quality of engagement that led to learning, even though diverse types of museum visitors were involved, from the visitor who browses through quickly but is still looking to be engaged, to the repeat visitor who experiences the audio information differently each time.

The evaluation did point out challenges and areas for further research. Some things we expected, such as the headphones were uncomfortable, yet to such a degree that we are currently rethinking the use of personalized spatial audio and headphones. Other results point to a threshold in the balance between levels of abstraction and local information, since visitors had difficulties at times connecting what they were listening to and what was in front of them (in part this was an inherent challenge in the exhibition since the display cases had from dozens to over a hundred artifacts). In many respects this points to the finding that the semantic technologies approach did not always provide a clear enough contextual link between the artifacts and the audio information. In addition, we see both a threshold point between play and focused attention on the exhibit. For example, one user's enthusiasm for the game-like quality led her to at times pay more attention to the interaction with the system than the exhibition. This raises the issue of balance in play and the possibility to shift attention away from the environment rather than play as a means of further exploring the environment.

Conclusion

Ec(h)o is an augmented audio reality system for museum visitors that uses a tangible interface. We developed and tested the prototype for the Canadian Museum of Nature in Ottawa. The findings of this project are positive, while also calling for more research in several areas. We conclude that learning effectiveness and functionality can be balanced productively with playful interaction through an adaptive audio and tangible user interface approach and that diverse ecology models help define the imaginative space and contextual aspects of play.

References

Bell, G. (2002). Making Sense of Museums: The Museum as "Cultural Ecology." Intel Labs.

Benelli, G., Bianchi, A., Marti, P., Not, E. and Sennari, D. (1999). "HIPS: Hyper-Interaction within the physical space." *IEEE Multimedia Systems '99*. Florence, Italy.

Bjork, S., Holopainen, J., Ljungstrand, P. and Akesson, K.-P. (2002). "Designing Ubiquitous Computing Games—A Report from a Workshop Exploring Ubiquitous Computing Entertainment." *Personal and Ubiquitous Computing*, 6, 443–458.

Brewster, S., Lumsden, J., Bell, M., Hall, M. and Tasker, S. (2003). "Multimodal 'Eyes-Free' Interaction Techniques for Wearable Devices." *CHI 2003*. Fort Lauderdale: ACM Press.

Hatala, M. and Wakkary, R. (2005). "Ontology-Based User Modeling in an Augmented Audio Reality System for Museums." *User Modeling and User-Adapted Interaction*, vol. 15, 3/4, 339–380.

Marti, P. (2001). "Design for Art and Leisure." *International Cultural Heritage Informatics Meeting: Proceedings from ICHIM01*. Milan, Italy. Archives and Museum Informatics.

Nardi, B. A. and O'Day, V. (1999). *Information ecologies: using technology with heart.* Cambridge, MA: MIT Press.

Oppermann, R. and Specht, M. (1999). "A Nomadic Information System for Adaptive Exhibition Guidance." In Bearman, D. and Trant, J. (Eds.). *Cultural Heritage Informatics: Selected Papers from ICHIM99.* Washington, D.C.: Archives and Museum Informatics.

Petrelli, D., Not, E., Zancarano, M., Strapparava, C. and Stock, O. (2001). "Modelling and Adapting Context." *Personal Ubiquitous Comput.,* 5, 20–24.

Pirhonen, A., Brewster, S. and Holguin, C. (2002). "Gestural and Audio Metaphors as a Means of Control for Mobile Devices." *Proceedings CHI 2002.* Minneapolis, MN: ACM Press.

Proctor, N. and Tellis, C. (2003). "The State of the Art in Museum Handhelds in 2003." In Trant, D. B. A. J. (Ed.) *Museum and the Web 2003.* Pittsburgh: Archives and Museums Informatics.

Semper, R. and Spasojevic, M. (2002). "The Electronic Guidebook: Using Portable Devices and a Wireless Web-Based Network to Extend the Museum Experience." In Trant, D. B. A. J. (Ed.). *Museum and Web 2002.* Toronto: Archives and Museum Informatics

Wakkary, R. (2005). "Framing Complexity, Design and Experience: A Reflective Analysis." *Digital Creativity,* Volume 16, 2, 65–78.

Wakkary, R. and Evernden, D. (2005). "Museum as Ecology: A Case Study Analysis of an Ambient Intelligent Museum Guide." In J.Trant, D. B. A. (Ed.) *Museums and the Web 2005 Selected Papers.* Vancouver, British Columbia, Toronto: Archives and Museum Informatics.

PART EIGHT

The Electronic Space

The challenges in the electronic environment are many, partly because of the novelty of its existence for most of us, and partly because of its inherent opacity. Developing intuitive cues for users to be able to navigate its corridors and understand its codes, and tapping the enormous potential of the medium, are major tasks that require wide interdisciplinary resources and a variety of sensitivities and forms of intelligence. This is a good time for inquisitive designers to build an understandable and useable electronic space.

CHAPTER TWENTY-THREE

Information Modeling

Charles Field

Modestspectacle, San Francisco, California, USA

I have been working for the past six years or so as a Creative Director making Web sites and applications, and it has been a time of ferocious innovation; an explosion of ideas, methodologies, and techniques of development.

Every team I joined or led tended to develop its own methods. The goal was clear in all cases, to record decisions and determine scope so that something appropriate could be built. But the variety of methods undermined the long-term goals and made knowledge transfer to succeeding teams partial at best.

There are sitemaps, layer diagrams, Booch method diagrams, data flow diagrams, Universal Modeling Language diagrams of a number of vintages. . . . The Internet, and the mix of disciplines that came together to form collaborative teams through the late nineties caused a multiplication of forms and methods.

Because all computer spaces are digital, they are inherently abstract. Therefore any communicational space we construct is a combination of cultural and engineering codings. In this new brand world, it is the intersection of software architects, usability engineers, information architects, and designers that are in both collaboration and occasional conflict.

What the field needs is a common language for development to begin to create an environment where we can communicate with each other. Better yet, a scaleable set of methodologies to respond to constantly shifting environments. However, simplistic solutions will fail in complex scenarios, so we must develop an extensible way of describing these ideas. To that end, I have noted a few of the kinds of diagrammatic spaces that people are currently building and using, and mapped them to assumptions of usage based in practice. Perhaps this can form the beginning of a debate on a unified understanding and use of these tools.

The two kinds of diagrams most useful for this kind of structural planning are hierarchical and event based drawings. To place them in their cultural encodings, let's call these a site map and a Universal Modeling Language use case record.

All of these kinds of diagrams have specific strengths and weaknesses. Data flow charts and sitemaps assume time, and pretend that users only travel in a single goal-specific direction. That is not necessarily the case, but the mechanisms for showing the narrative idea of wandering or surfing through a site is a communication challenge in a single surface sitemap.

Having watched teams search for utility in these situations, we see a plethora of reasons why communication can be difficult. The different notions of what constitutes creativity, different ideas on what is useful as structure and different views on what is an appropriate level of analysis, as well as vastly different educational preparations, lead to cycles of confusion and failed projects. All of these factors meet in a culture that aspires to invention.

Proposal

Given these variables, it is a useful strategy to codify some essential tools for developing these kinds of projects.

Sitemaps

Sitemaps were developed in a couple of places, but championed by Vivid Studios in the early 1990s. Nathan Shedroff and Drue Miller are the two names primarily associated with them, but they have become a common development tool. The advantages are a kind of generalization that allows basic decisions to be made, particularly in terms of logical groupings of information.

These maps can be rapidly produced, and articulate initial concepts with simplicity. Basic divisions of information can be recorded and agreed on with clients. They facilitate agreement on scope, as well.

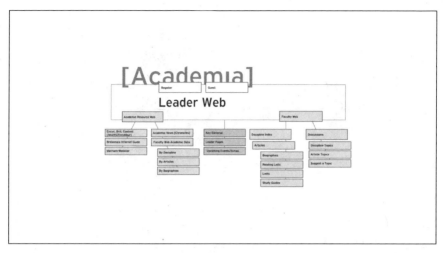

Figure 23.1: Sitemap for Encyclopedia Britannica, showing a registration gateway and basic structure underneath.

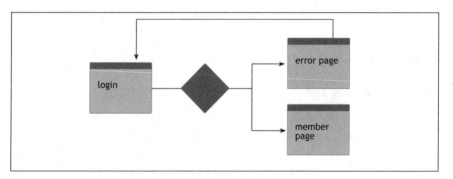

Figure 23.2

Problems arise when these diagrams are asked to accomplish more than the form can hold. Attempts to stretch the form into events based thinking change the paradigm from a hierarchical drawing, quickly adding uninterpretable complexity. Jesse James Garrett is associated with current hybrid developments of this form. Below is an example of Garrett's methodology. He attempts to synthesize recognition of events as part of his schema. This is an interesting notion but it doesn't scale with the same fluidity as use cases. It quickly reaches a level of complexity that is too specific for clients but too vague for programmers.

The problems become clearer with increasing complexity. Beyond double functions, he resorts to a cluster symbol, which is an umbrella term for not fitting in the system.

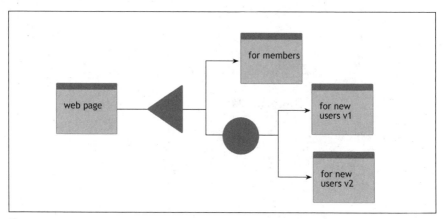

Figure 23.3

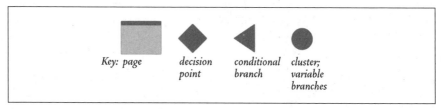

Figure 23.4

Universal Modeling Language

UML diagrams were developed in the software industry, originally by Grady Booch, James Rumbaugh, and Ivar Jacobsen starting in 1967. Through many years of development, this evolved into Rational Rose and the Unified Software Development Process. While use case diagrams are but a small part of a larger object modeling system, they represent the users' view. Thus they become the designer's bridge into programming, allowing recognition of human factors in a development process.

This is a requirements based process used with different levels of sophistication depending on the scale and budget of the project. The investment necessary for Rational Rose software starts big and continues skywards. While Rose is a useful system, the idea structures represented are of general applicability and can be effectively employed without the software. Consequently, many use UML diagramming techniques in programs like Visio and Omnigraffle. This allows the depiction of events based cases, but not the kind of sophisticated change management of Rose.

Elements of this kind of development have filtered down to smaller shops through the construction of user scenarios and the development of personas, a narrative

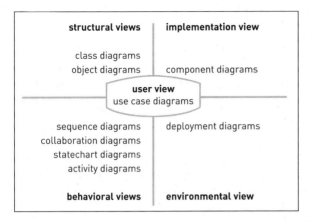

Figure 23.5: The components of the Universal Modeling Language arranged from the users' point of view.

version of an actor. Alan Cooper, for instance, outlines a process based on developing a cast of representative users and privileging one of them as the lead user. This keeps teams from endlessly debating an ambiguous "user" whose requirements can easily shift over the course of a few meetings.

By assigning a primary personality to the audience, he is able to be specific about their needs. This prevents two common development errors: diffusing the strategic purpose of the tool through the endless addition of features, and the creation of jackalopes that are useful to no one. Of course all this is changing with advances in genetics, but we will ignore that here.

Smaller shops also use UML as a tool to develop smaller scale database sites. Because these are tied to the requirements created in the use case, they record and track specific issues through the life of the project. This begins to build a knowledge base, the first step in a change management system.

To a designer/information architect, this is often seen as counter-intuitive and overly specific. To a software architect, it is the only path worth traveling.

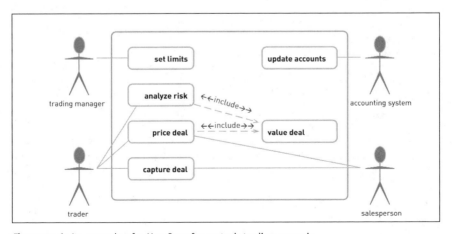

Figure 23.6: An example of a Use Case for a stock trading scenario.

Which Version of the Truth?

Both kinds of diagrams are useful, but at different stages of the process. Let's define these diagrams in terms of their goals to clarify things. The goal of a sitemap is to provide a general view of how conceptual chunks of the site or application relate. Their advantage is that they are inherently general; broad strategic goals are related to the medium.

Below is an example produced by the author in 1998. While Adobe's site was 13,000 pages—like many first generation Internet sites of large Silicon Valley organizations—it was composed of flat pages. This was true until 2001, when they began a transition to a database site that continues today.

This map clarifies strategic priorities while eliminating the distractions of detail. Maps like this become a bridge between the marketing department and site designers.

It is of limited use to a database programmer, however, as it does not describe the specific transactions that need to be designed for each page. The reductive

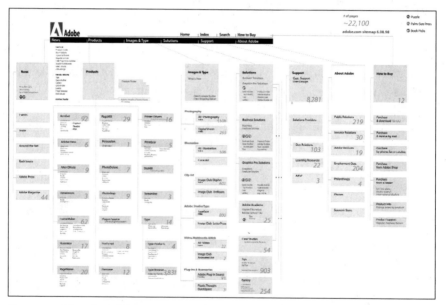

Figure 23.7: Though useful as an overview, these kinds of maps are of little value in showing a history of changes. (The purpose of this figure is to show the structure of the map, not all its details, which the reproduction size does not allow.)

generalizations it employs become a limitation, rather than a clarification.

This would apply to any problem over about 100 to 200 screens in size. Around this stage it becomes more time effective and scalable to design "types of cases" and "kinds of responses" rather than individual instantiations. This is true particularly for an initial stage, when a marketing or design direction evolves.

There are some limitations to use cases. It is an engineering culture specific set of procedures that clients find inaccessible. Some clients struggle with sitemaps; any of these tools, and the amount of energy devoted to planning a Web or application process need careful introduction and explanation. The technical specificity of use cases, however, is also their strength; a correctly formed set of use cases leads directly to the generation of classes and table structures for a database.

A mixed blessing of use cases is that they start at an extremely specific level; there is danger of even experienced software architects falling into a bog of minutia. They are often resistant to brainstorming, or forming a concept. But for change management of iterative software projects, particularly at large scale, they are an extremely powerful set of tools.

Depending on the type of problem this may not be an issue. For instance, when inventing a new product, service, or conceptualization, being able to brainstorm structures and test general strategies is paramount. For iterating software, conceptualization is minimized, and logical progression and consistent tracking is key.

Application

Any tools we devise must be outlines, as most problems, if handled well, have specific requirements or contextually sensitive demands. For instance, if one is making an instant messenger, most of the criteria of these are known, and an instant messenger is a series of events where the context changes little. Use cases and events diagramming are the most useful record here.

Conclusion

The primary advantage of a site map is its ability to show a heuristic view of the structure. The primary advantage of a use case is that it is a structure built on events. The emphasis is on collaborative systems here, but I include Web sites because these are the cultural root of sitemaps.

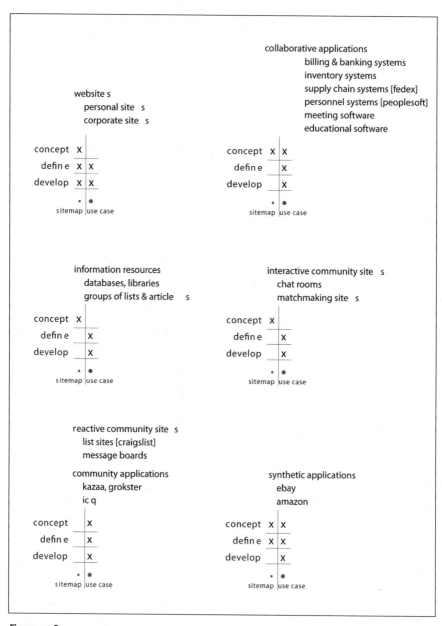

Figure 23.8

References

Alhir, Sinan Si (1998). *UML in a Nutshell*. Cambridge, MA: O'Reilly.

Cooper, Alan (1999). *The Inmates Are Running the Asylum*. Indianapolis: SAMS

Fowler, Martin (2004). *UML Distilled*. Addison Wesley Object Technology Series.

Garrett, Jesse J. (2002). *The Elements of User Experience: User Centered Design for the Web*. Indianapolis: New Riders

Landauer, Thomas K. (1995). *The Trouble with Computers*. Boston, MA: MIT Press.

Manovich, Lev (2002). *The Language of New Media*. Boston, MA: MIT Press.

Norman, Donald (2002). *The Design of Everyday Things*. New York: Basic Books.

Rumbaugh, James, Jacobsen, Ivar and Booch, Grady (1998). *The Unified Modeling Language Reference Manual*. Addison Wesley Object Technology Series.

Schneider, Geri and Winters, Jason P. (2001). *Applying Use Cases: A Practical Guide*. Addison Wesley Object Technology Series.

Tufte, Edward (2001). *The Visual Display of Quantitative information*. Cheshire, CT: Graphics Press.

All figures by the Author.

Charles Field can be contacted at charles@modestspectacle.com, www.modestspectacle.com.

CHAPTER TWENTY-FOUR

The Experiential Interface:
Creating Emotionally Engaging Spaces

Doreen Leo and Jim Budd
Simon Fraser University, Surrey, BC, Canada

There are fundamental differences in approach to interface design between the technically oriented disciplines of computer science and engineering and the socially-oriented disciplines of industrial design and communication design. The engineering approach tends to focus on technology . . . utility, efficiency, and performance. The design approach on the other hand tends to focus on social issues—the relationship between people and technology . . . helping people use technology to enhance life experience.

Technology Versus People: the Evolving Digital World

In his book *Interface Culture: How New Technology Transforms the Way We Create and Communicate*, Steven Johnson argues that due to the rapidly increasing adoption of the Internet, interface is emerging as a profoundly important medium in its own right (Johnson). Unfortunately up until the mid to late 1990s the people-based design perspective had largely been ignored . . . technology ruled and it seemed we all had to live with that. But we felt there were opportunities to change all that.

Engaging the Audience

In the late 1990s, my students at Georgia Tech became intrigued by new Web sites that were beginning to experiment with animation using Macromedia Flash. The implications for our work seemed obvious and we began to explore the potential to incorporate these new interactive digital tools to help us communicate more effectively by building on the visual skills we were most familiar with. The following series of visually based examples are presented to highlight the key developments in the evolution of our thinking and understanding of the techniques and methods that could help us foster audience engagement and facilitate a deeper level of understanding through emotionally engaging communicational spaces. The examples used are drawn from the work of graduate students who have helped me explore the role of interactivity in interface design over the past five years.

Case #1: The "ilab" Interface

The "ilab" was created to support collaborative interdisciplinary design research at Georgia Tech. This presentation was our first attempt to embody meaning in the design of the interface and our first attempt to work with Macromedia Flash.

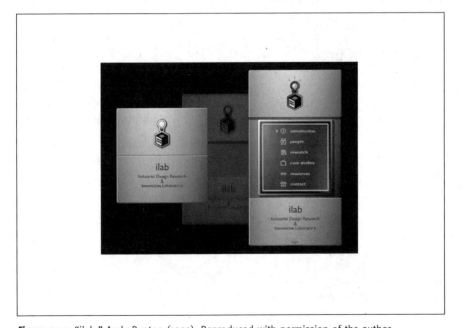

Figure 24.1: "ilab," Andy Runton (1999). Reproduced with permission of the author

Figure 24.2: "ilab," Andy Runton (1999). Reproduced with permission of the author

The initial challenge was to develop new techniques to engage the audience. We began focusing on the technical issues. How could we develop a stronger sense of personality? How could we incorporate animation to reinforce meaning? How could we organize and/or present information in a more effective and easy to navigate format?

The ilab interface is a virtual device, a non-linear presentation that promotes user interaction. The graphic imagery, animated effects, and sounds provide an appropriate context (secretive, high tech, innovative, and playful). The iconography simplifies navigation and the presentation communicates the concepts and culture of the lab in a meaningful way by embodying a sense of the "approachable, innovative personality" of the lab.

Case #2: "iComic"

iComic is an exploration of a potential interface for an interactive comic book. The prototype uses the metaphor of a book as a building block, and mimics elements of the printed page. The pages "turn" with a rustling sound providing a

Figure 24.3: "iComic," Andy Runton (1999). Reproduced with permission of the author

familiar frame of reference for the audience. However, iComic was conceptualized as more than a story and takes full advantage of the power of hyperlinks to provide biographical information on the authors as well as "behind the scenes" details on the development of the storyline, the origins of the characters, as well as a glimpse of the sequential iterative process leading to the final production of the comic artwork.

"Design serves as a form of expression and communication from the designer, through the (work) to the user. In order to communicate effectively . . . designers use a visual language, using shape and form instead of words. . . . This language is also responsible for generating that elusive, but critical emotional connection" (Runton, 10).

Case #3: "E-binder"

E-binder is a prototype tool developed to assist designers too quickly and easily present a complete project or work in progress to others via the Internet. The E-binder project builds on lessons learned from "ilab" and the "iComic" projects. E-binder helps the designer to actively engage the audience in the design process by providing an emotive context for the project being presented.

"Everybody understands how a book works . . . the book metaphor supports a user's sense of agency giving them control over the presentation itself. They are able to experience the presentation in any manner they choose: they can move through it linearly or non-sequentially as they see fit. This perception of agency is reinforced through the use of both sound and visual effects. Buttons click as users

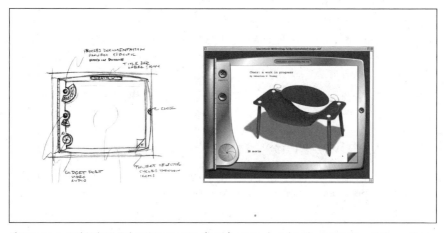

Figure 24.4: "E-binder," Sebastian Toomey (2000). Reproduced with permission of the author

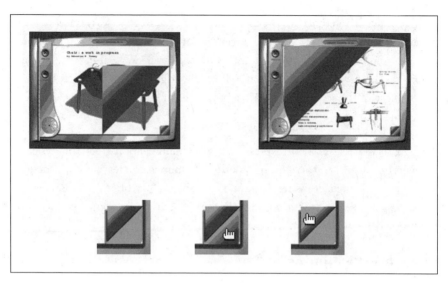

Figure 24.5: "E-binder," Sebastian Toomey (2000). Reproduced with permission of the author

'push' them and pages rustle as they are 'turned.' Actions are confirmed not only through sound but also through blinking lights, animated title bars, and the actions of dynamic media widgets that scurry across the screen in response to the user's actions" (Toomey, 28).

Exploring Context in Interface and Navigation

Through the work of Andy Runton and Sebastian Toomey at Georgia Tech, we had been able to demonstrate that the design of the interface could significantly affect audience interpretation and understanding of content . . . in other words thoughtful design of the interface itself could enhance communication. This observation is consistent with Brenda Laurel's reference to the work of Tom Bender: "Information communicated as facts loses all of its contexts and relationships, while information communicated as art or experience maintains and nourishes its connections" (Laurel, 119). The next step was to explore the potential to reinforce the role of context.

Case #4: "Qing-Ming-Shang-He-Tu"

The work of Cheryl Qian at Simon Fraser University Surrey helped consolidate much of our previous thought by demonstrating the potential to generate a contextually based interactive multimedia presentation . . . with a level of sensitivity not previously associated with digital materials seen on the Internet.

Figure 24.6: "Qing-Ming-Shang-He-Tu," Cheryl Qian (2001). Reproduced with permission of the author

"This project intends to provide a path for the (audience) to navigate inside this ancient Chinese environment . . . the design is not only an attempt to show the ancient arts but also a new approach to preserve, represent and research ancient art works by electronic methods" (Qian, 1).

Transferring Qing-Ming-Shang-He-Tu to a digital environment presents a number of interesting challenges. The scroll painting measures 5.35 meters x 0.25 meters. The painting portraits a linear piece of the huge kermis along a river of the Song Dynasty's capital, Bian Liang, during the Qing Ming festival. It captures the cultural, economic, and architectural aspects of the period. A typical solution based on existing Web-based models would have been to zoom in and out of various sections of the painting . . . but as we have learned, information

Figure 24.7: "Qing-Ming-Shang-He-Tu," Cheryl Qian (2001). Reproduced with permission of the author

out of context loses much of its meaning. Cheryl's solution was to implement her Web-based version of the painting as a virtual scroll that unrolls on the screen accompanied by background music of the era. Once the scroll is open the scene begins to pan from right to left . . . effectively allowing us to traverse the entire painting. Navigation is similarly implemented in a subtle fashion—a menu bar is visually integrated into the border of the scroll painting allowing the audience to change the direction of the pan or immediately jump to either end of the painting.

Another challenge was to provide a sense of life in China at this point in time. The solution was to create a series of "sliding" menus along the primary menu bar to provide access to special features. These unobtrusive, transparent, sliding menus, modeled after ancient Chinese screens, allow the viewer to explore key architectural, cultural, and social aspects of the painting. For example, on selecting the "Rainbow Bridge," the scroll immediately pans to the location of the Rainbow Bridge in the painting. As the audience rolls the cursor across the scene an outline of the bridge illuminates to identify the feature. On a mouse click, a 3-D animation of the bridge begins to emerge from the painting to show us magnified architectural details. As the animation ends, the 3-D model merges back into the painting and the painting begins to scroll once more. This same technique is used to depict social life of the time. If you select the City Gate from the special features menu, the painting immediately scrolls to that location. On a mouse-over an outline of the City Gate illuminates. On a mouse-down a real-time video clip emerges from the painting complete with sound to provide a depiction of life in China at that time. This subtle exploitation of technology serves well to enhance context and continuity, contributing to the creation of an engaging virtual space for the viewer.

Figure 24.8: "Qing-Ming-Shang-He-Tu," Cheryl Qian (2001). Reproduced with permission of the author

An Experiential Approach to Storytelling

Our work to this point was still very technical in nature. So far we had developed an understanding of the importance of reflecting personality; we had begun to demonstrate the value of interactivity; and we had a sense of the importance of context. Doreen Leo's work represents progress in an important new direction.

"My particular interest in design methodologies led me to further investigate the how of experience design. The process began with my involvement in 'Interface and Navigation,' a course designed by Jim Budd at Simon Fraser University. My objective was to use the digital medium and interface to support an understanding of individual personality and emotion. Along the way I discovered narrative to be an important component of experience design, instrumental in achieving the *how*" (Leo, 2).

Hillary McLellan, in her survey of the key concepts and theories relevant to experience design, notes the importance of stories as a central element in the design of experiences (Leo). Using narrative enabled me to give practical effect to the AIGA definition of experience design—I succeeded in creating a relationship with individuals and invoking and creating an environment that connects on an emotional or value level to them. The experience design community is apparently catching on to what storytellers have known all along, that is, that stories have the power to command emotion and involvement, and to transport us into other places. Stories foster a way of thinking, and are the soul of a culture, and of a people. Stories help us know, remember and understand (Johnson).

The Work

Emotion drives the human experience. We tend to revisit spaces that have engaged us emotionally. Interface has the potential to be a powerful tool for creating an emotive experience. In *Computers as Theatre* Brenda Laurel talks about engagement as a desirable and essential human response to computer-mediated activities. Jacobson proposes that engagement has cognitive components, but that it is primarily seen as an emotion. Interface mediates the creator's intent and is the point of interaction with the user. Creating an enjoyable and engaging interface is possible and essential. Designing for usability alone is insufficient. In the experience economy Pine and Gilmore claim that consumers unquestionably look for experiences.

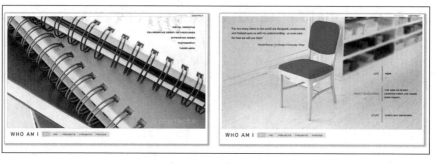

Figure 24.9: Portfolio, Doreen Leo 2002

In trying to reach my goal in interface and navigation I used the conventional space of the portfolio Web site to create an emotive experience. A portfolio site seemed a good place to begin a dialogue with my audience because it is understood as a space where one communicates with others through the display of one's personal artifacts and thoughts. The first design of my portfolio site is illustrated in figures 24.9 and 24.10. I thought I would immediately connect with people based on the sentimental quality of my artistic work and the thoughtfulness of my writing. It did not occur to me to design navigation in a way that would help people make this connection and so the navigational structure emphasized the organization of artifacts. Initial reactions from Jim and my classmates made me realize I had built a beautiful container for my things that could be appreciated for its aesthetic quality but did little to express my personality, or induce a flow response. Flow, a term used by Mihalyi Csikszentmihalyi to describe an optimal experience, can occur in practically any activity, including browsing the Web. In a flow state time seems to stand still, distractions are excluded form consciousness, there is no worry of failure and self-consciousness disappears. Although flow can occur anywhere, certain activities like rock climbing, playing chess, and composing music, lend themselves to this state of almost automatic, effortless, but highly focused attention. Responsive, engaging Web sites can also induce flow in their users. To effect flow is to create an engaging experience.

I revamped the initial design for my Web site based on the feedback I received. Without realizing I was beginning to add narrative elements to my work, I wrote

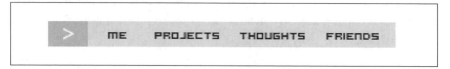

Figure 24.10: Portfolio, Doreen Leo 2002

a short blurb about my friends and myself (figure 24.11) to give people a glimpse into my life. In addition, I created mini-interfaces (figure 24.12) that asked my audience to tell their stories. The text on figure 24.12 reads: "Dear Friend, I have been trying to find out who I am my entire life. Perhaps you have been on the same quest. I invite you to participate in a process of self-discovery. Do so as honestly as you can." This first attempt at storytelling, however, was still somewhat superficial and seemed like a last minute, obligatory add-on; the story of "me" functioned like a resume, and I did not know what to do with the mini-interfaces. At this point my story was still taking a backseat to the traditional portfolio structure of links leading to a collection of artifacts.

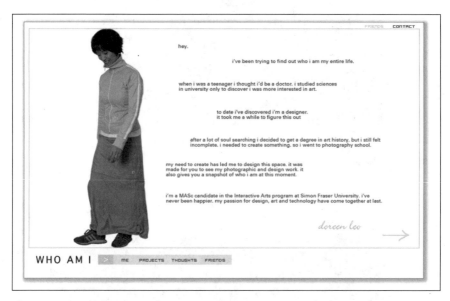

Figure 24.11: Portfolio, Doreen Leo 2002

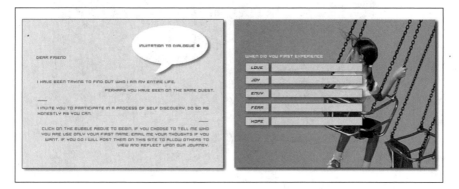

Figure 24.12: Portfolio, Doreen Leo 2002

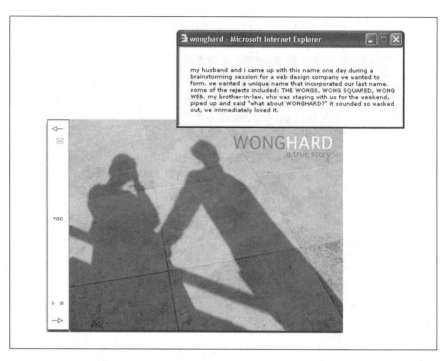

Figure 24.13: Portfolio, Doreen Leo 2002

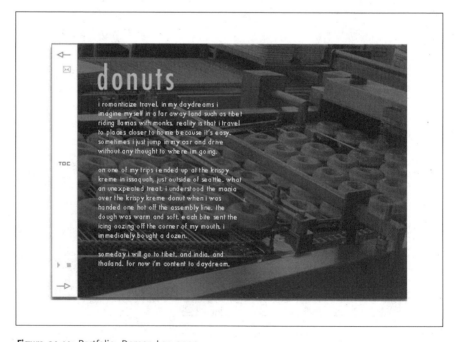

Figure 24.14: Portfolio, Doreen Leo 2002

A third reworking of the site privileged storytelling. Gone are the headings organizing personal artifacts. Navigation has been designed to help the reader move through the narrative: directional arrows move the reader forwards and backwards while a table of contents allows the reader to jump to any part of the site she chooses. Hyperlinks lead to pop-up windows (figure 24.13) and to a video clip that expands the narrative. Titled "Wonghard: A True Story," the work tells the story of particular events in my life through photographs merged with text. A page titled "donuts" (figure 24.14) relates my desire to travel around the world, which inadvertently leads me to a Krispy Kreme donuts store. Focusing my efforts on storytelling provided me a means to establish an emotional rapport with my audience. One viewer e-mailed me to tell me: "Doreen, I felt as though I was sharing a very personal experience with you as I traveled through your site. Your choice of music added to the site's intimacy, but clearly, your story telling involving family is what defines the experience."

Narrative, when combined with the power of the digital medium, results in a richer, more interactive experience. Livo and Reitz's book discusses how computers can become the next great medium for storytelling, arguing that the computer offers writers the opportunity to tell stories from multiple viewpoints. They allow one to offer intersecting stories that form a dense and spreading web. They suggest that when the writer expands the story to include multiple possibilities, the reader takes a more active role. Before the computer the art of telling a story was fairly straightforward. A writer would organize his narrative with a beginning, middle, and end, and a reader would read the story in the way the writer intended. The concept of a narrative having a fixed structure, however, has been challenged by the rise of the Internet and hypertext articles. As a result, readers can now decide how they want a story to be organized by clicking on links.

The present work evokes a more intuitive approach to the design of the interface. It has no obvious widgets, or at least none that gets in the way. Such an interface can be described as transparent. Transparency aims to create the sense of immersion, facilitating a feeling of being lost in a story. The less the audience is aware of the technology, the easier it is to engage them. According to Jay David Bolter and Richard Grusin, professors in the School of Literature, Communication and Culture at Georgia Institute of Technology, designers often say that what they want is an "interfaceless" interface, one with no recognizable electronic tools. Instead they want the user to move through the space interacting with the objects "naturally," as one does in the physical world. In this sense, a transparent interface would be one that disappears from sight, and stands in an immediate relationship to the contents of the medium.

Future Directions

In the new discipline professionals need to use a range of skills that stretch the preconceptions of design. Among these skills is storytelling, because one cannot underestimate the importance of this skill, since experience is about a journey occurring over time (Csikszentmihalyi). Stories stimulate dialogues, which in turn build a bond between reader and writer. At the level of interface design narrative supports the goal of providing the audience with an interactive, absorbing, and memorable experience.

The nascent field of experience design excites some and baffles others. Part of this frustration stems from a lack of attributes and methods of practice. This chapter has begun to address this issue by proposing narrative as a key factor of experience design. Further investigation in these areas will go a long way to legitimizing experience design as a discipline in its own right, as opposed to being a new label that describes what many designers have been doing for a long time.

References

AIGA. *What is Experience Design?* <www.aiga.org/content.cfm?CategoryID=479>

Bolter, J. D. and Grusin, R. (2000). *Remediation: Understanding New Media*. Cambridge, MA: MIT Press.

Csikszentmihalyi, M. (1996). *Creativity: Flow and the Psychology of Discovery and Invention*. New York: Harper Collins.

Grefe, R. (2000). "(Form+Content+Context)/Time= Experience Design." *Gain: AIGA Journal of Design for the Network Economy*, 1.1.

Johnson, S. (1997). *Interface Culture: How New Technology Transforms the Way We Create and Communicate*. New York: Basic Books.

Laurel, B. (1993). *Computers as Theatre*. Reading, MA: Addison-Wesley.

Leo, D. (2003). "Narrative as a Key Factor of Experience Design." Unpublished manuscript.

Livo, N. J. and Reitz, S. A. (1986). *Storytelling: Process and Practice*. Littleton, CO: Libraries Unlimited.

McLellan, H. (2000). "Experience Design." *CyberPsychology and Behaviour*, 3.1, 59–69.

Pine, B. J. and Gilmore, J. H. (1999). *The Experience Economy: Work is Theatre and Every Business a Stage*. Boston, MA: Harvard Business School Press.

Qian, C. (2001). "Qing Ming Shang He Tu: A Design Brief." Unpublished manuscript.

Rettig, M. et al. (2001). "What is Experience Design." *AIGA Advance for Design Summit*: AIGA.

Runton, A. (2000). *Products with Personality: Using the Language of Character Design to Create Emotional Products*. Thesis; Georgia Institute of Technology.

Toomey, S. (2000). *E-Motional Interface: Meaningful Interface for Web-Based Industrial Design Presentations*. Thesis; Georgia Institute of Technology.

CHAPTER TWENTY-FIVE

Traces of Previous Use:

The Communicational Possibilities of Interaction Histories

Stan Ruecker
University of Alberta, Edmonton, Canada

In the digital environment, human presence leaves no trace; every user of an electronic collection is in effect an isolated user. Some researchers in computer interface design have suggested that a useful strategy for reducing this isolation might be to provide a means for a collection to retain an interaction history. If the system creates and makes accessible a record of activity, subsequent users may be able to derive meaning from the record. One well-known implementation of this strategy is in the Amazon.com lists of books that were also bought by people who bought the book currently shown. This strategy holds promise for a wider implementation, and is particularly promising as a tool for interfaces designed for information browsing, where user structuring of the items represented can be a significant indication of how users have interpreted the collection. Issues include the role of intention in communication—clearly purchasers at Amazon.com are not buying books primarily to create a message for subsequent users—and the significant effects of presuppositions in any communication process—subsequent users must assume, for example, that previous buyers were not collecting a set of "worst books" on the topic. Drawing on previous research on interaction histories, as well as Suchman's ideas on situated activity and the phenomenological approach to interface design proposed by Winograd and Flores, this paper examines the means by which interaction histories might be designed specifically to play a role as a communication tool between users of rich-prospect browsing interfaces to electronic document collections.

Interaction Histories

Some of the actions that people perform in the analog world result in visible consequences that persist beyond the action. There is a sense in which this observation, if taken in its largest scope, can serve as the definition of human culture. However, in its more limited sense, it draws attention to the fact that it is normal for action—or at least some action—to leave a trace. The actions can be further divided according to the intention to leave a trace or not. Clearly, people engaged in constructing or demolishing the built environment are engaged in an act of intention to leave a record of their activity: the point of the activity is to create the record, which in this case takes the form of either a new building or other object, or the removal of a building or object where one previously existed.

There are also unintentional traces of activity, as when students at a college climb the stone stairs for some hundreds of years, and the steps wear in a pattern that reflects their footsteps. In this case the intention of the action has nothing to do with the trace that remains: the students weren't climbing the stairs in order to wear them out—they were climbing the stairs in order to go to class.

A third class of actions are those in which an artifact or some other visible trace is established, but is subsequently revisited in order to modify it or re-purpose it for some secondary intention. An example of this kind of action is the work of people who create graffiti, where an existing wall or other surface is taken as the basis for a subsequent public statement. Graffiti is usually the work of a third party, but it is also possible, of course, for the re-purposing to be done by the owner of the original artifact, as when landowners use their property during the period preceding an election to post political campaign materials.

Each of these three kinds of actions that result in traces of human activity have analogs in the digital environment. Previous research on interaction histories has tended to focus on the creation of traces of user activity that are outside user intention and control, paralleling the situation where people walking on the stairs are leaving wear that can be discerned by subsequent visitors to the university.

However, the visible evidence of previous users in a digital environment can be contextualized in such a way that the information is more directly useful in the execution of other activities.

People Who Purchased this Book also Purchased . . .

An example that will be familiar to many people are the lists displayed on Web sites that retail books, where retrieval of information about a given title will also retrieve information about related titles. The related titles are not established by the designers of the collection, but have been associated with each other by the activity of previous purchasers, who have bought the books in a single batch. It wasn't the primary intention of the people buying the books to make a record for subsequent researchers to examine, but the information is nonetheless often interesting and occasionally useful, in suggesting new authors or titles to consider on a given topic.

One shortcoming of this approach is that because the information does not reference the original purchaser's intention in buying the books, there are many presuppositions in place that might not be true. For example, it may be the case that everyone purchasing the current book of interest already owns the important books on the topic, and is simply filling out a collection. If this were true, the interaction history would not suggest the most important books.

A similar scenario would be the situation where books purchased in groups tend to be less significant in a given field because they are less expensive, whereas primary titles need to be more durable and are therefore more expensive, with the result that people tend to purchase them as individual titles rather than as part of a set.

A third and fairly common possibility is that the titles ordered as a set are actually heterogeneous, representing different areas of interest or the interests of different people, as when purchasers order some books for themselves and some as gifts. It is possible, of course, for the system to filter these kinds of problems by relying on some additional information about the titles in a set, such as cataloguing information or meta data.

Digital Wear and Tear

Another form of unintentional interaction history that has been widely discussed in the literature is related to previous document access, either for reading or for editing. In this case, some visual mechanism is used to retain a record of document use by previous readers. Hill et al. created a scrollbar, which is visually associated with the entirety of a document, and applied black horizontal lines associated with locations in the document where previous editors had concentrated their efforts. The visual presentation of this kind of edit wear allows people collaborating on documents to quickly identify those areas which have received the most attention.

One of the shortcomings of visual presentation of edit wear is that some edits may radically alter the document. In order to make the algorithm for applying marks to the scrollbar intelligible, it is therefore necessary to determine what is most appropriate in cases where substantial parts of the document have been removed or relocated. Within the constraints of a relatively stable document that is nonetheless undergoing occasional revision, the display of edit wear may, however, prove very useful.

An example of this situation might be in computer mainframe software, where the code that has been placed in production may need to be modified periodically but generally tends to be fairly static. Another example might be in product technical documentation, which in the case of complicated systems such as a commercial airliner can extend to entire technical libraries. In these cases it may be useful to provide an analogous collection wear indicator that could be used to show at a glance which parts of the library tend to be subject to frequent revision.

Systems that automatically record user interaction therefore have some potential to provide useful information to subsequent users. However, there is also the opportunity to extend the process of creating user interaction histories by making them accessible to the users who create them, for the purposes of editing, annotating, or discarding the record.

Editable Interaction Histories

However, whereas in the analog world the unintentional traces of activity arise as a consequence of the physical, in the digital environment they must be deliberately recorded and displayed. Since digital trace-making is subject to deliberate control, it can also be subjected to re-purposing, either according to the intentions of the owners of the collection or under the control of the users of the material. There are inevitably costs in both time and effort to the users who are willing to edit and store these latter kinds of interaction histories, but the opportunities for useful communication with a larger community of subsequent users also expand significantly.

In short, interaction histories that are accessible to the user as editable artifacts have the potential to be a communication method specifically suited to communicating from one user to subsequent users about acquired knowledge of a digital collection, and in particular, about its contents, structure, and strengths. The benefits of user-editable interaction histories are likely to be seen at their most marked in conjunction with rich-prospect browsing interfaces to relatively homogeneous digital collections.

Rich Prospect Browsing Interfaces

The most common form of collection interface provides retrieval functions, but is not particularly well suited to tasks related to browsing. That is, if the user has a target document in mind, a retrieval interface is a good tool, because it is possible to quickly identify the search target and find out whether it is available in the collection. However, for cases where there is no initially well-defined search target, retrieval interfaces pose an obstacle to people attempting to access the collection. In these cases, it is better to allow the user to interact with the collection through some form of meaningful representation of every item in the collection, presented as an intrinsic part of the interface. When the representations are combined with tools for manipulating the display, I call an interface of this kind a rich-prospect browsing interface, because it allows the user to obtain prospect on the entire collection at an early point of interaction (Ruecker).

Once the interface displays some meaningful representation of the items in a collection, it is also necessary to provide a number of tools that can be used to manipulate the display, either through searching, sorting, grouping, or subsetting the items. Criteria not originally involved as part of the meaningful representation of collection items, but nonetheless derived from the collection, can then be brought into play as the basis for the various manipulations.

For example, in the Orlando collection, which is an integrated history of women's writing in the British Isles, the textual material is largely associated with individual authors. The names of the authors can therefore be used to represent the documents. One obvious means of sorting author names is alphabetically. However, because the Orlando collection has been interpretively tagged, it is also possible for the system to identify the date of birth of the majority of the authors in the collection. This date information could then form an alternative basis for sorting the display. The Orlando tagset contains several hundred tags, which in turn reference over six hundred tag attributes. Methods of sorting, grouping, and subsetting the documents in the collection could draw on many of these tags or tag attributes, or on combinations of tags.

One possibility is for the designers of the collection to create pre-existing methods of this kind that the user would be able to access, through selecting appropriate tags and developing interface choices that draw on the information. This would be equivalent to the book retailers creating lists of related books. As a design strategy, it has the disadvantage to the collection designers of requiring a non-trivial amount of effort. From the perspective of the user, it may also restrict the choices available to those that were within the discourse of primary interest to the collection designers, which may not be shared by all the users. An alternative strategy is therefore to provide the users with the necessary information and tools, and allow them to construct their own sorting and subsetting instructions, in much the same way that retrieval interfaces allow users to construct queries, without the system constraining them to making a selection from a pre-defined list of those queries constructed by the collection designers.

If these choices could be edited, annotated, and stored by the user for subsequent access by other users, they could form a dynamic interaction history that would allow communication of a growing body of insights into how the material might be organized and understood. If the history itself is amenable to subsequent editing and annotation, it may become a forum for communication between people accessing the collection.

Structuring Coupling

The concept of user-editable interaction histories derives in part from the principles of interface design popularized by Winograd and Flores, who suggest that an interface is a form of communication between the collection and the user. The design of the interface should therefore reflect both the underlying structure of the information in the collection and the task domain of the user. One of the difficulties with the communication paradigm proposed by Winograd and Flores is that both the collection and the interface are under the control of the designers, and there has traditionally been no method for the subsequent users of the installed system to contribute to the conversation in a way that left traces.

However, in the case of the dynamic creation of interaction histories, the domain of the interests of the users of the collection would add a third and vital component to the equation. Given the right interface design and an appropriate set of tools, it would become possible for the system to grow in functionality as the users engage in the activity of identifying and using various strategies for grouping and structuring material. These strategies might be based on various features of the collection, ranging from automatically generated topic maps or other indexes to manually applied interpretive tagging, as in the Orlando Project.

Situated Activity

The other theoretical principles that are strongly associated with the creation of interaction histories relate to the concept of situated activity. The idea behind situated activity is that it is not normal for people to make plans and carry them out, but that instead the vast majority of human work takes place through people simply doing what comes next, or what comes to hand. In this paradigm, planning takes place when the usual processes of doing what comes to hand break down and the work begins to fail (Suchman).

By creating records of people working with the display of a collection, interaction histories are a means of capturing the situated activity of the user in the process of coming to understand and access the material. If those records are made available to the user as a subsequent opportunity to edit, annotate, and store as a concurrent part of the session, there are likely to be some people who undertake the additional effort, not only because they recognize its potential value, but also because it is what comes to hand.

Quality Control

Whenever anyone works with digital information, there are questions of quality control. When the people creating, editing, and annotating the information are the users, it is possible to obtain a wide range of results in terms of quality and potential usefulness. An initial level of quality is inevitably going to depend on the amount of intelligence, skill, experience, and work the users are willing and able to bring to bear.

However, once the various forms of interaction are created and stored, it is possible for the designers or maintainers of the system to review them before they are released to the public. If these people pursue some particular agenda in their choices, the resulting list of interaction histories might contain material that is reduced in terms of possible scope, which in a sense may partially defeat one purpose of providing editable interaction histories in the first place.

On the other hand, if the people tasked with monitoring the history list are willing to accept a wide range of possibilities, then they can also provide a safety net of sorts in terms of ensuring that labelling and annotation are done in such a way as to make the history as useful to others as possible.

Individual Versus Public Histories

In addition to issues of effort and quality, there is also a possible concern about the rights of the user to intellectual privacy. In the case of academics working with text collections related to their field of expertise, it may be possible that activities such as sorting, grouping, and subsetting the material are a form of professional engagement that should not by default be made available to subsequent users, since these actions may provide insights into the collection that could prove of value, and their introduction into an interaction history may constitute a form of public release that is inappropriate. In this case, the ability of the user to decide whether or not to store the interaction history may prove to be a necessary feature for these kinds of collections.

On the other hand, it may also happen that people who are recognized authorities in a given field are willing to create, edit, annotate, and store interaction histories that are in some way associated with them as scholars. Such activity would then become part of the public record of the work of these people, and could be duly noted within the collection. A parallel example in the analog world exists in the form of library catalogs of personal libraries of famous writers or academics.

An alternative strategy is to provide the user with a method that allows for personal storage and re-access of the interaction history, without making the record public. For this to be possible, it would also be necessary to store enough information about the user to secure subsequent access, either through a password system or a browser cookie or some similar method.

Conclusion

Although there is a body of existing research and some notable commercial examples, the role of interaction histories in the work of people accessing digital collections has yet to be fully explored. One particularly promising avenue of further investigation has to do with the value of such histories as tools in working with rich-prospect browsing interfaces, where some meaningful representation of every item in the collection is an intrinsic part of the interface, and tools exist that allow the user to manipulate the display in various ways as a means of coming to understand the structure, scope, and significance of the available materials.

Acknowledgments

The author wishes to acknowledge the generous support of the Social Sciences and Humanities Research Council of Canada, the Killam Trust, the Orlando Project, and the Departments of English and Film Studies, and Art and Design at the University of Alberta.

References

Brown, S., Clements, P. (Project Director), and Grundy, I. (Forthcoming). *The Orlando Project: an Electronic History of Women's Writing in the British Isles.*

Frascara, J. (1997). *User-Centred Graphic Design: Mass Communications and Social Change.* London: Taylor & Francis.

Gibson, J. J. (1979). *The ecological approach to visual perception.* Boston: Houghton-Mifflin.

Grundy, I., Clements, P., Brown, S. Butler, T., Cameron, R., Coulombe, G., Fisher, S., and Wood, J. (2000). "Dates and ChronStructs: Dynamic Chronology in the Orlando Project." *Literary and Linguistic Computing.* 15:3 (2000), 265–289. http://www.ualberta.ca/ORLAN-DO/Chronolpaper.htm

Hill, W. C., Hollan, J. D., Wroblewski, D., and McCandless, T. (1992). "Edit Wear and Read Wear." *Conference proceedings on Human factors in computing systems,* 3–9. http://doi.acm.org/10.1145/142750.142751

Ruecker, S. (2003). *Affordances of Prospect for Academic Users of Interpretively-Tagged Text Collections.* Interdisciplinary PhD in Humanities Computing. Edmonton: Departments of English and Art and Design, University of Alberta.

Suchman, L. A. (1987). *Plans and Situated Actions: The Problem of Human-Machine Communication.* Cambridge: Cambridge University Press.

Wexelblat, A. and Maes, P. (1999). "Footprints: History-Rich Tools for Information Foraging." *Proceedings of the CHI 99 conference on Human factors in computing systems: the CHI is the limit.* Pittsburgh, PA, 270–277. http://doi.acm.org/10.1145/302979.303060

Winograd, T. and Flores, F. (1986). *Understanding computers and cognition: a new foundation for design.* Norwood, NJ: Ablex.

Biographies

Jim Budd

Jim Budd is an Associate Professor in the Interactive Arts and Information Technology program at Simon Fraser University. He has a Master in Industrial Design from the University of Alberta (1982). He has been working as a practicing designer since 1975 and has been actively engaged in research and teaching since 1995 in both the United States and Canada.

Jim teaches design-oriented courses at both the graduate and undergraduate levels, and his research interests focus on design management and the use of digital technologies in all aspects of the design development process. Jim has co-authored three highly customized Asynchronous Learning Networks (ALN) to support collaborative design initiatives—the first at the University of Illinois at Urbana-Champaign, the second at Georgia Tech, and the third at Simon Fraser University. He has published works related to digital literacy, rapid prototyping, and manufacturing, interactive digital tools for design collaboration, and interactive products.

Sauman Chu

Sauman Chu is an Associate Professor at the Department of Design, Housing, and Apparel at the University of Minnesota. She received her PhD from the University of Minnesota in Design Communication with an emphasis on Educational Psychology in 1996. Her research focuses on multiculturalism and its influence on design education. Research projects include cross-cultural comparisons of visual perception and understanding of symbols, design variables in multilingual printed materials, design of symbols in computer games, and classroom teaching strategies. Her articles have appeared in *Visible Language, Journal of Visual Literacy, Multicultural Education, Journal of Applied Communications*, and *Journal of Family and Consumer Sciences*. Chu has been practicing graphic design for fifteen years. Her creative production has received regional and national awards.

During the past seven years, as a result of her efforts, twenty-nine student projects were completed for twenty-seven different organizations. Approximately sixty student designs have been published and are being used by various community organizations and University clients.

Susan Colberg

Assistant Professor and Coordinator of Visual Communication Design in the Department of Art and Design at the University of Alberta, Susan Colberg teaches typography, information design, and the practice of graphic design.

Her practice is focused on book and publication design. She has won national and international awards for her work and has had work published in *Graphis* and in *Communication Arts*.

She is Past-President of the Society of Graphic Designers of Canada, Alberta Chapter, and is currently the Canadian Representative to Icograda (International Council of Graphic Design Associations).

She has presented and published papers based on her Master's thesis (University of Alberta, 1991), entitled "The Graphic Presentation of Language for Dyslexic Children: Typographic Design to Facilitate Beginning Reading."

Charles Field

Former Creative Director of Adobe.com and head of Brand and Interactive departments at frogdesign SF. Designed community sites for Encyclopedia Britannica and Customer Support applications for Genesys Labs, among others. Broadcast design at RGA/LA, CD covers for Chameleon Records Ethyl Meatplow and editorial illustration for the *LA Times Sunday Magazine*. Design historian, educator, and typographer. Currently collaborating on an interdisciplinary Design History database. Charles has an MFA from CalArts, and a BFA from the University of Alberta.

Rubén Fontana

Rubén Fontana started out his long professional career working for various advertising agencies, before joining the established team of the Design Department at the Instituto Torcuato Di Tella, one of the most important centres of visual experimentation in the Argentina of the sixties. He is responsible for the articulation and introduction of Typography as a subject in the Graphic Design program at the University of Buenos Aires (UBA), where he held the Typography Chair for ten years. He is the Director of Fontanadiseño, and also the editor and founder of *tipoGráfica* magazine. Among others, he designed the Fontana tpG font and he is the Argentine representative of the Association Typographique Internationale (ATypI).

Jorge Frascara

He is Professor Emeritus, Department of Art and Design, University of Alberta; Fellow, Society of Graphic Designers of Canada; International Fellow, Society for the Science of Design (Japan); Board of Governors Member, Communication Research Institute of Australia; and Advisory Board Member, Design Department, Doctoral Program, University of Venice, Italy. He was Chairman, Art and Design, University of Alberta (1981–1986); President of Icograda (International Council of Graphic Design Associations, 1985–1987); and Chairman of Icograda/Education (1994–1999). He has seven books to his credit, among them, *Communication Design*, New York: Allworth Press, *Design and the Social Sciences*, London: Taylor & Francis, and *User-Centred Graphic Design*, London: Taylor & Francis. He has written more than fifty articles, has led several major research projects, and has organized conferences in Canada, Latin America, and Africa. His professional practice is dedicated to research and planning of communications for traffic safety and information design.

Joan Greer

Joan Greer, Associate Professor in the Department of Art and Design at the University of Alberta, received a PhD from the Free University of Amsterdam (2000). She currently teaches courses in the History of Art, Design and Visual Culture, focusing on Europe from the eighteenth century to the present. Her research, which she has published in various languages, deals in particular with aspects of late-nineteenth- and early-twentieth-century visual culture with a special focus on Holland, Belgium, and France. Areas of concentration include constructions of genius and of artistic identity, the relationship between artistic and religious discourses, representations of Christ, the mythologizing and reception of Vincent van Gogh, art and design periodicals and the private press movement, the convergence of the fine and applied arts and the history and theory of sustainable design.

Marek Hatala

Dr. Marek Hatala is a professor at School of Interactive Arts and Technology at Simon Fraser University Surrey in British Columbia, Canada. Before this appointment Dr. Hatala was a Research Fellow at the Knowledge Media Institute at The Open University, UK, and an Assistant Professor at The Technical University of Kosice, Slovakia. Dr. Hatala holds a PhD in Cybernetics and Artificial Intelligence. His main research interest areas are knowledge representation, ontologies and semantic web user modeling, intelligent information retrieval, organizational learning and eLearning. His current research projects look at how semantic technologies can be applied to achieve interoperability in highly distributed and heterogeneous environments, what are the social and technical aspects of building a distributed trust infrastructure, and what role the user and user group modeling can play in interactive and ubiquitous environments.

Zalma Jalluf

Jalluf is a graduate of the University of Buenos Aires where she has been instructor and adjunct in Typography, Graphic Design, and Information Design. She has also taught at the University of Arts of Oberá in the northeast of Argentina.

Since 1989 she has worked as a designer and Project Director in Fontanadiseño in Buenos Aires, leading teams specialized in the field of corporate identity. She has directed projects for large corporations such as Telecom, Supermarkets Disco, Disco Virtual, and the newspapers *La Nación* and *Le Monde Diplomatique*, amongst others. She is also a member of the Advisory Board of the journal *tipoGráfica*.

She has participated as a speaker in conferences and schools of Argentina, Chile, and Paraguay, and has been an invited lecturer at the University of the Americas Puebla in Mexico and at the Instituto Superior de Diseño of Havana, Cuba. She has written instructional materials on graphic design for the University of Buenos Aires and the Gutenberg Foundation of Argentina.

Doreen Leo

Doreen Leo is a MSc candidate at the Interactive Arts Program at Simon Fraser University. She holds a BA degree in Art History from The University of British Columbia and an Applied Information Technology Diploma from the Information technology Institute of Vancouver. She is a practicing photographer and designer and works as a critic of New Media. She is a researcher for a SSHRC research grant titled "Managing E-Loyalty through Experience Design," working with an interdisciplinary group formed by experts in management, technology, communications, statistics, and design.

Doreen's research interests intersect at design processes and experience design. She has received a Graduate Fellowship from Simon Fraser University to develop her current projects, which include the exploration of interface as art and prototyping a development environment for designers. She heads the Experience Design Research Cluster at Simon Fraser University.

Stefano Maffei

Stefano Maffei is an architect (graduated with Tomas Maldonado) and designer. He holds a PhD in Industrial Design (with Ezio Manzini), and is Associate Professor at the Design Faculty of Politecnico di Milano. He is also a member of the Master in Strategic Design-Design Faculty, where he coordinates and teaches in the Local Development Area.

He researches in the Design Research Agency SDI (Sistema Design Italia)-INDACO Department-Design Faculty of Politecnico di Milano, and in DESIGNfocus, the Observatory of Milan-Lumbardy's Design System. He also directs the design and exhibit activities of OPOS Design Foundation, Milan.

His designs have been published by *Modo*, *Domus*, *Abitare*, and *Interni*, and his writings have been published by Electa, Scheiwiller, Abitare Segesta, Editoriale Sole 24 Ore, Lupetti, Eleuthera, and Alinea. His current research and work interests are: theory of innovation, design driven innovation in local productive systems, activity system design, design for local development, ethnographic research methods, and action research methods.

Barbara Martinson

Dr. Barbara Martinson is an Associate Professor in the Department of Design, Housing, and Apparel at the University of Minnesota. She is currently the Buckman Professor of Design Education and Director of Graduate Studies. Martinson is both a researcher and designer. Research areas include design history concentrating on nineteenth-century illustration, design education, multicultural design, and design process. Recently her research has been published in *Visible Language*, *Journal of Visual Literacy*, and *FATE in Review*.

Both her graphic design and fiber work has been exhibited and published nationally, and has received national awards. Martinson has advised twelve

PhD students and numerous MFA/MA students. She teaches courses in Design, Planning, and Analysis; Design History, Color and Design, and Human Factors for Graphic Designers. She is the curator of the Electronic Gallery, the National Art Education Association's annual members exhibition. She received her PhD in 1991 in design from the University of Minnesota.

Simona Maschi

Simona Maschi holds a PhD from the Politecnico di Milano, Milan, Italy, where she was Researcher at the Faculty of Industrial Design, and Coordinator of design workshops at the Master Course in Strategic Design. From 1998 to 2003, she was assistant to Professor Ezio Manzini. She was a Researcher for project HiCS (Highly Customized Solutions) funded by the European Union; participants in the project were four corporations, four research institutions, and one consumer association. She was a guest lecturer at the Rhode Island School of Design, and has been a design consultant for DeSter.ACS (Belgium), a leading company for food packaging. She was an award-winning project designer at the Young Designers and Industry Contest, promoted by The Netherlands' Institute of Design (NL) 2000. She has worked on interior design and architecture for residential and commercial clients and now teaches design at the Ivrea Design Institute.

Bernd Meurer

Bernd Meurer is Professor Emeritus in design at the Fachhochschule Darmstadt and Director of the Laboratorium der Zivilisation, Darmstadt, Germany. He has taught at universities in Germany, the United States, and Japan. He is member of the Deutscher Werkbund; of the City Development Council of the City of Darmstadt; of the Scientific Committee of the Istituto Europeo di Design at Cagliari, Italy; of the foundation committee for the Bauhaus Kollege Dessau; of the European Committee "The New Academy" at the European League of Institutes of the Arts (ELIA); and founding member of The Society for the Science of Design Studies in Tokyo. He has published several books and articles, most notably for English readers *The Future of Space*, a book produced as a result of one of a series of conferences Meurer organized around interdisciplinary cooperation, technology, and sustainable development.

Thomas M. Nelson

Dr. Nelson is Professor Emeritus and was Chair of Psychology for nineteen years at the University of Alberta. In recognition of his many achievements he was awarded the title of University Professor in 1986. He has more than one hundred articles to his credit published by refereed journals in the field of psychology. Dr. Nelson's research interests exhibit a wide range of expertise, from geriatrics, traffic safety, Scandinavian history, music appreciation, environmental concerns, child education, art and architecture, agriculture and political science, to the more traditional psychological pursuits of perception, cognition, and sensory physiology. His research has encompassed theoretical contributions, basic research, and extensive applied research endeavors. He has frequently collaborated with other researchers in such diverse disciplines as Engineering, Art and Design, Medicine, and Education, both nationally and internationally.

Kenneth Newby

Kenneth Newby, BA, MFA, is an Assistant Professor in the School of Interactive Arts and Technology at Simon Fraser University. His research interests focus on the development of interactive and generative techniques for the composition, sonification, visualization, and spatialization of multimodal displays and installations, as well as theorizing the role of encoded practices in new media. Kenneth has worked as an interactivity consultant for Pixar Animation Studios, and an interactive audio software engineer at Electronic Arts. His creative output includes works for responsive kinetic materials, sound sculpture, interactive audiovisual performance works, and compact disc editions of music and spoken word. Kenneth has received a number of arts awards and commissions from the Canada Council for the Arts and research grants from Social Sciences and Humanities Research Council and Canarie Inc.

Guillermina Noël

Noël is a Master of Design student at the University of Alberta. She graduated in visual communication design from the Universidad Nacional de La Plata, Argentina, in 1997, has followed several graduate courses in Argentina, and has delivered presentations in Argentina, Cuba, and Spain. She was instructor in design studio and in the History of Design at the Universidad Nacional de La Plata, where she also participated in several research and design projects. She worked in the practice of design for government and businesses in the city of La Plata until 2002, the year in which she emigrated to Canada. She was curator for the show "The metal era," one of ten exhibitions organized by the magazine *tipoGráfica*, at the Borges Cultural Centre in Buenos Aires in November 2001, on the occasion of the international conference "Tipografía para la vida real/Type for real life".

Sharon Helmer Poggenpohl

Sharon Helmer Poggenpohl is Professor and Co-coordinator of the PhD in Design Program, Institute of Design, Illinois Institute of Technology, Professor of Design at the School of Design, Hong Kong Polytechnic University, and Editor and Publisher of *Visible Language* since 1987. Her research interests include new structures for information delivery in digital media, such as motion, search strategies, interface, and interaction—all from a user-centered or perceptual point of view. A recipient of three teaching awards, she is also concerned with learning strategies in design and beyond.

Recent writing includes: "Interaction as an Ecology: Building a Framework" in *Foundations of Interaction Design* (New York: Lawrence Erlbaum, in press); with Chujit Jeamsinkul and Praima Chayutsahkij, "Language Definition and Its Role in Developing a Design Discourse," *Design Studies* 25, 579-603; "The Invisibility of Design Research in Practice" in *Proceedings of the DRS Future Ground Conference*, Melbourne, 2004.

Stan Ruecker

Dr. Stan Ruecker is an Assistant Professor of Humanities Computing in the Department of English and Film Studies at the University of Alberta. He is a graduate of the University of Regina (BA Hons English 1985, BSc Computer Science 1988), the University of Toronto (MA English 1989), and the University of Alberta (MDes 1999, PhD 2003). His PhD research was on the affordances of prospect for computer interfaces to large, interpretively tagged text collections. His postdoctoral research dealt with browsing interfaces for electronic documents. His current research interests are in the areas of computer-human interfaces, text visualization, and information design.

Bonnie Sadler Takach

Bonnie Sadler Takach is an Assistant Professor at the Department of Art and Design, University of Alberta, Canada. She was a co-recipient of an international teaching award for the collaborative exhibition project, Thoughtprints, and served for seven years as a member of the Alberta Government's Design Focus Group, helping to develop design curriculum for the Career and Technology Studies program in high schools. She has served on the executive of the Alberta chapter of the Graphic Designers of Canada.

As a partner in the communications firm, Real-Life Comedia, she specializes in the design of informational and educational media. She has received numerous national and international awards for her design work for public and private clients, including a tactile map designed for Parks Canada as part of an award-winning interpretive centre for the visually impaired. A coauthored article, published in *Information Design Journal,* was based on her Master's thesis on the development of tactile map symbols for visually impaired people. She is working towards a PhD in Psychology in Applied Developmental Science (Instructional Technology). Her interests include research literacy for designers, knowledge translation, and the design of interactive learning media involving children as research and design partners.

Elizabeth B.-N. Sanders

Liz Sanders pioneers new tools and methods for understanding the unmet needs and dreams of people. She then applies these insights to the development of future products, services, and environments. Some of her clients have included Apple, AT&T, Coca Cola, Compaq, IBM, Intel, Johnson Controls, Kodak, Microsoft, Motorola, Procter & Gamble, Steelcase, Thermos, Thomson Consumer Electronics, 3M, and Xerox. Liz co-founded SonicRim, a design research consultancy, and has more recently founded MakeTools in order to explore generative tools for collective creativity. Her current focus as a consultant is to bring human-centered design to the architectural community.

Liz speaks about and teaches human-centered innovation to clients, colleagues, and students around the world. She is a member of the Board of Advisors for the School of Design at Carnegie Mellon University. She also serves as an Associate Editor for CoDesign: Collaboration in Design. Liz is a Senior Lecturer in the Department of Industrial, Interior, and Visual Communication Design at The Ohio State University (OSU) where she teaches the required Design Research courses to the undergraduate and graduate students. She is also an Adjunct Faculty Member in the Industrial and Systems Engineering Department at OSU. Liz has a PhD in Experimental Psychology with a minor in Quantitative Psychology and a BA in both Psychology and in Anthropology.

Daniela Sangiorgi

Sangiorgi holds a PhD in Industrial Design from the Politecnico di Milano. Her thesis dealt with service design, and was titled "Service Design as the Design of Activity System. The Activity Theory Applied to Service Planning."

She currently works as a researcher at the SDI Research Agency (Italian Design System) of the Industrial Design Department (INDACO), Politecnico di Milano, doing research and educational activities in the field of service design. She is researcher within the European research MEPSS Product Service Systems Methodology, development of a toolkit for industry while she teaches "service design" within the Master in Strategic Design of the consortium POLIdesign, Politecnico di Milano. She worked in national research projects on the relation between design and local productive systems.

Rosemary Sassoon

Dr. Rosemary Sassoon has specialized in the educational and medical aspects of handwriting since 1980. The University of Reading awarded her a PhD for "The Effects of Models and Teaching Methods on the Joining Strokes in Children's Handwriting."

At the Medical Research Council Applied Psychology Unit, Cambridge, she worked on writer's cramp and techniques to help stroke patients regain the use of their writing hand. She has designed the Sassoon family of typefaces, now used for teaching handwriting as well as reading and for maximum legibility on screen.

Her publications include: *Handwriting; the Way to Teach it, The Art and Science of Handwriting, Handwriting of the Twentieth Century, The Acquisition of a Second Writing System, Signs Symbols and Icons,* and two volumes of *Computers and Typography*. Her latest book, *Understanding Stroke,* resulted from her having a stroke in 1998, and becoming aware of the necessity to change many of the entrenched attitudes to the condition.

Ronald Shakespear

Ronald Shakespear is the founding director of Diseño Shakespear, in Buenos Aires, Argentina, one of the most influential design studios in Latin America dedicated to signage and identity. He now directs the studio with his sons Lorenzo and Juan, and his daughter Bárbara.

His large projects of urban signage and visual identity—Buenos Aires Signage System (1971), Buenos Aires City Hospitals (1978), the Buenos Aires Subway (1975), the Tren de la Costa (1996), and Temaiken Zoo (1999)—have been reproduced in several design books and magazines. His last book, *Señal de Diseño, Memory of a Practice,* was published by Ediciones Infinito in 2003, and is the most comprehensive documentation of the work of Diseño Shakespear.

He has been Professor at the National University of Buenos Aires (1985/1990); Past President of the Association of Graphic Designers of Buenos Aires

(1984/1986); and founder of Espacio Diseño (1984), the first permanent design exhibition in Buenos Aires (Centro Cultural Recoleta).

He has been a speaker at several international congresses and guest lecturer at many institutions, and has as well served as a member of the International Jury at the Art Directors Club of New York, and several other design competitions.

David Sless

Professor David Sless is Director of the Communication Research Institute of Australia. He graduated from Leeds University in 1965. In 1975 he was awarded an MSc by Durham University for his research in communication and information design. In 1976 he became the Foundation Chairman of the Standards Australia Committee on Signs and Symbols. In 1985 he was invited by Industry and Government to set up the Communication Research Institute of Australia. Under his direction the institute has provided advice and advanced communication and information design services to over 200 large organizations in government and industry. In 1995 he was Foundation Director of the Advanced Studies Program at the International Institute of Information Design.

He is Professor in Science Communication at the Australian National University, and Senior Research Fellow at the Information Design Research Centre at Coventry University. In 2001 he became Co-Chairman of the Information Design Association in the UK, and in 2002 he was elected as a Fellow of the Royal Society of Arts. He is the author of over 180 publications.

Zoe Strickler

Zoe Strickler is a visual communication designer with a research interest in communication design for health behavior change. She holds the MDes from the University of Alberta, Edmonton, and the BFA from the Minneapolis College of Art and Design. Since 1990 she has collaborated on studies related to injury prevention and health that involve communication interventions, including work in the areas of traffic safety, prevention of drug interactions, and interactive interface design for seniors, and adherence to antiretroviral medications for HIV positive populations. During the 1980s she worked as a graphic designer in Minneapolis for the firms Eaton & Associates Design Company and Cohen Little Design, where her design work won national awards for excellence. She has held academic appointments at the Minneapolis College of Art and Design and the University of Connecticut. She is currently at the Center for Health/HIV Intervention and Prevention (CHIP) at the University of Connecticut, Storrs, CT.

Barbara Sudick

Barbara Sudick is Associate Professor in the Department of Communication Design at California State University, Chico. She received a BFA in arts and crafts from Kent State University (1976) and an MFA in graphic design from Yale University (1981) where she studied with Paul Rand. She also studied graphic design in Switzerland with Armin Hofmann and Wolfgang Weingart. From 1983 to 1998, Barbara Sudick was a principal and partner in Nighswander Sudick, designing for corporate identity, signage, and communications programs. Her work for the Yale Repertory Theatre has received awards from distinguished professional organizations and publications.

Barbara's clients has included IBM, ITT, Champion International, United Technologies, The New York Public Library, and the Taunton Press. Her work has been published by the American Institute of Graphic Arts, *Graphis*, and *Print*. She has received awards from The Connecticut Art Directors, Boston Arts Directors, Los Angeles Art Directors Club, International Festivals Association, and the American Association of Museum Publications.

Rosalind Sydie

Ros Sydie is Professor and Chair at the Department of Sociology, University of Alberta. She is primarily a theorist with interests in art, culture, and gender. Her interest in the phenomenology of space and the built environment is long standing, and in part arises from early associations with some architects during her time at the University of Liverpool.

Karel van der Waarde

Karel van der Waarde studied graphic design in the Netherlands (Eindhoven) and in the UK (Leicester Polytechnic, Reading University). He received his doctorate in 1994 for a dissertation entitled "An investigation into the suitability of the graphic presentation of patient package inserts." In 1995, he started an information design-research consultancy in Belgium specializing in contextual enquiries and usability testing of visual information. Typical products in the medical area are leaflets for patients, information about medicines for doctors and pharmacists, and medical labelling. Projects outside the medical domain are, for example, the development of user manuals, readability research, and information architecture for Web sites.

Karel van der Waarde frequently teaches and publishes about medical information design. He was editor of *Information Design Journal* between 2000 and 2004 and is moderator of the InfoDesign and InfoDesign-Café discussion lists. He is also the co-owner of the InformationDesign.org Web site.

Ron Wakkary

Ron Wakkary is Associate Professor in the School of Interactive Arts and Technology at Simon Fraser University in British Columbia. His research includes design theory, design methods, and interaction design in mobile and ambient intelligent environments. He has presented and published widely, including Computer Human Interaction ACM, Siggraph, Interact, and Consciousness Reframed. He was cofounder of Stadium@Dia in New York where he collaborated and co-developed pioneering projects in art and the Internet. He has led technology research and design projects for the Nature Museum of Canada, Nokia Research, Museum of Modern Art, the Guggenheim Museum, and Electronic Arts Intermix.

Dietmar R. Winkler

Educated in Germany, Winkler is an emeritus professor at the University of Massachusetts Dartmouth. Since 1960, he has been combining professional design practice with teaching design and communication, as well as interdisciplinary research with the goal to expand traditional design literacy to include user-based methods to explore behavioral, social, and cultural contexts.

He taught for twenty years in the Design Department of the University of Massachusetts Dartmouth, holding simultaneously an adjunct appointment in the Cognitive Science Program. For seven years he taught at the School of Art and Design at the University of Illinois at Urbana-Champaign. He also taught at the Institute of Design in Chicago, and at the Kansas City Art Institute in Missouri, where he held an endowed chair and directed the Center for the Study of Form, Image and Text.

His design work has been awarded, exhibited, and published in the international professional media. He has presented his concepts at many prestigious American universities and at national and international symposia. He is a member of the editorial board to *Visible Language*. His papers have appeared in publications of AIGA, ICOGRADA, and *Visible Language*.

Index